WALLACE STEVENS
A Poet's Growth

# WALLACE STEVENS

 *A Poet's Growth*

GEORGE S. LENSING

LOUISIANA STATE UNIVERSITY PRESS

BATON ROUGE AND LONDON

Designer: Albert Crochet
Typeface: Linotron Bembo
Typesetter: G & S Typesetters, Inc.
Printer: Thomson-Shore, Inc.
Binder: John H. Dekker & Sons, Inc.

*Library of Congress Cataloging-in-Publication Data*

Lensing, George S., 1943–
    Wallace Stevens : a poet's growth.

    Includes index.
    1. Stevens, Wallace, 1879–1955—Criticism and
interpretation.  I. Title.
PS3537.T4753Z6745    1986        811'.52        86-7280
ISBN 0-8071-1297-6

Published with the assistance of a grant from the National Endowment for the Humanities.

For permission to reproduce Stevens' notebooks *Schemata* and *From Pieces of Paper,* the author is grateful to the Huntington Library, San Marino, Calif. For permission to quote from correspondence and other unpublished materials, the author gratefully acknowledges Holly Stevens; Theodore Weiss; the Huntington Library; Joseph Regenstein Library, University of Chicago; and Wallace Stevens Collection, Special Collections and Rare Books, University of Massachusetts/ Amherst Library. Grateful acknowledgment is made to Alfred A. Knopf, Inc., for permission to quote from the copyrighted works of Wallace Stevens and for use of unpublished correspondence from Stevens to Knopf. Previously unpublished letter by William Carlos Williams (to William Van O'Connor, August 22, 1949), Copyright © 1985 by William Eric Williams and Paul H. Williams; used by permission of New Directions Publishing Corp., agents.

Chapter 7 first appeared, in slightly different form, as "*From Pieces of Paper:* A Wallace Stevens Notebook," *Southern Review,* n.s., XV (Autumn, 1979), 877–920. Chapter 9 was first published, in slightly different form, as "Wallace Stevens' Letters of Rock and Water," in Thomas A. Kirby and William John Olive (eds.), *Essays in Honor of Esmond Linworth Marilla* (Baton Rouge, 1970), 320–30.

For
Anna Heim Lensing
(1892–1984)

# Contents

# Preface and Acknowledgments

When Wallace Stevens published "The Planet on the Table" two years before his death and with his poetic achievement all but complete, he set forth a glimpse at the origins and ends of the work that had occupied him for more than a half century:

> And his poems, although makings of his self,
> Were no less makings of the sun.
>
> It was not important that they survive.
> What mattered was that they should bear
> Some lineament or character,
>
> Some affluence, if only half-perceived,
> In the poverty of their words,
> Of the planet of which they were part. (*CP*, 532)

His makings derived from both self and world ("sun"), and they were also reduced to the inevitable insufficiencies ("poverty") of language. "What mattered," however, was something else. The lineament, character, and affluence of the poet's peculiar planet should survive in the poems upon his table.

The affluence of Stevens' world is preserved, not in the final poverty of language, though the popular deconstructionist readings of Stevens remind us of how intractable such language can be. Stevens' language, however, also partakes of an abundance, words "of ourselves and of our origins" (as defined in another poem) that comprise the nature of what it is to be human. The lineament and character of his world are harder to ascertain, in large part because Stevens was a stubbornly private person, and his poems in one sense are far more impersonal than those of T. S. Eliot, who championed that stance. After Howard Baker's essay on Stevens' poetry (1935), the poet told a correspondent that he thought it "striking," but that Baker had failed to see "the sort of world in which I am living" (*L*, 292). We who read the poems a half century after Baker find that world hardly less elusive. This book, then, is an investigation into the lineament and character of Stevens' planet of words.

The *how* of a poet's achievement is no less daunting than its *what,* but to understand the forces that shaped Wallace Stevens' art is to discover again and again its very nature. As a result, the motive of this study is not to rehearse yet another paraphrasing of the poems, but to delve beneath their surfaces to explore a poem's origin in Stevens' life as a "cry of its occasion" (*CP,* 473). Even in his letters and essays recommending the poems to his readers—beyond the immediate act of making—we come across other manifestations of the poems' lineament and character. Consequently, this study draws upon biography and history; it reproduces notebooks and examines sources; it is a development of appraisals, including the poet's own. Part I, through unpublished letters and other sources of personal history, considers the first half of Stevens' life, during which he moved slowly but ineluctably toward his primary vocation as a poet. Part II shows the poet in the exercise of making poems: how he found his way toward modernism; his peculiar habits of composition; and his use of notebooks, epigraphs derived from reading, and the extensive personal correspondence that brought the world to Hartford, from which Stevens only rarely strayed. Finally, Part III discusses two ways in which the poems were presented to their readers. The first is through the sponsorship of Harriet Monroe and her magazine at the beginning of Stevens' career. The other, representing a later and more retrospective stance, shows the poet as self-critic: his personal readings and paraphrases of his poems in his correspondence and essays. The growth of Wallace Stevens is traced from apprenticeship, to full engagement as a practicing poet, and to presenting and promoting his poems among publishers and readers.

From time to time material overlaps. For example, Stevens uses quotations from Eugène Lemercier's *Lettres d'un Soldat* as epigraphs in a series of poems with the same title. The first publication of "Lettres d'un Soldat" is also an important episode in Stevens' association with Harriet Monroe, who published the work in *Poetry: A*

*Magazine of Verse*. The sequence of poems is considered in each of the appropriate chapters. There is, however, a cumulative sense. A poem like "Thinking of a Relation between the Images of Metaphors" derives from Stevens' notebook *From Pieces of Paper* and from his correspondence with his genealogist as well as his memories of his father fishing for bass in the Perkiomen near Reading, Pennsylvania. "Sea Surface Full of Clouds" was written after the poet and his wife sailed from New York City to California by way of the Panama Canal. Mrs. Stevens' diary of that voyage discloses connections between her impressions of the trip and details in the poem. There is another context for "Sea Surface Full of Clouds," as Stevens indicated when he acknowledged that "when I wrote this particular poem I was doing a great deal of theorizing about poetry" (*L, 390*). After almost twenty years the self-critic could not (or would not) remember the theory, but surely it included in part his experiments in *la poésie pure*. In short, individual poems and even aspects of the poet's personality are approached from different perspectives.

*Wallace Stevens: A Poet's Growth* is not an introductory study, though certain chapters might serve that purpose. Rather, it assumes a familiarity with the *oeuvre* and an interest in the poet that is more than cursory. I hope that both the generalist and the specialist will find valuable the variety of material presented here. The Stevens archive at the Huntington Library yielded a wealth of heretofore unpublished papers. This book presents new information on Stevens, and I hope it will be not only absorbed but used as a base for additional application and speculation.

At the beginning of "The Planet on the Table" the hulking figure of the insurance executive–poet identifies himself as Ariel, proclaiming his gladness in writing the poems. "They were," he continues, "of a remembered time / Or of something seen that he liked." That statement is perhaps Stevens' most personal self-assessment in his verse. The poetry ratifies the joy that underlay the character of his own special world. If we can trace the "lineament or character" of Ariel's self and sun in his poetry, it is surely through the "something seen that he liked." "Natives of poverty, children of malheur, / The gaiety of language is our seigneur," he proposes in another poem. As that gaiety gathers toward a wholeness in his work, each reader will construct for himself that totality from the several patterns of Stevens' progress.

I owe a special thanks to the Huntington Library in San Marino, California, its former director James Thorpe, and all the staff who made my work there especially pleasant. For my readers Weldon Thornton, Martin Meisel, and Walton Litz, I am also grateful. Milton Bates and the late Peter Brazeau offered valuable suggestions. My editor, Barbara O'Neil Phillips, offered many improvements.

# Abbreviations

Wallace Stevens' works are cited as follows:

CP     *The Collected Poems of Wallace Stevens*. New York, 1955.

L       *Letters of Wallace Stevens*. Edited by Holly Stevens.
        New York, 1966.

NA     *The Necessary Angel*. New York, 1951.

OP     *Opus Posthumous*. New York, 1957.

PEM   *The Palm at the End of the Mind*. Edited by Holly Stevens.
        New York, 1972.

SP     *Souvenirs and Prophecies: The Young Wallace Stevens*.
        Edited by Holly Stevens. New York, 1977.

# I ✍ PREPARATION, 1879–1916

# 1 &#x270E; Early Life and College Years

Wallace Stevens was slow in his poetic development. It was not until he was about thirty-five that he found his authentic voice, and he was almost forty-four when his first volume, *Harmonium,* was published. Then twelve years elapsed before he issued a second collection. Various explanations have been set forth to account for the recalcitrant muse, including business ambitions and, later, his family. Yet Stevens committed himself to a poetic vocation by the time he was a student at Harvard, and, in spite of impediments, he never abandoned it. I want to examine here his exceptionally long gestation as a poet, a period of time, in fact, that absorbs the first half of his life. It includes his eighteen years in Reading, Pennsylvania, three years as a special student at Harvard, and then sixteen years in New York City as a newspaper reporter, law student, and unsettled attorney, followed by marriage and the beginning of a permanent affiliation with the insurance business. As Stevens himself once explained to Harvey Breit, poetry's attraction was continuous: "You said in your first letter something about a point at which I turned from being a lawyer to writing poetry. There never was any such point. I have always been intensely interested in poetry, even when I was a boy" (*L,* 413). How, we may legitimately ask, do these protracted apprentice years account for the birth of the modern poet in middle age? What were the forces of encouragement and distraction in his progress to that point?

Stevens' recorded memories of his early years rarely focused on parents, brothers or sisters; friends from his school days were all but forgotten. The town of Reading itself, industrially and agriculturally prosperous, is hardly noted. When he remembered home with warmest feelings, Stevens invariably conjured up the countryside, a world he explored usually on foot and often alone throughout his teens and later on trips home during vacations and on weekends. Mount Penn, Mount Neversink, the fields of Oley, the Schuylkill, Perkiomen, and Tulpehocken rivers—place names often reflecting the settlers' German and Dutch heritage—became for Stevens a personal arcadia, an inexhaustible pastoral landscape for the intrepid explorer and future poet. It is from this world, surrounding his family, church, and school, that Wallace Stevens' origins as a poet spring.

Stevens' home for eighteen years and the site of his birth was a three-story brown sandstone row-house at 323 North Fifth Street. When he was born on October 2, 1879, the Stevens family was growing rapidly. Garrett Barcalow, Jr., was almost two. A second brother, John Bergen, would follow a year later. His two sisters, Elizabeth and Mary Katharine, were born in 1885 and 1889. He once told his genealogist that he had been named after Wallace De La Mater, a prominent politician in eastern Pennsylvania during the 1870s.[1]

From his mother, Margaretha Catharine Zeller, a native of Reading and a descendant of an officer in the Revolution, Stevens once claimed to have inherited his "imagination" while his "practical side" derived from his father, Garrett Barcalow. After her death, he found himself "more like my mother than my father. The rest, I think, all resemble my father most" (L, 213–14). The few letters and items of information still available indicate that Mrs. Stevens—"Kate" to her friends—was absorbed in the lives of her husband and children; she "kept house and ran the family," Stevens remembered.[2] But she must have taken more than a passive interest in her children's education, for she had been a schoolteacher before her marriage.[3] She spoke Pennsylvania Dutch "rather imperfectly, but always when she went to market talked with the farmers' wives" (L, 417). Stevens' daughter recalls that both Wallace and Garrett, Jr., shared the family piano with their mother and learned to play the harmonium in the parlor of neighbors

---

1. Milton J. Bates cites the unpublished letter in "Selecting One's Parents: Wallace Stevens and Some Early Influences," *Journal of Modern Literature*, IX(May, 1982), 194.

2. Stevens quoted in Jerald E. Hatfield, "More About Legend," *Trinity Review*, VIII (May, 1954), 30.

3. Bates reports that "around 1869, she edited or helped to edit a literary publication of the annual Berks County Teachers' Institute" ("Selecting One's Parents," 185).

across the street.[4] Stevens also found support from his mother for his evolving interest in literature while he was at Harvard: she gave him the first volume of Emerson's *Works* at Christmas in 1898 and then Ernest Rhys' edition of *The Prelude to Poetry: The English Poets in the Defense and Praise of Their Own Art,* which she purchased in Boston the following October. When his mother was dying in 1912, the thirty-two-year-old Stevens returned to Reading for a final visit. The occasion rekindled memories for his journal: her strong Presbyterian faith and her reading a chapter from the Bible to her children every night; her piano playing and hymn singing on Sundays ("I remember her studious touch at the piano, out of practice, and her absorbed, detached way of singing"); the house and its arrangement, left totally to her, like "a huge volume full of the story of her thirty-five years or more within it" (*L,* 173). Whatever imaginative life Stevens inherited from his mother must have been rooted in her piety, love of music, and firm domestic affection.

His father had grown up near Reading and was a member of the Dutch Reformed church. Like his future wife, he was a teacher for a while, but then he read law for two years. In 1872, shortly after he met Margaretha, he was admitted to practice. They married four years later, and Garrett began a long career in Reading that combined law and business.

His correspondence with Wallace while the latter was an undergraduate indicates the hard financial combat by which he barely kept his bicycle and steel factories solvent. One particularly anxious letter in 1897 describes the strain:

> I note what you say about voyages and absences for weeks, & all that. That used to be a vision of my own before I married and babies came and expenses grew and bills multiplied. The expense is not great—but the stopping of the process of earning during an absence of even two weeks is more serious—and I sometimes despair of ever getting my affairs into such shape that I can have an opportunity to really enjoy leisure—When one is practically running things—when people depend on you to direct—when business ventures are saved from disaster

4. Holly Stevens quoted in Michael O. Stegman, "Wallace Stevens and Music: A Discography of Stevens' Phonograph Record Collection," *Wallace Stevens Journal,* III (Fall, 1979), 79.

only by constant watching—when you must stay home every day to
sign or endorse some new note the non attention to which would
bring disaster—when you must direct a half dozen Corporations—
you must forget Baddeck, London, Halifax, Jericho and hold your
hand on the nozzle all the time.

The bicycle factory burned in 1898, and the insurance was not totally adequate. Just after Wallace turned nineteen, his father asked
him for an "abatement in the general expenditures," though there
is no evidence that the young Stevens' tastes were extravagant. He
went on to explain: "I refer to the Steel plant and the Bike plant
both of which are costing me much money to hold and yet are
things I cannot sell without great loss."[5] By means of his pre-
carious business holdings and his position as a partner in the law
firm of Stevens and Stevens,[6] the elder Stevens grasped his bourgeois prize, but insecurely and only with hard attention to the
principles of the work ethic. There was a natural tendency for Garrett to sponsor frugality in his sons by reminding them of his own,
but his financial struggles were genuine, especially during the
years when Wallace and his two brothers were undergraduates and
law students. Garrett's skill as an attorney, however, was considerable. At his death in 1911 he was remembered for representing
"many of the largest business concerns in this section. When a firm
found its affairs tangled he was often called into consultation and
usually found a way to solve the difficulty in a manner satisfactory
to all interests."[7]

Garrett's manner was stern and solitary, as Stevens explained in a
letter to his niece many years later: "I think that he loved to be at
the house with us, but he was incapable of lifting a hand to attract
any of us, so that, while we loved him, as it was natural to do, we
also were afraid of him, at least to the extent of holding off. The
result was that he lived alone. The greater part of his life was spent
at his office; he wanted quiet and, in that quiet, to create a life of his
own" (L, 454).

But there was another side to Garrett—he valued occasional op-

5. Garrett B. Stevens to Wallace Stevens, November 12, 1897, October 10, 1898, both in
Huntington Library, San Marino, Calif. All correspondence to and from Wallace Stevens
cited herein is to be found in this archive, with exceptions as indicated.
6. His partner Kerper Stevens was not related to Garrett Stevens' family.
7. Reading Eagle, July 14, 1911, p. 1.

portunities both for reading and writing. Shortly after meeting his future wife he gave her *The Poetical Works of Alexander Pope* as a Christmas gift. In 1907, Wallace indicated that he possessed "my father's copy of Burns' poems" (*L*, 102). Garrett's fondness for solitary reading was one his second son would also indulge and remember: "We were all great readers, and the old man used to delight in retiring to the room called the library on a Sunday afternoon to read a five or six-hundred page novel. The library was no real institution, you understand; just a room with some books where you could go and be quiet." Garrett himself wrote and published poems in the Reading newspapers, usually anonymously. Some were reprinted in the Reading *Times* after his death. But poetry was a minor hobby and the results were not remarkable.[8]

Garrett Stevens prized the security of a comfortable income and a stable family life. His insistent recommendation of those values contributed to an early and important dilemma for Wallace, who could not escape his father's counsel even as he discovered a consuming interest in an aesthetic life that signaled like a siren out of range of his father's ear. The ensuing conflict within the young man would find resolution, as we shall see, only after an exacting ordeal that lasted several years.

Until he left Reading for Harvard, Stevens' life did not differ notably from those of other boys with whom he was growing up. As the second son in a family of seven, he must have enjoyed few opportunities for quiet and privacy, those amenities he subsequently treasured. In high school, he later told his future wife, he "played football" and there was a time when he was "distinctly a rowdy" (*L*, 126), involved in boyhood pranks. "Pat," as Wallace was known during these years, fell under three dominant influences, and each would assume a formative role in his adult life: a conventional but intense religious faith, a growing fascination with the Reading countryside, and a gift for writing, at this time almost exclusively prose, which won him minor recognition among family and friends.

Reflecting on his childhood to his fiancée several years later, Stevens concluded: "It seems now that the First Presbyterian church

<hr>

8. Stevens quoted in Hatfield, "More About Legend," 30. For Garrett Stevens' poem "A Foosganger's Evening," see Peter A. Brazeau, "'My Dear Old Boy': The Wallace Stevens–Arthur Powell Friendship," *Antaeus*, XXXVI (Winter, 1980), 151–52.

was very important: oyster suppers, picnics, festivals. I used to like to sit back of the organ and watch the pump-handle go up and down" (L, 125). Religion was central to life, not only in Bucks County with its strong Presbyterian and Lutheran roots, but on both sides of the Stevens family. When he undertook his extensive genealogical search in the 1940s and 1950s, Stevens prepared a collection of photographs of the region with a brief introduction. "Epitaphiana" was published for himself and his surviving family, and in his preliminary remarks he recorded: "The first Stevens in Bucks County, Abraham, was active in the church. His son John (recorded as Johannes) married Saartje Stoothof there in 1763. Their grandson, Benjamin Stevens, was superintendent of its Sunday School for forty years. Benjamin Stevens' grandson, also Benjamin Stevens, had the gold-headed cane that was presented to his grandfather when he gave up his work in the Sunday School, and this is now in the possession of his daughter. The church was a vital center for all of them."[9] Stevens wrote about his mother's ancestors, the Zeller family, in his 1948 essay "About One of Marianne Moore's Poems":

> I visited the old Zeller house in the Tulpehocken, in Pennsylvania. This family of religious refugees came to this country in 1709, lived for some fifteen or twenty years in the Scoharie region of New York and then went down the Susquehanna to the valley in which the house was built. Over the door there is an architectural cartouche of the cross with palm-branches below, placed there, no doubt, to indicate that the house and those that lived in it were consecrated to the glory of God. From this doorway they faced the hills that were part of the frame of their valley, the familiar shelter in which they spent their laborious lives, happy in the faith and worship in which they rejoiced. Their reality consisted of both the visible and the invisible. (NA, 99–100)

Stevens was baptized in the Reading First Presbyterian Church on June 20, 1880. He and his brothers were enrolled in a Lutheran school in Reading, and Wallace spent a year at a school attached to St. Paul's Lutheran Church in the Williamsburg section of Brooklyn, where his uncle Henry Strodach was pastor. Stevens' early training in Christian doctrine and morals was obviously thorough.

---

9. "Epitaphiana," reproduced in J. M. Edelstein, *Wallace Stevens: A Descriptive Bibliography* (Pittsburgh, 1973), 53.

In Reading he sang in Christ Church choir, "soprano and, later, alto" (*L*, 126), and there is a photograph of him in cassock and surplice when he was about fourteen years old. From family history and family practice, through school and church and friends, religious faith was at the heart of Stevens' earliest environment. What is equally important, the church stirred a personal temperament that thrilled to a reality removed from the ordinary, where devotion, song, and ritual fed the spirit. Stevens' first experiences of the imagination's life originated in German and Dutch Protestantism. Later, he would identify "the supreme poetic idea" with the "idea of God" (*NA*, 51). How to reconcile a naturally pious disposition with what became an equally natural skepticism was another conflict that was gradually resolved in the New York years.

I have already noted Stevens' fondness for the Reading countryside. Although his father's businesses and the Stevens home were in the center of town, one might easily form the impression that his youth was spent in a rural setting. The country was easily accessible, especially after he acquired a bicycle. The image Stevens painted, whether in one of his later journals or even in comments years afterward, does not seem excessively idealized, even as it takes on the color of a personal Eden: "Then I took to swimming. For three or four summers I did nothing else. We went all morning, all afternoon and all evening and I was as black as a boy could be. . . . I could swim for hours without resting and, in fact, can still. . . . . We used to lie on the stonewalls of the locks and bake ourselves by the hour, and roll into the water to cool. —I always walked a great deal, mostly alone, and mostly on the hill, rambling along the side of the mountain" (*L*, 125). His reverential love of religion and his robust love of nature, both ripening simultaneously, were not unrelated in his mind. When he was about twenty-two, as we shall see, he reflected in his journal on "an old argument with me": "the true religious force in the world is not the church but the world itself: the mysterious callings of Nature and our responses" (*SP*, 104).

Stevens' studies at Reading Boys' High School were in the classical curriculum. His training in Greek (Xenophon, Homer, Herodotus) and Latin (Virgil, Cicero, Livy) was extensive, and Stevens kept improving as a student. He was held back his freshman year because of what his daughter identifies as "a serious bout with typhoid fever,"[10] but graduated "with merit" in 1897. Two special academic interests were honed during these years—one in elocution, the other in writing. When he told his fiancée that he "took *all* the prizes at school!" (*L*, 125), he was not exaggerating. He won a prize sponsored by the Reading *Eagle* for an essay he wrote during his junior year. Just before Christmas in his final year he took a gold medal on Alumni Night for a speech on the "greatest need of the age." His remarks on that occasion were reprinted in the *Eagle*, and though the content is unoriginal, even conventional, the speech must have pleased his father—Garrett Stevens' letters to his son in the ensuing years might have been extracted from the speech itself. For this reason, it is helpful to imagine the seventeen-year-old orator winning a spirited response from his fellow students ("a favorite in the school, as was proven by the send-off his classmates gave him") and seeing his picture in the *Eagle* the next day. In his speech he said: "There is one triumph of a republic, one attainment of Catholicism, one grand result of Democracy, which feudalism, which caste, and which monarchy, can never know—the self-made man. We cannot help but admire the man, who with indomitable and irrepressible energy breasting the wave of conditions, grows to become the concentration of power and worth. . . . Believe me, among men there is no need like an opportunity. It is all we ask, it is all we ever achieve in peace, in war."[11] Stevens gave another speech, "The Thessalians," at the commencement exercises.

Stevens also had a chance to be a columnist for the short-lived high school newspaper *Dots and Dashes;* his name was listed as part of the staff in 1895. By the time he left Reading, Stevens had earned a minor fame as a writer. One of Garrett's first letters to his son in Cambridge requested some writing for his law partner: "You must write me something that I can turn over for Kerper's inspection. His admiration for you borders on idolatry!" (*L*, 15).

Our earliest examples of Stevens' prose are letters to his mother written from a resort in Ephrata, Pennsylvania, when he was fifteen and from his grandmother's home in Ivyland, Pennsylvania, the following summer. The letters have an air of amused de-

---

10. Holly Stevens, "Bits of Remembered Time," *Southern Review*, n.s., VII (1971), 656.
11. Reading *Eagle*, December 23, 1896, p. 5.

tachment from the more mundane concerns of his brothers and peers, though he confesses to enjoying girls and, at cards, "a royal straight." For all their adolescent posturing, they are remarkable nonetheless, showing Stevens' delight in verbal swagger. In one, for example, he describes the Ivyland homestead and his relatives, and he indulges in a descriptive catalog: "Red geraniums, sweet-lyssoms, low, heavy quince trees, the mayor's lamps, Garrett play-ing on the organ, water-lilies and poultry—that is Ivyland." Later in the same letter, he manages a striking simile: "Emma—well Emma reminds me of a tub of lilies—you must pull aside the leaves to see the flowers." The previous summer he had captured the sound of his brother's mandolin playing, "the keen, splattering, tink-a-tink-tink-tink-tink-a-a-a" (*L*, 8, 9, 6).

Edwin De Turck Bechtel, a classmate of Stevens' during these years, recalled him as "a whimsical, unpredictable young enthusi-ast, who lampooned Dido's tear-stained adventures in the cave, or wrote enigmatic couplets to gazelles" (*SP*, 11). Lampoons and couplets to gazelles smack of the hyperbolic insouciance that char-acterized the letters. Stevens' earliest writing, slightly arch, just as his speeches were more than slightly orotund, was calculated to garner approval through wit. There is a curious journal entry in which he blamed a personal weakness for the absence of authentic emotion: "Those cynical years when I was about twelve subdued natural and easy flow of feelings" (*SP*, 50). At sixteen, he wondered half jokingly to his mother if his cynicism had embittered him be-cause the resort he was visiting was "dead" (*L*, 5). Whatever his irreverences, they were nurtured by the discovery that deprecating humor was common among the young, but few were as gifted at it as he.

During his last years in Reading, Stevens' budding interest in literature was far from cynical. He later remembered his fondness for reading at home in the third-floor front room that was his: "Those were the days when I read Poe and Hawthorne and all the things one ought to read" (*L*, 125). A close friend, Edwin Stanton Livingood, became his principal confidant, and during his last months in Reading and later on visits home from Harvard, the two were partners in hikes, red wine, and literary talk. In the margin of his copy of Wordsworth's poems, Stevens jotted in his own hand beside "Earth has not anything to show more fair": "Livingood recited this as we were crossing Mt. Penn one morning last summer. Looking back of me how I felt 'the beauty of the morning'!" [12]

"My first year away from home, at Cambridge, made an enormous difference in everything" (L, 126), Stevens recalled almost twelve years later. A gradual estrangement from his family began almost immediately, and he would never again live permanently in Reading. During his years at Harvard, from 1897 to 1900, the world of art unfolded before Stevens: questions of aesthetic theory and practice preoccupied him, French and English literature, especially of the nineteenth century, waited to be tapped, and Harvard extended the opportunity for him to edit and write poetry himself. Stevens, however, did not win his vocation as a poet immediately or easily. His social and economic future could not be ignored, especially in the wake of his father's tireless promptings. The mauve world of literary "decadence," at its apex in this decade, was never a serious temptation, but the pleasures of literature and the prospect of a literary life after Harvard took a firm hold. Stevens knew at the outset that compromises and deferments would be necessary, but he made them reluctantly and, at times, with pain and confusion.

Stevens spent but three years at Harvard as a special student. His brother John had matriculated at the University of Pennsylvania at the same time, and it was determined, according to Holly Stevens, that "there was not enough money for the full degree program." In a biographical summary prepared for his genealogy many years later, his wife justifed the shorter curriculum on grounds of his "not having been prepared in High School for a college entrance." She also claimed that sixteen courses were required in a four-year term, and Stevens had completed sixteen and a half during his time there. [13]

Stevens' instructors are not known, though it appears that

12. *The Lyric Poems of William Wordsworth,* ed. Ernest Rhys (London, 1897), 62. Stevens' copy in Huntington Library. Stevens' marked books are all to be found there, with exceptions as indicated.

13. Holly Stevens, "Bits of Remembered Time," 657; Elsie Stevens, "A Branch of the Bright Family" (1945) (Typescript, in Huntington Library), 25. Robert Buttel, *Wallace Stevens: The Making of Harmonium* (Princeton, 1967), 251, reproduces Stevens' Harvard transcript. There are a total of nineteen courses, though they may not all have had equal academic weight. Milton Bates has recently shown that Stevens received a scholarship from Harvard for his second year (*Wallace Stevens: A Mythology of Self* [Berkeley, 1985], 5).

Charles Townsend Copeland taught one of his survey courses in English literature.[14] He did not have a course with George Santayana, but Stevens came to know him "quite well" (L, 637). In the curriculum itself one notes the concentration on French and German language and literature, as well as a thorough three-year exposure to the history of English literature. There were no courses in mathematics or the natural sciences, and only two outside the humanities—a course on constitutional government that he took his first year and an economics course in his second. From the time of his arrival at Cambridge, Stevens' dedication to literature, languages, and history was fixed, although he did not pursue his high school studies of Greek and Latin. The eighteen-year-old freshman was already confident enough of his own interests to elect academic depth in a more narrow curriculum over a more typically general one. Here is the first solid evidence that the young Stevens preferred a literary to a commercial agendum. His courses were not shaped around a profession, no matter how seriously he contemplated a career in journalism or law. For these few years, at least, he indulged in a concentrated review of English and French literature for no other reason than the pleasure it inspired.

The "Pat" Stevens of Reading became "Pete" when he moved into the rooming house at 54 Garden Street in Cambridge, his home for the next three years. Another undergraduate living there was Arthur Pope, the future chairman of the art department at Harvard. The poet Russell Loines, a recent graduate of Columbia, was a law student who had a room there as well.

Loines, though older than Stevens, made a lasting impression. Exactly a half century later Stevens remembered him in a letter to William Carlos Williams: "In those days Loines was very much of a poet, not that he wrote a great deal of poetry—but he was intensely interested in it and thought about it constantly" (L, 588). Seeking employment in journalism in New York City, Stevens dined with Loines shortly after leaving Cambridge in 1900, and as late as 1906, Loines was commending writers to his friend's attention (SP, 163). During Stevens' first year at Harvard, Loines was teaching a literature course to a small group of workingmen in

14. When Stevens arrived in New York City, he presented his letter of recommendation from Copeland to the *Commercial-Advertiser* (SP, 71).

Cambridge and completing his third year in the Harvard Law School. Over six feet tall, gregarious, and endlessly energetic, he was also editing a literary magazine called the *Shadow*. Loines' surviving correspondence does not mention Stevens, though he boasts of a "beer and song night" in his room for the "men in the house" in December and his private reading of Marcus Aurelius and Tennyson the next day.[15] When Loines gave up his attic room the following spring, Stevens took it as his own. With the possible exception of his association with Santayana, Stevens' friendship with Loines, at least during his first year in Cambridge, was the most important for the future poet while he was an undergraduate.

The house on Garden Street offered a steady colloquium on poetry and art, and, what was more, Stevens found that his own opinions carried weight. Milton Bates has demonstrated the role of club life at Harvard generally and for Stevens specifically. He joined a literary club called the Signet at the end of his second year and the O.K., Santayana's preferred society, in his final semester. In addition, Stevens' friend from Reading, Ed Livingood, returned to Harvard for graduate work in 1898 and was in a position to introduce Stevens to students and faculty who made up the Santayana circle. Stevens' confidence in his developing literary taste grew rapidly.[16] Pope, in a 1964 letter to Holly Stevens, looked back more than sixty-five years: "I recall especially his bursting out of his room to recite a new combination of words or a new metaphor that he had just invented, and to share his delight which was most infectious" (*SP*, 15). A letter to her from Murray Seasongood, one of Wallace's colleagues from the *Harvard Advocate,* confirms Pope's impression. It is obvious that he had outgrown the cynicism of his adolescence: "He was modest, almost diffident, and very tolerant and kindly towards, alike, his colleagues and contributors of manuscripts. Even then a magnificent craftsman, he could write noble sonnets, odes and mighty lines in the traditional forms of poetry" (*SP*, 37). Diffidence notwithstanding, Stevens put both his wit and his training in elocution to work when he recited an ode at the junior class dinner. Floyd Du Bois recalled the occasion to the poet

15. Russell H. Loines to Mrs. Stephen Loines, December 12, 1897, in *Russell Hillard Loines, 1874–1922: A Selection from His Letters and Poems with Biographical Sketch and Recollections by His Friends* (New York, 1927), 171.
16. Bates, *Wallace Stevens,* 24–25.

in a 1942 letter: "I remember when you wrote and read the most humorous poem I ever heard in my life. You drank a whole bottle of King William scotch just before spouting it at the class dinner, then, after reading it, you promptly passed out, and I had to take you home, and missed the rest of the dinner" (*SP,* 63).

Both his "mighty lines" and his avid interest in poetry must have recommended him for a staff position on the *Advocate.* Stevens' first published poem, an eight-line lyric entitled "Autumn," appeared in his high school's new journal, the *Red and Black,* four months after his arrival at Harvard. (Loines had written a more ambitious poem called "Invocation to Autumn—October 10, 1897" at approximately the same time.) By the time he was leaving Harvard, he succeeded in placing a sonnet in a New York publication called *East & West.* Loines may have introduced him to the magazine, which published a lyric by Loines two months before Stevens' appeared. Between these two publications, there were prose sketches, sonnets, and other poems for the *Advocate* and the *Harvard Monthly.* Stevens became a member of the *Advocate*'s literary board in the spring of his second year and its president for a few months before his departure. His success as a literary personality at Harvard was complete.

Throughout his time in college, though, there were steady reminders of the world beyond Harvard. In the more than forty letters Garrett wrote his son, he spoke tenaciously and sometimes tendentiously of the future and Wallace's obligations. The letters, and the confident if sometimes ungrammatical counsel, sharply checked his avowed intention to become a poet.

Stevens' family noticed a change when he arrived home at the end of his first year; for one thing, he had lost his Pennsylvania Dutch accent. Garrett, Jr., his older brother who was in school at Yale, had failed after four months, and it had been arranged that he would enroll in law school at Dickinson College. But he dropped out in May, 1898, to enlist in the Spanish-American War. If the Stevenses were also apprehensive about Wallace's academic stability, his grades, all A's and B's, must have reassured them. There were other causes for worry, however. The boy's head was obviously turned—he had declined to return home for various holidays. A minor but stubborn rebellion was under way. Stevens later remembered that 1897 Christmas alone at Harvard as a "forlorn experience." His purported justification for staying was his desire to attend a reception given by Charles Eliot Norton, but "when the time came to go to the reception I said to myself the hell with it and spent the time sitting by the fire" (*L,* 575). Garrett's letter to his son earlier in the month had been artful: "Of course if you think you'd be just as happy in making them wonder what you look like after a longer stay I will understand you and not take it to mean that you have forgotten us—and that you mean to have a good time anyhow. But let me know what you decide." A discreet inquiry was added at the end: "Are the other Reading boys coming home[?]"[17] In spite of his loneliness on this occasion, Stevens' isolation in Cambridge signaled the attraction of solitude and independence that were to become so large a part of his temperament. He would never again take his place easefully in the Reading family circle.

In a brief prose sketch by Stevens that appeared in the *Advocate* at the end of his second year, he presented a character named Bernard Travers as a student at Harvard who aspires to fame as an opera singer. He awaits a visit from Rose, Lily, and May, friends he scornfully associates with his life before college. Travers' hauteur is unmistakable, but just how much irony Stevens was willfully investing in this character in "The Higher Life" is not clear: "And I—six months of college and enlightenment go a long way. In another year I shall be able to gabble your French and bluster your German—and perhaps the newspapers will have a column for 'Bernard Travers, opera singer,' where they had a line for 'B. Travers, juggler.' Then my world will be full of 'monsieur et mademoiselle,' instead of Rose—and Lily—and May."[18]

Garrett's strongest fears for his son, however, were based on the possibility, as he saw it, that the benefits of Harvard would be squandered. There had been no Harvard or Yale or University of Pennsylvania for him; at the age of seventeen, he left the family farm in Feasterville and went to Reading to become a schoolteacher. At twenty he began the study of law in a private office in Reading, and his granddaughter believes that he taught himself Greek and Latin in order to pass the bar examination (*SP,* 6). His ambition was as vaulting as his self-discipline was exact. He care-

---

17. Garrett B. Stevens to Wallace Stevens, December 8, 1897.
18. Wallace Stevens, "The Higher Life," *Harvard Advocate,* LXVII (June 12, 1899), 124.

fully fed his profits, which gradually increased, into the bicycle and steel plants, and Stevens once spoke of his being an officer in the Reading Hardware Company (*L*, 126). A self-made entrepreneur who managed to support with reasonable comfort a family of seven, he naturally expected equal success for his "boys": "You will be like I was myself at 16—bound to 'paddle your own canoe' without help from home of any substantial character" (*L*, 18).

Garrett was not insensitive to his son's interest in writing, for Stevens had spoken with some enthusiasm about journalism before he left home. Garrett also knew the attractions that art held for Wallace, an interest he shared in his own inchoate fashion. The father of Wallace Stevens could hardly have written a more auspiciously contrived letter than the one he sent just after his son arrived at Harvard:

> A little romance is essential to ecstasy. We are all selfish—Self Denial doesn't seem to be a good thing excepting in others—the world holds an unoccupied niche only for those who climb up—work and study, study and work—are worth a decade of dreams—and romantic notions—but I do not believe in being so thoroughly practical that what is beautiful, what is artistic—what is delicate or what is grand—must always be deferred to what is useful. And there is no better exercise than an effort to do our best to appreciate and describe to others the beauties of those things which are denied to the vision of the absent. . . .
>
> When we try to picture what we see, the purely imaginary is transcended, like listening in the dark we seem to really hear what we are listening for—but describing real objects one can draw straight or curved lines and the thing may be mathematically demonstrated—but who does not prefer the sunlight—and the shadow reflected.
>
> Point in all this screed—Paint truth but not always in drab clothes. Catch the reflected sun-rays, get pleasurable emotions—instead of stings and tears. (*L*, 14–15)

The statement remarkably anticipates aspects of Stevens' later poetics, the contrast between "real objects" and "the shadow reflected," for example. It is also prophetic: "And who knows but bringing to its [his Cambridge "cloister"] description your power of painting pictures in words you make it famous—and some Yankee old maid will say—it was here that Stevens stood and saw the road to distinction" (*L*, 14).

During his second year as an undergraduate, Stevens mailed back to Reading a copy of one of his own poems. His father's response was sportive but encouraging: "Your lines run prettily in the Stanzas sent and we may soon expect the shades of Longfellow to seem less grey. —I'll talk it over prosily with you when I see you" (L, 21). That prosy exchange during the Christmas holidays is unrecorded, but the elder Stevens' counsel two months later must have been dispiriting: "I am convinced from the Poetry (?) you write your Mother that the afflatus is not serious—and does not interfere with some real hard work" (L, 23). In May his father sent a punning paragraph to congratulate him on his election to the Signet Society, but concluded more soberly: "Keep hammering at your real work however my boy—for a fellow never knows what's in store—and time mis-spent now counts heavily" (L, 26). About the same time Garrett had to insist that copies of the *Advocate,* where Stevens was now on the board and in which his prose and poetry were appearing, be sent home: "I do not get any copies of your esteemed publication."[19] Even in the magazine, his poems were published under pseudonyms—R. Jerries, Carrol More, Henry Marshall, Kenneth Malone, John Morris 2nd, Hillary Harness—and under his own name as well. Although most appeared before his brief tenure as president, he later claimed that as editor he was forced to come up with poems to fill space.[20] His father's suspicions about the opposition between poetry and "real hard work" do not account entirely for this reticence and self-camouflage; Wallace was shy and uncertain about the merit of his work.

The father hoped that all three of his sons would become lawyers, and in this he ultimately succeeded. Of the three, however, Wallace was the most intractable. It must have been with some relief that he noted Wallace's study of English history and constitutional government: "You will be ready for old Blackstone when you shall have swallowed their [Dicey and Pomeroy] panegyrics on the English Constitution." And as Stevens later told Henry Church, Garrett gave a specific assignment: "Many years ago, when I was at Harvard, my father asked me to procure legal material for him on the origin and administration of the Peabody Insti-

19. Garrett B. Stevens to Wallace Stevens, April 18, 1899.
20. "Verlaine in Hartford: An Interview with Wallace Stevens by Charles Henri Ford," *View,* I (September, 1940), 1.

tute."[21] But Garrett did not press the matter too heavily, and he suggested a summer job more in keeping with Stevens' avowed intentions: "If your aim is still journalism—a summer on a Boston or N.Y. large Daily in almost any capacity—would be of greatest value as a stimulus or to cure you" (*L*, 19). Stevens, however, would be "cured" only after his education had ended; he returned to Reading for another summer job arranged by his father.

Whatever his expectations for his son's future, Garrett was convinced that academic success was imperative. His expatiations on the subject were constant, a contemporary primer of Puritan virtues. The tone is consistently affectionate but unwavering, not so much that of a taskmaster as a Polonius of the post:

*November 2, 1897:* A lot of the fellows from here that are monkeying with study at U of Pa [where John was enrolled]—are absolutely no good anywhere and a great deal better would be at some honest labor—They are simply having a picnic and acquiring habits that absolutely unfit them for the real battle that is right in front of all us.

*February 1, 1898:* I am betting high on you and nothing is too good for you if you get right down to the essential work.

*March 6, 1898:* Glad to get your encouraging reports—and shall be happy always to get the substantial evidence of your progress, for, as you are aware—you are not out on a pic-nic—but really preparing for the campaign of life—where self sustenance is essential and where everything depends upon yourself. (*L*, 18)

*November 13, 1898:* Our young folks would of course all prefer to be born like English noblemen with Entailed estates, income guaranteed and in choosing a profession they would simply say—"How shall I amuse myself"—but young America understands that the question is—"*Starting with nothing, how shall I sustain myself and perhaps a wife and family—and send my boys to College and live* comfortably in my old age." Young fellows must all come to that question for unless they inherit money, marry money, find money, steal money or somebody presents it to them, they must *earn* it and earning it save it up for the time of need. How best can he earn a sufficiency! What talent does he possess which carefully nurtured will produce something which people want and therefore will pay for. This is the whole problem! and to Know Thyself! (*SP*, 71)

21. Garrett B. Stevens to Wallace Stevens, February 22, 1898; Wallace Stevens to Henry Church, April 17, 1940.

*May 3, 1899:* Glad to hear from you and that you are improving your present opportunity to prepare for the darned serious task of supporting yourself, and the rest of us if need be.[22]

In terms of immediate academic success, the exhortations were wasted: Stevens' grades were consistently good (*L,* 17, 23, 33–34). For his future, however, the summons to "battle" and the "campaign of life" by "earning" a way to "sustain myself" defined the quandary of the young Stevens. "Honest labor" was preferable to "monkeying with study." And, what must have struck at the heart of Stevens' own doubts about his future, Garrett insisted that an individual talent should be nurtured, not for its own sake or the pleasure to be derived in exercising it, but to "produce something which people want and therefore will pay for."

Garrett was plainly baffled by the behavior of his second son. He could hardly fault the young man for academic failure in the manner of Garrett, Jr. But of all his children, Wallace remained the most independent from the rest of the family, the most suspicious in his literary disposition, and the most elusive when it came to paternal influence. Garrett's only mode of confrontation was polite but firm admonition. In this there was no relaxation. The result was a powerful psychological battle between father and son, the consequences of which would be long lasting. One sees its subtlety in the remark cited earlier about Garrett's own dream of travel and adventure, a dream aborted by the very circumstance of his son's existence and the very expenses his studies were incurring: "That used to be a vision of my own before I married and babies came and expenses grew and bills multiplied." It is less subtle in the charge that he should prepare to support not only himself but also "the rest of us if need be."

As Stevens wrestled with possible ways to reconcile the aesthetic and commercial applications of his talent, relief, such as it was, was found in falling back upon a commitment to journalism, where one wrote for money. That intention had already been announced to his father. But Stevens knew next to nothing about journalism; his only practical experience was his work on the *Advocate* and possibly a part-time job in Reading (*SP,* 18). There is no mention of it

22. Garrett B. Stevens to Wallace Stevens, November 2, 1897, February 1, 1898, May 3, 1899.

in his journal. As a resolution of his problem, it was tentative at best.

Nowhere is his personal tension better expressed than in a Petrarchan sonnet he wrote in his journal on February 23, 1899:

> Come, said the world, thy youth is not all play,
> Upon these hills vast palaces must rise,
> And over this green plain that calmly lies
> In peace, a mighty city must have sway.
> These weak and murmuring reeds cannot gainsay
> The building of my wharves; this flood that flies
> Unfathomed clear must bear my merchandise,
> And sweep my burdens on their seaward way.
>
> No cried my heart, this thing I cannot do,
> This is my home, this plain and water clear
> Are my companions faultless as the sky—
> I cannot, will not give them up to you.
> And if you come upon them I shall fear,
> And if you steal them from me I shall die. (*SP*, 29–30)

In the octave, palaces, city, wharves, flood, and merchandise all but destroy "These weak and murmuring reeds" by which the speaker endures his "burdens." The struggle is set against a masculine power that leaves him all but defenseless: the city is "mighty"; the flood "flies" and "must . . . sweep" everything in its way. The sestet's answer is a plaint of desperation. It is his home itself that is threatened. The first word is one of resistance, but the means of resistance are unproved—stubborn will, but also fear and death.

In retrospect, it is easy to see that the father's influence prevailed. Stevens would be a poet, at least that was his hope, but the serious writing of poetry would be postponed indefinitely. The sacrifice would have to be endured. In the troubled words jotted in his journal the last summer before he left Harvard, he settled upon a compromise, one he would cherish both consciously and unconsciously for the next decade and a half: "One *must* make concessions to others; but there is never a necessity of smutching inner purity. The only practical life of the world, as a man of the world, not as a University Professor, a Retired Farmer or Citizen, a Philanthropist, a Preacher, a Poet or the like, but as a bustling merchant, a money-making lawyer, a soldier, a politician is to be if unavoidable a pseudo-villain in the drama, a decent person in private life" (*SP*, 53). Those to whom concessions had to be made included his father. The "practical life of the world" would have to exclude both the "Poet," at least for the near future, and the "University Professor," the life of his mentor Santayana. A full year before undertaking his experiment in journalism, the idea of being a "bustling merchant" or a "money-making lawyer" was no longer implausible. The compromise, founded on "villain" versus "inner purity," has an innocent simplicity, which nevertheless suggests that Stevens viewed the conflict as a moral one, a crisis of concession to villainy.

Stevens' most self-consciously meticulous preparation for the life of an artist was concentrated in the Harvard years; it was the only period of his life when he was free to pursue it exclusively. His journal is a demonstration of that preparation, for as the first page announces:

> *Varii Imagorerum.*
> If I live I ought to speak my mind.
> Jowett.

Stevens' lively pleasure in the issues and principles of literary theory is found on the pages of the journal he began at the start of his second year at Harvard.

The journal is itself incomplete—there are unexplained excisions—and it includes only the last two years at Harvard, as well as his idyllic summer at Wily's farm in Berkeley, Pennsylvania. The prose documentation of a practicing poet, it contains, in fact, a few of his poems, mostly sonnets, some of which were published at Harvard; it includes ideas for poems and rough sketches that became short prose narratives. In the main, however, it is a collection of impressions and ideas, all of which eventually return to the value of art and the role of the artist. In a sense, it is Stevens' private shield against his father.

The poetics of Wallace Stevens emerges from the pages of the Harvard journal—not complete or final, but as another manifestation of apprenticeship. One sees its origins in his reading of Benjamin Jowett, Francis Palgrave, Barrett Wendell, Walter Pater, Edward FitzGerald, Thomas De Quincey, John Keats, Matthew

Arnold, James Russell Lowell, as well as Santayana. The topics spilled over into debates with Livingood and Christopher Shearer, his friends back in Reading, and must have been further debated with his companions on Garden Street and around the *Advocate.*

The issue that dominates the journal is whether art should concern itself with facts, the immediate data of the senses, or should look beyond them toward some spiritual ideal. The question itself was commonplace, provoked anew by the Naturalists, whose novels were appearing at that very time. Stevens was not interested in Crane or Dreiser, however. He shaped his ideas around Pater's aestheticism and the poems that were coming from the latter-day Pre-Raphaelites. Behind the debate lay another and even more personal preoccupation: the conflicting claims of his father's pragmatism and his own idealism, his unsmutched "inner purity" as an aspiring artist.

Early in 1899, Stevens drafted an objection to Pater in his journal that unintentionally betrays an unwitting alliance. Art as "sensuous for the sake of sensuousness" is "the most inexcuseable rubbish." But art in the service of beauty is otherwise: "To say that stars were made to guide navigators etc. seems like stretching a point; but the real use of their beauty (which is not their excuse) is that it is a service, a food. Beauty is strength" (*SP,* 38). With words like *use* and *service,* Stevens reaches for a pragmatic application of beauty and a repudiation of Pater's airy aestheticism. But the true service he finally endorses is that of beauty as a food for the interior self and a form of aesthetic compensation after all.

The tension between fact and ideal would find reformulation in his later poetics of reality and imagination; there would also be a reconciliation in what he would term their "interdependence." Initially, however, Stevens' instincts led him to prefer the ideal because of its identity with beauty and moral perfection. Early in the journal he quoted approvingly from Abbott and Campbell's *The Life and Letters of Benjamin Jowett, M.A.* "'True poetry is the remembrance of youth, of love, of the noblest thoughts of man, of the greatest deeds of the past.—The reconciliation of poetry, as of religion, with truth, may still be possible. Neither is the element of pleasure to be excluded. For when we substitute a higher pleasure for a lower we raise men in the scale of existence'" (*SP,* 20). On October 5, 1898, Stevens purchased Arnold's *Essays in Criticism.* In the margins of "The Literary Influence of Academies," Stevens responded personally to Arnold's plea for "balance of mind and urbanity of style": "By not setting up some ideal such as urbanity etc we never attain any, except by chance; and if there is anything noticeable among those I know and I wonder whether it is not the same with the world as a whole it is the lack of ideals." On November 7, Stevens dated and signed his copy of Pater's *Appreciations* and marked thoroughly the essay "Style." "Here he found further confirmation of his growing belief in the inadequacy of "mere fact." He drew a vertical line beside these words: "Such is the matter of imaginative or artistic literature—this transcript, not of mere fact, but of fact in its infinite variety, as modified by human preference in all its infinitely varied forms."[23] In Jowett's "noblest thoughts of man," Arnold's idealistic "urbanity of style," and Pater's facts "modified by human preference," Stevens found reinforcement for his early belief that art ought to espouse the discovery of the spiritual in place of the reproduction of facts. That theory, however, was about to be further tested.

In the summer of 1899, Stevens lived at the Wily farm in nearby Berkeley and worked sporadically in the hay fields. The journal contains a summary of these idyllic weeks. Although the impressions were now more consciously those of a poet, he welcomed the opportunity to indulge again his affection for the natural world around Reading. Berkeley, in fact, became his Grasmere, though he was carefully reading Keats's *Endymion* at the time. The summer was crucial for Stevens in many ways: he was facing his last year at Harvard and a decision about his future would have to be made. It was at Berkeley that he came to his "pseudo-villain" compromise. But the conflict between fact and ideal also took on a new intensity. In the fields and mountains, facts were not the gray configurations of a remote and hostile world, but the immediate landscape that he had loved since childhood. Facts in themselves ironically approached the ideal in the gratifications they offered: "The first day of one's life in the country is generally a day of wild enthusiasm. Freedom, beauty, sense of power etc. press one from all sides. In a short time, however, these vast and broad effects lose their novelty and one tires of the surroundings. This feeling of having exhausted the subject is in turn succeeded by the true and lasting

23. Matthew Arnold, *Essays in Criticism* (London, 1895), 69 and inside back cover; Walter Pater, *Appreciations with an Essay on Style* (London, 1897), 7.

source of country pleasure: the growth of small, specific observation" (*SP*, 48). What remained a problem for Stevens was how to exalt "small, specific observation" as the ideal.

He argued a defense of the ideal early in the summer with Christopher Shearer, a young painter who lived nearby and whose canvases would later be displayed in the Reading Museum:

> Walked over to Christopher Shearer's and had him show me his pictures. He said that after all nature was superior to art! Is this delayed conclusion not consistent with his belief that, when we are dead, we are gone? He does love nature, but from this point of view how much of it he must love. I said that the ideal was superior to fact since it was man creating & adding something to nature. He held however that facts were best since they were infinite while the ideal was rare. Now compare his hesitancy in putting nature above art, his materialistic religion and beliefs, and does it not seem as if he were unaware of anything divine, anything spiritual in either nature or himself? If this be so do his pictures possess humanity? Are they not so much mere paint: sky and trees and blank places holding a bird or two?

Shearer's unchristian materialism obviously disturbed Stevens; for Stevens, the infinite and the ideal were one, but here was his friend insisting that facts were themselves infinite. Was there not some way to reconcile the two? The entry for the same day continues, leading Stevens indirectly back to the same question:

> In the afternoon I sat in the piano room reading Keats' "Endymion," and listening to the occasional showers on the foliage outside. The fronds of a fern were dangling over my knees and I felt lazy and content. Once as I looked up I saw a big, pure drop of rain slip from leaf to leaf of a clematis vine. The thought occurred to me that it was just such quick, unexpected, commonplace, specific things that poets and other observers jot down in their note-books. It was certainly a monstrous pleasure to be able to be specific about a thing.
>
> Shearer may be right about the infinity of facts—but how many facts are significant and how much of the ideal is insignificant? (*SP*, 45–46)

The intended reply (that few facts are significant, while the ideal always is) rescued a victory for him over Shearer. But his painter-friend's observation about the infinity of facts was not forgotten.

His journal indicates that within a few days he had worked his way to a reconciliation with his friend: "I believe, as unhesitatingly as I believe anything, in the efficacy and necessity of fact meeting fact—with a background of the ideal" (*SP*, 53–54). The relocation of the ideal as a "background" for fact instead of its antithesis allowed for Shearer's position as well as his own: infinitude could be attributed to both fact and ideal; rather than contending, they could be joined. This conclusion occurs in the same entry and immediately after his "pseudo-villain" compromise. Resolving his debate with Shearer had dovetailed with the resolution for his future life.

The union of fact and ideal placed Stevens firmly on the Emersonian track. The previous Christmas his mother had presented him with a copy of Emerson's *Addresses and Lectures*. Stevens read it carefully, marking it throughout. In the section "Language" from "Nature," Emerson defines the transparency of the natural world: "For the universe becomes transparent, and the light of higher laws than its own shines through it. It is the standing problem which has exercised the wonder and the study of every fine genius since the world began; from the era of the Egyptians and the Brahmins, to that of Pythagoras, of Plato, of Bacon, of Leibnitz, of Swedenborg. There sits the Sphinx at the roadside, and from age to age, as each prophet comes by, he tries his fortune at reading her riddle." Stevens marked the last sentence with a vertical marginal line.[24] The same journal entry attributing a "background" of the ideal to the real went on to proclaim more boldly his own transcendentalism: "I'm completely satisfied that behind every physical fact there is a divine force. Don't, therefore, look *at* facts, but *through* them" (*SP*, 54).

Seen in theological terms, the ideal could then be reconciled with his own religious disposition—"The feeling of piety is very dear to me" (*SP*, 53). Communion with the divine could as well be effected in the natural world as in the Presbyterian church, and, what Stevens was coming to appreciate, the former could even be superior. His first step away from orthodoxy was accomplished, and the poem he had written for Santayana the previous March was validated:

> Cathedrals are not built along the sea;
> The tender bells would jangle on the hoar

---

24. Ralph Waldo Emerson, *Nature, Addresses and Lectures* (Boston, 1897), 35. In Emerson's *Essays* (Cambridge, 1898), which Stevens signed on the flyleaf in 1898, he drew a line beside these words from "Compensation": "The soul strives amain to live and work

And iron winds; the graceful turrets roar
With bitter storms the long night angrily;
And through the precious organ pipes would be
A low and constant murmur of the shore
That down those golden shafts would rudely pour
A mighty and a lasting melody.

And those who knelt within the gilded stalls
Would have vast outlook for their weary eyes;
There, they would see high shadows on the walls
From passing vessels in their fall and rise.
Through gaudy windows there would come too soon
The low and splendid rising of the moon. (*SP*, 32–33)

Wind, storms, waves lapping the seashore, and moonlight—the facts of the natural world—better appease the weary churchgoers than does the church itself.

Stevens' preoccupation through 1899 with the relation between fact and ideal may have included discussions with Santayana, who befriended promising undergraduates, took them to dinner and invited them to his rooms for cigarettes and drinks. Stevens' journal describes one such episode in which he participated (*SP*, 68). A letter many years later recounts the well-known exchange of sonnets: "Once he asked me to come and read some of my things to him. I read one of them in which the first line was 'Cathedrals are not built along the sea.' He must have spent the evening writing his reply because the next morning in my mail there was a sonnet from him entitled 'Answer to A Sonnet Commencing Cathedrals Are Not Built, etc.'" (*L*, 637).

In Stevens' last year at Harvard, Santayana's *Interpretations of Poetry and Religion* was published. Stevens must have known it well, and Santayana may even have shared some of its formulation with him. The Preface takes up the same fact-ideal debate: "All observation is observation of brute fact, all discipline is mere repression, until these facts digested and this discipline embodied in humane impulses become the starting-point for a creative movement of the imagination, the first basis for ideal constructions in society, religion, and art." Here Santayana approaches Stevens' own resolution of the dichotomy: the mind begins with facts but proceeds to

---

through all things. It would be the only fact. All things shall be added unto it,—power, pleasure, knowledge, beauty" (87).

"ideal constructions." Another part of his theory, however, was less consistent with Stevens'. While Stevens would go "through" facts to discover the imaginative ideal, Santayana insisted that the alliance between the real and the imagined was in the end an unholy one: "It would naturally follow from this conception that religious doctrines would do well to withdraw their pretension to be dealing with matters of fact. . . . For the dignity of religion, like that of poetry and of every moral ideal, lies precisely in its ideal adequacy, in its fit rendering of the meanings and values of life, in its anticipation of perfection; so that the excellence of religion is due to an idealization of experience." The identity of poetry and religion with the "anticipation of perfection" to the *exclusion* of facts would have taken Stevens back to Jowett and his own starting point. Although Stevens would later share Santayana's notion that the imagination was "unreal," leading to "purities beyond definition" (*OP*, 241), he would hold more firmly than Santayana to the role of facts as not only a "starting-point" but also a pervasive and continuing presence in the exercise of the imagination. For Santayana, the imagination itself, the source and sustenance of religious promulgations, should acknowledge its discrete efficacy apart from "brute fact" and thus resist the temptation to validate itself in the name of empirical truth.[25]

Still adhering to the Christianity of his boyhood, Stevens could not accept the reality of God's existence merely as a "symbolic truth." He was willing to accept Santayana's enfolding of religious and imaginative life, and it is precisely here that *Interpretations of Poetry and Religion* is a watershed in Stevens' personal history and evolving poetics. But, unlike Santayana, he could neither then nor later dissociate the imagination from a "conformity with existence," whether that existence was the reality of God or, later, the elusive reality of sense-data in the process of perception. The truest exercise of the imagination lay in the marriage of the "prophetic" and the "literally valid." To effect what he would call in "The Comedian as the Letter C" the "blissful liaison," he was more than willing to embrace the imagination as the "flatterer of things." But the imagination is escapist in a "pejorative sense," he later argued in "The Noble Rider and the Sound of Words," "where the poet is not attached to reality, where the imagination does not adhere to

25. George Santayana, *Interpretations of Poetry and Religion* (London, 1900), viii–ix, v–vi, 11.

reality, which, for my part, I regard as fundamental" (*NA*, 31).

The validation of empirical data as the veil behind which the ideal, or divine, emanates had the effect of upgrading facts for Stevens. Toward the end of his summer in Berkeley, there was an outing with Shearer and Levi Mengel: "Most of the day however was taken up with conversations about gale-bugs or gale-flies, ichneumon bugs, tiger bugs, the argymous Cybele, mandibles, thoraxes of butterflies, birds: kingbirds, etc. etc. You felt in the two men an entire lack of poetic life, yet there was an air of strict science, an attentiveness to their surroundings which was a relief from my usual milk and honey" (*SP*, 49). The function of the real in the province of art had advanced markedly from Jowett's "noblest thoughts of man" and "greatest deeds of the past."

Stevens welcomed his return to Harvard in the fall of 1899 after his stay at Wily's. The notebook was full of ideas for poems and sketches; later in the year he would assume the presidency of the *Advocate* and in May the writing and reading of the class ode. The relation between poetry and study was a happy one, as he had determined after a conversation with Livingood early in the summer: "There must exist a place to spring from—a refuge from the heights, an anchorage of thought. Study gives this anchorage. . . . Study is the resting place—poetry, the adventure" (*SP*, 41). But for all the value and pleasure afforded him by his books and writing, Stevens knew that these years were no more than an interlude in his life. He was about to leave his classmates after their third year, his own Harvard days over. The "pseudo-villain" compromise was already resolved. At the end of the year he reminded himself: "I must try not to be a dilettante—half dream, half deed. I must be all dream or all deed" (*SP*, 71). His father had said in a letter two years earlier: "For life is either a pastoral dream—the ideal of the tramp, or superannuated farmer—Or it is the wild hurly burly activity of the fellows who make the world richer and better by their being in it" (*SP*, 17–18). The commitment to something more than mere dream had now become his own injunction.

Again and again in his studies, Stevens chanced upon a ratification of his resolve to make a life of deeds rather than dreams. In his immediate case, this meant establishing a professional career before turning to his own poetry. Emerson's "Nature" prophesied a life of steady discipline, and this too Stevens had marked in his copy: "What continual reproduction of annoyances, inconveniences, dilemmas; what rejoicing over us of little men; what disputing of prices, what reckoning of interest,—and all to form the Hand of the mind; —to instruct us that 'good thoughts' are no better than good dreams, unless they be executed!"[26] In November, 1898, "instead of going to New Haven to see the Harvard-Yale Football Game" (as he inscribed on the flyleaf), Stevens purchased a two-volume edition of *The Letters of James Russell Lowell*. A letter of 1849 to Charles R. Lowell spoke determinedly of the work ethic: "Talents are absolutely nothing to man except he have the faculty of work along with them." Stevens' marginal note agreed: "Nul bien sans peine." He also purchased *The Letters of Thomas Gray* in January, 1900, and checked in the margin Gray's strong conviction voiced in a 1760 letter to Thomas Wharton: "To find oneself business (I am persuaded) is the great art of life; and I am never so angry as when I hear my acquaintance wishing they had been bred to some poking profession, or employed in some office of drudgery, as if it were pleasanter to be at the command of other people, than at one's own; and as if they could not go, unless they were wound up." Finally, he adopted Keats as a model after reading Arnold's remarks in *Essays in Criticism*. Keats's own principles of idealism had remained intact, despite a hostile world. He had succeeded in preserving the values of the inner life. Keats's avowals of independence from public opinion prompted Stevens to write in the margin: "Myself, and I believe most college men like me, are still 'avid of praise.' We are young and are looking for encouragement. Keats was alone and bold. What we need, and are soon to have, is our entrance into the world away from instructors and examiners. Then, perhaps, like Keats we may become truly absorbed in the beauty and nobility of literature for itself."[27]

At least in part because the demands of deed were at hand, Stevens appears to have undergone a period of acute anxiety during his final months at Harvard. To what, he must have worried, was he committing himself in the name of deeds? And at what cost to the aesthetic values he had come to cherish? Could he, like Keats, move through his entrance to an uncertain world and on to the

---

26. Emerson, *Nature, Addresses and Lectures,* 37.
27. *Letters of James Russell Lowell,* ed. Charles Eliot Norton (2 vols.; New York, 1894), I, 165; *Letters of Thomas Gray,* ed. Henry M. Rideout (Boston, 1899), 116; Arnold, *Essays in Criticism, Second Series* (London, 1898), 111.

"beauty and nobility of literature"? He was by no means confident. A journal entry at the end of the year, we know from other evidence, is overstated, but perhaps not by much: "Nine months have been wasted. In the autumn I got drunk about every other night—and later, from March until May, and a good bit of May, I did nothing but loaf" (SP, 70). The dilemma posed by dream and deed was an extension of the aesthetic conflict between ideal and fact that had so absorbed him the previous year. But the situation had become intensified emotionally: the claims of deed and fact had moved to the forefront of his life. Having elected the world of deeds, however, he did not abandon his ambition to be a poet. Witter Bynner, a classmate, was present at his last meeting with Copeland: "I remember Copey's asking him just before he left Cambridge what he was going to be and when the undergraduate answered, 'A poet,' Copey's exclaiming, 'Jesus Christ!'" (SP, 68).

By the end of his college career, Stevens' personal dedication to poetry was no ignis fatuus, whatever the delay and cost. "It is a great pleasure to seize an impression and lock it up in words: you feel as if you had it safe forever" (SP, 48), he had noted the previous summer. He would not speak of his literary ambition often, not even in the journal, though he would continue reading poetry, debating its issues, and writing it casually in the next few years. As he was bidding his farewells to his Cambridge friends in June, he set down his state of mind and his plans for the immediate future:

> I am going to New York, I think, to try my hand at journalism. If that does not pan out well, I am resolved to knock about the country—the world. Of course I am perfectly willing to do this—anxious, in fact. It seems to me to be the only way, directed as I am more or less strongly by the hopes and desires of my parents and myself, of realizing to the last degree any of the ambitions I have formed. I should be content to dream along to the end of my life—and opposing moralists be hanged. At the same time I should be quite as content to work and be practical—but I hate the conflict whether it "avails" or not. I want my powers to be put to their fullest use—to be exhausted when I am done with them. On the other hand I do not want to have to make a petty struggle for existence—physical or literary. (SP, 70–71)

# 2 ✍ Career and Marriage

From June 14, 1900, the date of Stevens' arrival in New York City, to May, 1916, when he and his wife Elsie took up residence in Hartford, Connecticut, the poet was absorbed in carrying out the terms of the vocational compromise he had settled upon as an undergraduate. As the twenty-year-old Stevens embarked on his new life just before the turn of the century, he could not have foreseen the years of unsettledness, of false starts and temporary setbacks, of financial precariousness and personal solitude. He could not have known that his dedication to poetry would be continually tested and that his serious writing of it would suffer an indefinite postponement. He did possess an extraordinary faith that the compromise could be achieved, for his journals and letters make clear that the values derived from art, literature, and the pastoral beauty of the land outside New York City and back in Reading were still his great interior wealth. Another beauty, in the person of Elsie Viola Kachel, whom he met in 1904 but could not marry for five years, brought a different happiness in spite of her staying in Reading during the long delay before marriage. The compensations notwithstanding, Stevens' sixteen years in New York were turbulent. Although marrying Elsie helped ease the tension, he was not fully settled until he began writing his mature verse in 1913–1915 and then went to work for the Hartford Accident and Indemnity Company in 1916 and moved to Connecticut.

His interest in journalism as a career dated back at least to his first year at Harvard, when Garrett had offered to help his son locate a summer job with one of the dailies in New York or Boston. Offering a natural alliance with literature, journalism was also a career in the "practical life of the world," with which Stevens had determined to be reconciled. It promised an ideal union of personal predilection and practical exigency, the very compromise he had made as one of the "concessions to others." But within days of his arrival in New York, Stevens had not escaped the anxiety that had plagued his final months at Harvard: "Have been wondering whether I am going into the right thing after all. Is literature really a profession? Can you single it out, or must you let it decide in you for itself? I have determined upon one thing, and that is not to *try* to suit anybody except myself" (*SP*, 74). Stevens had a letter to the editor of the *Evening Post* from Barrett Wendell, who had taught the first course in American literature at Harvard in 1898 and who had published his American literary history the year Stevens left. Wendell's letter said Stevens had shown "marked literary aptitude in college, and has been for some time in charge of the *Advocate*. He would like, if possible, to engage in some occupation related to journalism or to literature."[1] The letter earned for Stevens a place on the *Post,* but it lasted only a few days. He then became a cub reporter with the New York *Tribune,* a position he was to hold until the following spring. In July he took a room on West Ninth Street and, depending upon copy published, was earning between $16 and $26 a week within a few months. The new position guaranteed his freedom from Reading, and after his first few weeks in the city he could boast in his journal that he had "not yet written father for money" (*SP*, 80). "Hang it," he pounded out in August, "—a fellow must live with the world—& for it and in it" (*SP*, 85). Three months later he reaffirmed: "We cannot deny that on the whole 'money is our object.' We all get down to that sooner or later. I won't cross this out either" (*SP*, 90). The young journalist was now boldly adopting his father's idiom.

There was occasional levity in his life, in spite of parsimony. William Carlos Williams recalled Stevens' stories of the first months in New York: "He used to tell stories of the gay life of those days among the other kids, especially of certain hilarious evenings when the crowd would be high. They had a little nondescript orchestra and little or no instrumental ability and would indulge themselves none-the-less until the early hours of every Saturday

---

1. Barrett Wendell to Oswald Villard, June 4, 1900, in University of Massachusetts Library, Amherst.

morning. Stevens would look forward to these jam sessions with
passionate interest."[2]

The work for the *Tribune* was far from "literary" in comparison
to the essays he had submitted to the *Advocate*. An early assignment apparently included an account of Stephen Crane's funeral—
"The whole thing was frightful" (*SP*, 78), he wrote in his journal.
He heard "4 speeches in 3 hours" (*SP*, 88) by William Jennings
Bryan, who was beginning his second presidential campaign
against McKinley. There was an interview with the mother of a
"two headed Hebrew child—Horrible sight" (*SP*, 101). Although
his pieces were accepted for publication by the *Tribune* and his
wages guaranteed subsistence, Stevens quickly saw that the desired
compromise-career would evolve slowly, if at all, and the work itself was more burdensome than he had anticipated.[3]

His disenchantment with newspaper work led to a final coming
to terms with Garrett, Sr. In these exchanges, Stevens gradually
came to the knowledge that his father's solution, the study and
practice of law, would prevail. His visit to Reading at Christmas
lasted only "a few hours," but his intent was clear: "Talked with
father—who is kept busy holding me in check. I've been wanting
to go to Arizona or Mexico, but do not have any good reason for
doing so. I am likely to remain here [New York City] until Spring,
at least" (*SP*, 94). In February, Garrett called upon his son and took
him to dinner at the Astor House. The journal reports laconically,
"We remarked that we looked well" (*SP*, 97). But the long-standing
and troubling issue of his professional future was moving toward
resolution. A recent interview for a job with a publishing house
had not proved encouraging. In March, there was another visit to
Reading and another conversation with Garrett: "I had a good
long talk with the old man in which he did most of the talking.
One's ideas don't get much of a chance under such conditions.

2. William Carlos Williams, "Wallace Stevens," *Poetry: A Magazine of Verse*, LXXXVII
(January, 1956), 236–37.
3. Williams reported on Stevens' despondency as a journalist: "There is also the story of
the down and out Stevens sitting on a park bench at the Battery watching the outgoing tide
and thinking to join it, as a corpse, on its way to the sea (he had been a failure as a reporter).
As he sat there watching the debris floating past him he began to write—noting the various
articles as they passed. He became excited as he wrote and ended by taking back to the
Tribune office an editorial or 'story' that has become famous—in a small way among newspaper offices" (William Van O'Connor, *The Shaping Spirit: A Study of Wallace Stevens*
[Chicago, 1950], 14–15).

However he's a wise man. We talked about the law which he has been urging me to take up. I hesitated—because this literary life, as it is called, is the one I always had as an ideal & I am not quite ready to give it up because it has not been all that I wanted it to be" (*SP*, 100). The journal entry for the next day discloses a final and somewhat desperate appeal to his father. He wanted to leave the *Tribune* and devote himself fully to writing: "This morning I heard from him &, of course, found my suggestion torn to pieces. If I only had enough money to support myself I am afraid some of the tearing would be in vain. But he seems always to have reason on his side, confound him" (*SP*, 101). After leaving the *Tribune*, Stevens tried briefly an editing job for *World's Work*, a publication of Doubleday, Page and Company.

The triumph of his father's reason led to Stevens' enrolling in the New York Law School the following October. It had taken the better part of a year to disavow his first compromise-career, journalism. Law, though more remote from literature, was an inevitable choice, largely because his father had advocated it so persistently and strenuously. His brothers Garrett, Jr., and John were already law students. Russell Loines, too, was a practicing attorney who had not abandoned his interest in poetry. His best friend back home, Ed Livingood, had just returned from the West to take up the practice of law in Reading. Livingood's history, in fact, paralleled his own. Seven years Stevens' senior, he graduated from Harvard in 1895 and studied law in Reading and then at the Dickinson School of Law in Carlisle, Pennsylvania. In 1897 and 1898 he was in Wyoming and Nebraska, ranching and farming, but returned to Harvard as a graduate student in Arts and Sciences during Stevens' second year there. Stevens reported in his journal on October 5, 1900, that Livingood had "just come back from the West—where he did not prosper" (*SP*, 86). At the very time that Stevens was deciding on a legal career, Livingood, having exhausted his own alternative, had come home to be an attorney. Stevens had himself concluded during the summer at Wily's farm that "a money-making lawyer" was another of the acceptable concessions for a "man of the world."

By an irony that is not completely incongruous, Stevens' estrangement from his Reading family was all but final after his deference to his father's urgings in 1901. Though he returned occasionally, and even regularly between 1904 and 1909 when he was courting Elsie, Reading itself "got quite on my nerves" and was seen as "a terrible place except to the native" (*SP*, 168). The family, meanwhile, was "to be candid, insuperably dull" (*SP*, 143), "about as depressing as usual" (*SP*, 174). In November, 1908, his mother reported to his sister that "Wall was in town, didn't come home" (*SP*, 196). Some later correspondence between Garrett and Wallace survives, but it consists of legal matters on which the father sought his son's assistance. Garrett's hopes for his second son were at last being realized, but there is a poignant note of personal distance in a 1907 letter: "I am glad you feel strong and self reliant."[4] The estrangement from home had begun during the first year in Cambridge, but now it became virtually complete. Had his father, the "wise man" with "reason on his side," not triumphed? Stevens retaliated by retreating from the family field. His compromise with the literary "ideal" seemed shattered in 1901, but it would, in fact, only be postponed.

Stevens' impressions of law school are not recorded in his journal and extant letters. One infers a tolerance rather than an avid engagement. The evidence is indirect, but the two years of legal study must have been an ordeal, an exercise of will over propensity.

Possibly because both had had associations with the *Advocate* at Harvard, Stevens met W. G. Peckham, an attorney in New York with whom he began a clerkship in the vacation periods from his studies. One of the founders of the *Advocate* in 1866 when he was a student, Peckham was later remembered by a co-founder as "a boy of fourteen when he entered, a precocious scholar, too critical to be popular, but full of driving Yankee energy."[5] Just when Garrett's influence was receding, Peckham, a year younger, was for Stevens a new and enviable exemplar. Here was a Harvard man who had already combined successfully a prosperous legal career in New York with a vital and continuing interest in literature and art. Their friendship included weekend visits to the family homes in New Jersey and in the Adirondacks. Stevens was visiting the Peckhams when he encountered "this angel," Sybil Gage, whose beauty had captured his attention in Cambridge. (W. S. Gage, her father, had

4. Garrett B. Stevens to Wallace Stevens, November 17, 1907.
5. F. P. Stearns, "The Founding of the Advocate," in Richard M. Smoley (ed.), *First Flowering: The Best of the Harvard Advocate* (Reading, Mass., 1977), 4.

joined Peckham in inaugurating the Harvard *Advocate* when they were undergraduates.) At the time of their meeting, Sybil was reading Froebel and Pestalozzi on the education of children; Stevens, on the other hand, was more interested in her and said as much in "To Miss Gage":

> Froebel be hanged! And Pestalozzi—pooh!
> No weazened Pedagogy can aspire
> To thrill these thousands—through and through—
> Or touch their thin souls with immortal fire.
>
> Only in such as you the spirit gleams
> With the rich beauty that compassions give:
> Children no science—but a world of dreams
> Where fearful futures of the Real live. (*SP*, 103)

Peckham and Stevens also went on a memorable hunting trip to British Columbia in the summer of 1903. With a note of affectionate forbearance, Stevens captured in his journal the personality of his mentor in the Canadian wilds: "W.G.P. sits up with his lamp translating Heine aloud endlessly; or else retelling his eternal cycle of stories" (*SP*, 119–20).

Three months before his bar examination, still clerking with Peckham, Stevens wrote of a new despondency. His loneliness was acute, and there was a natural anxiety as he faced the imminent demands of his chosen career. "Here am I, a descendent of the Dutch, at the age of twenty-five, without a cent to my name, in a huge town, knowing a half-dozen men & no women. God help us, what a lark!" (*SP*, 128). A week later he was in "the Black Hole again" (*SP*, 128), yearning for companionship. There was relief in long walks, a series of Shakespeare plays, or an evening on the town with his friend Charles Dana, but the sense of dislocation was as painful as were the final months at Harvard when another transition loomed.

Stevens was admitted to the bar on June 29, 1904. His career did not begin auspiciously. The practice itself he found taxing and tedious; the financial rewards were sparse, requiring him to live austerely in various boardinghouses around the city. To his future wife he wrote in 1907 that the practice of law was "surely the quaintest way of making a living in the world. Practicing law is only lending people the use of your bald-head. It is silly" (*L*, 124). He had met

Elsie Kachel in Reading in the summer of 1904, and his letters indicate that he was deeply in love by the time he returned to New York
and his new office.

Lyman Ward, a casual acquaintance from Harvard, joined Stevens in setting up a partnership in September. The firm, Ward and
Stevens, was not a success. Stevens remembered Ward more than
thirty years later in a letter to his business associate Philip May: "At
that time he had a good deal of money at his disposal; at the same
time he was inclined to believe what people said to him (as a
gentleman should do) with the result that he had to confess, rather
sadly, one day that he needed a job" (*L*, 318). So, of course, did his
partner, whose own inexperience cannot have aided the situation.
His journal, which captures the activities of his evening hours and
weekends, is totally reticent on the firm's collapse. On the last day
of 1905 he found himself "frightened at the way things are going,
so slowly, so unprofitably, so unambitiously" (*SP*, 156). Four
months later he found it a "splendid melancholy" to "get my pipe
going well, and meditate on suicide." Far from utter despair, however, Stevens found his gloom "mixed with a little beer and whiskey—divine" (*SP*, 164).

It is not easy to assess the degree of Stevens' depression, especially during the years he was courting Elsie. The letters to her are
hardly self-pitying, and the journal itself was given over to activities in which he took a positive interest. It is only the occasional
entry that undisguises the quiet desperation in which he lived the
first decade of the new century. On September 15, 1906, for example, he notes tersely: "Out of work" (*SP*, 171). Another brief
entry six weeks earlier may account as much as anything for
his need to go job-hunting: "Engaged at the office all day on a
sonnet—surreptitiously" (*SP*, 170). His employment had been
with Philbin, Beekman, and Menken, and then with Eaton and
Lewis. "I am drifting" (*SP*, 175), he appreciated in April of the
next year, and in October he reported "three months of idleness"
(*SP*, 185). He began an association with Eustis and Foster in late
1907, but it lasted only three months. In the three years since passing the bar, Stevens had witnessed the failure of his partnership,
followed by a rapid shuttle through three other firms. The prospects for his own desire to write, not to mention his future with
Elsie, must have seemed shadowy indeed. "I do not know what to
think," he wrote toward the end of 1907. "I am intent on getting

something of consequence, and it seems to be impossible. But I'll get it or leave New-York" (*SP*, 185).

Much of the work was dull. "My office [at Eaton and Lewis] is dingy, and I go to and from it, underground," he wrote without elaboration in 1907 (*SP*, 171–72). In addition, he was not earning much more than he had as a *Tribune* reporter. During his clerkship with Peckham he had recognized that he was "starting at the bottom" and it made him aware of "millions of fellow-men struggling at the same point, of whom one previously had only an extremely vague conception" (*SP*, 114). Although he could scrape together enough money to buy books, see an occasional play, or enjoy an evening out eating and drinking, he was parsimonious. Shortly after the commencement of his partnership with Ward, he wrote: "Living a strange, insane kind of life. Working savagely; but have been so desperately poor at times as not to be able to buy sufficient food—and sometimes not any" (*SP*, 142). Six months later he confessed an inclination "toward deviltry now and then, but *only* a little. I have money in pocket but not in bank & I pay most of my bills promptly & all of them eventually. Still my hands are empty" (*SP*, 144–45).

From his arrival in New York until the time of his marriage, Stevens' professional instability was paralleled by his changes of residence. His frequent moves are another indication both of his rootlessness and his solitude. He lived in boardinghouses, usually in a single room that held bed, chair, table, and lamp. He carted around a growing library, many of the books from his classes at Harvard as well as more recent acquisitions. Meals were served in common to boarders in several of the houses. Stevens quickly grew restless in such establishments; he could move from one to another, but he could not escape them. His journal indicates that a change in season was frequently an invitation to find a new place. After inhabiting several houses in Manhattan, he shared rooms for a while in 1904 with Arthur Clous, an old classmate from Reading, but soon moved to East Orange, New Jersey. A year later he was back in Manhattan at Fordham Heights. There were regular moves until he settled at 441 West Twenty-first Street with Elsie after their marriage.[6] In one of his last temporary locations one of

---

6. Stevens later spoke to his mailboy, Richard Sunbury, of his unhappiness during these years: "He said he despised living in a hall bedroom. . . . I guess for a while there he was

the "old maid" European schoolteachers living there wrote a short verse and presented it to her fellow tenant:

> He shakes his head, this stalwart chap,
> And says he doesn't care a rap,
> Nor give a single finger snap,
> For all this wearisome clap-trap.
>
> just beware for you will find
> He's pessimistic still in mind.
> Is there a cure for Mr. S—?
> We all smile in saying "Yes!" [7]

Although Elsie accepted the indefinite delay before marriage, the long courtship proved troublesome. Wallace found her "unmanageable" (*SP,* 174) midway through it, and there was a time in the summer of 1906 when they apparently came near breaking it off. A year later he redefined their dilemma: "This morning, on the train, I thought that we were like two people in a dark room groping for each other. Once in a long while our hands touch and we get a glimpse of each other. Then we are lost again. —It is very hard to lose you this time, harder than ever before, because we both feel that we are becoming 'all letters,' as you said." [8] The strains were inevitable, given their separation and the uncertainty of their future.

Only eighteen at the time of their meeting in 1904, Elsie was seven years younger than Wallace. She was small and delicate in frame and had strikingly beautiful eyes. She lived with her mother and stepfather in an area of Reading that was socially inferior to the part of town where the Stevenses resided. She was born only a few months after her parents' marriage, and her father died a year later. Holly Stevens believes she "suffered from a persecution complex which undoubtedly originated during her childhood" (*SP,* 137). She was inveterately shy all her life. Her formal education consisted of grammar school and less than a year of high school. She was an accomplished pianist and went to work in a department store where she sold sheet music by playing the songs on the pi-

obliged to just secure that sort of accommodation" (Peter Brazeau, *Parts of a World: Wallace Stevens Remembered* [New York, 1983], 36).

   7. Wallace Stevens to Elsie Moll [Kachel], July 9, 1909.
   8. Wallace Stevens to Elsie Moll [Kachel], April 3, 1907.

ano. Stevens' introduction to Elsie is described in one of the genealogical notes she wrote in 1945. Although she is uncertain about
the year, the note recaptures scenes of the blossoming courtship:

> On July 7th 1903? in 1904? Mr. John Repplier (then a slight acquain-
> tance of the writer, and a neighbor of the Stevens family) brought
> Mr. Wallace Stevens to her parents home, and at this time introduced
> Mr. Stevens to her, and to three friends who were spending the eve-
> ning with her; the sisters Misses Alice and Clare Tragle, and Miss Har-
> riet Heller. Mr. Stevens had been away from home a number of years,
> and was in his 25th year of age when he came to Reading to spend the
> summer with his parents. On returning to Reading, he found that his
> friends were either married, or had left Reading, so he made friends
> with their younger brothers, and Johnny Repplier was one of them.
> That evening, the six of us had a pleasant time on the front porch,
> and singing Gilbert and Sullivan songs at the piano. During the re-
> maining summer Mr. Stevens spent many evenings and Sunday after-
> noons with the Tragle sisters, as well as with the writer, until Septem-
> ber, when he returned to New York City to begin the practice of law.[9]

The courtship, as it is described through those letters by Stevens
that Elsie did not destroy after his death, was filled with moral ear-
nestness and discreet affection, as well as a playful banter and teas-
ing. Stevens nicknamed her "Bo," himself "Buck."

In an excerpt from an early letter, preserved in a notebook by
Elsie, Stevens alluded to his economic aspirations in New York: "I
mean to keep as busy as I can, so that in the end I shall have something to show for the trouble of keeping alive" (L, 79). What was
not said, though clearly implied, was that their own future depended upon the successful realization of that goal. One can only
speculate at the anxiety the young attorney suffered as a result of
his early professional setbacks. At about the same time, he introduced his still unquenchable goal to her: "I should like to make a
music of my own, a literature of my own, and I should like to live
my own life" (L, 79). Elsie may have paid little attention to his occasional hints at literary ambitions, though she was sympathetic
enough at the time. In later years she separated herself almost entirely from that part of her husband's world. Stevens shared with

9. Elsie Stevens, "A Branch of the Bright Family" (1945) (Typescript, in Huntington
Library), 24–25.

her his intentions, saying in one of the excerpts she preserved: "I feel as if I could begin to write all over again—it is almost self communion with me."[10]

By March, 1907, after the several job changes, he confessed his sense of continuing futility, again implying that their own plans were no nearer a fixed settlement: "Sometimes I think that if things do not go well soon, I'll pack up and go to California or some other outlandish place. There is so little in New-York that I desire enough to work for: certainly I do not desire money, and yet my thoughts must be constantly on that subject. It is active, gay (at times), powerful, interesting and full of people who say that they would rather be lamp-posts on the Bowery than cedars in Lebanon. But, of course, I'm of the cedary disposition" (*L*, 100). Even a few months before their marriage, he wrote to Elsie: "I wish I could spend the whole season out of doors, walking by day, reading and studying in the evenings. I feel a tremendous capacity for enjoying that kind of life—but it is all over, and I acknowledge 'the fell clutch of circumstance.' —How gradually we find ourselves compelled into the common lot!" (*SP*, 217).

At the beginning of 1908, Stevens joined the New York branch of the American Bonding Company of Baltimore. It marked the beginning of what was to be his permanent work with the legal staff of large insurance companies. He would hold the position for the next six years, eventually becoming resident assistant secretary and participating in various settlements around the country. His prospects must have heartened him at once, though his income remained modest. For his fiancée's birthday in June of that year he undertook his first extensive gathering of poems since his time at Harvard. The twenty short lyrics copied out in what he called the "Book of Verses" are slight and unexceptional, but his sheer delight in their composition, releasing the long-deferred pleasure of "song," is apparent:

> A month—a year—of idle work,
>     And then one song.
> Oh! all that I am and all that I was
> Is to that feeble music strung,
>                 And more. (*SP*, 193)

10. "Excerpts from Letters of Wallace Stevens from 1904—" (Notebook, in Elsie Stevens' hand, in Huntington Library), 5.

Only one other poem in the sequence points autobiographically to his toleration of urban life and labor, "In Town":

It's well enough to work there,
When so many do;
It's well enough to walk the street,
When your work is through.

It's night there that kills me,
In a narrow room,
Thinking of a wood I know,
Deep in fragrant gloom. (*SP,* 195)

After a year with the American Bonding Company, Stevens was formally engaged to Elsie, the wedding set for the following autumn.

A genuine pleasure and satisfaction in his legal responsibilities, even after assuming his new position in 1908, seem to have eluded Stevens until he moved to Hartford. In July of that year he purchased a copy of Herbert W. Paul's biography of Matthew Arnold and marked these words: "Matthew Arnold was as sociable as Browning, and as genuine a poet. But he had to work for his living, and either the Education Department or the critical faculty almost dried up the poetic vein." The demands of his own business routine sapped his energies in a similar fashion. In the summer before his marriage he complained to Elsie: "And promptly at nine o'clock to-morrow the stale round of the office will commence all over again and I must grind for six days before I can get back to the sun."[11] Stevens' despondency in the years before his marriage was the most acute of his life: not only was the wedding itself indefinitely postponed but the professional and financial rewards he had come to expect now eluded him. Only the occasional walks that led him outside city and office offered respite. The ethic of work seemingly had betrayed him; the aesthetic of art offered occasional solace, but his own art had found little outlet in the years since he left Harvard.

After a courtship of more than five years, they were married in a private ceremony in Reading on September 21, 1909. A week before, Stevens wrote that he had "decided to get along without a

11. Herbert W. Paul, *Matthew Arnold* (New York, 1903), 175; Wallace Stevens to Elsie Moll [Kachel], July 18, 1909.

best man. There is no one at home whom I should care to ask, or, in fact, of whom I can think. And if I asked any one from New York, we should have to come back with them-him." Elsie described the ceremony in a terse note written many years later: "We were married by Rev. William H. Myers, in Grace Lutheran church in Reading, attended by the bride's parents and two bridesmaids, Miss Anna Rigg, and Miss Mary Stoner." The Stevens family's absence suggests that gradual dissociation had become a complete break. With one of his business associates, John Ladish, Stevens once discussed the occasion from the perspective of many years. Ladish recalls, "He'd [Stevens] rush over to the girl's [Elsie's] place, and the family would never see him until it was time for him to leave. After that had gone on for some time, his father said, 'If you're going to consider our home just a hotel, just a place to bring your laundry, you might as well not come at all.' They had words, and this was the last he saw of his father. He regretted this very much, because the father died [in 1911] without ever having spoken to him. He brooded over that over the years." When Elsie visited the Stevens' home during the courtship, there was further unpleasantness. Stevens' niece recalls the event: "Mamma said that Wallace was so proud. She [Elsie] came in, so elegant-looking dressed that way. Just didn't work out too well. Wallace said, 'I'll never come back. I'll never come back into this house!' That's what Mamma told me, 'cause she was there." The wedding announcement in the Reading *Eagle* states that the ceremony "was witnessed only by immediate relatives." Stevens had asked Elsie a week before the wedding if her stepfather would be present: "It would be pleasant to have him—for then I should not feel so much like the captive of four ferocious women—and he and I could support each other."[12]

He and Elsie lived on the top floor of a house across the street from the General Theological Seminary and owned by the sculptor Adolph Weinman. It was Stevens' first true sense of home since he left Reading as a Harvard freshman twelve years earlier. The forty "June Book" poems—there had been a second collection in 1909—had pleased both Elsie and himself. But Stevens was still

12. Wallace Stevens to Elsie Moll [Kachel], September 13, 1909; Elsie Stevens, "A Branch of the Bright Family," 25; Brazeau, *Parts of a World*, 256, 262; Reading *Eagle*, September 21, 1909, p. 5; Wallace Stevens to Elsie Kachel, September 13, 1909.

several years away from the satisfactory compromise between a steady professional income and his serious dedication to poetry.

Stevens' father died in the summer of 1911, and there is no record of his son's reaction. Garrett's influence over Wallace's decision to enter law school had occurred a decade earlier. And, as Stevens later explained to his niece, it was John, his younger brother, who had looked after Garrett in his declining years:

> About ten years before his death (you may or may not know of this) he had nervous prostration, and John took him to the Adirondacks, where they had made a long stay. After some six months or so he returned to Reading, and, little by little, got back into practice. For a while he seemed to have been completely remade, but he took no exercise and, while the complete change in his habits, as, for example, going to bed early instead of late, kept him going, it failed to keep him in good shape, so that, by the time the photograph that the people in Reading have was taken, he had become flabby and must have been very unhappy about it.
>
> Personally, I intend to forget all that because I think that we have to take him as he wanted to be. (*L,* 454)

It is obvious that Stevens can only imagine his father's unhappiness over his physical decline. Garrett's psychological victory in the matter of his second son's future had been accompanied almost simultaneously by physical collapse. It left the son with ambivalent emotions, but there was no real reconciliation with his father. Garrett's ideals, however, his hardy conservatism, his principles of work and sacrifice, had gradually become Stevens' own and would remain a permanent part of his identity. Thirty-three years later, in writing "Esthétique du Mal," Stevens added these lines:

> It may be that one life is a punishment
> For another, as the son's life for the father's.
> But that concerns the secondary characters.
> It is a fragmentary tragedy
> Within the universal whole. The son
> And the father alike and equally are spent,
> Each one, by the necessity of being
> Himself, the unalterable necessity
> Of being this unalterable animal.
> This force of nature in action is the major
> Tragedy. This is destiny unperplexed,
> The happiest enemy. (*CP,* 323–24)

Within days of his father's death, Stevens learned that a hoped-for promotion was stymied by the choice of another, a man named J. Collins Lee. He admitted his disappointment to Elsie, who was back in Reading: "You will recall that I always said that Lee stood in my way—and I know that they are all loyal friends of mine. Only now that Lee is taken care of, I should be next in line." He added his determination to carry on: "I fully intend to continue along my present line—because it gives me a living and because it seems to offer possibilities. I am far from being a genius—and must rely on hard and faithful work" (L, 170).

His mother, whom he had "not been able to see . . . often for ten years or more" (L, 172), began to fail the following year. Stevens returned to Reading to visit her in May of 1912 and again two weeks before her death in July. In *Schemata,* a notebook with short entries for future poems, he included "The mother, the one unknown." Perhaps because he was absent from work after his mother's death, he wrote to Elsie, who was vacationing at a resort in Vinemont, Pennsylvania, that "the events of July set me back so much that even as it is I shall be able to make progress only by making use of every dollar." [13]

In spite of his protestations, Stevens' steady application to his work was paying off. In the spring of 1914 he left the American Bonding Company to become New York resident vice-president of the Equitable Surety Company of St. Louis. This would be followed two years later by the move to Hartford and the permanent association with the Hartford Accident and Indemnity Company.

13. Wallace Stevens to Elsie Kachel Stevens, August 11, 1912.

# 3 ✐ Toward *Harmonium*

In all likelihood it was because the practice of law was in his own mind removed from "the great things in life" (*L,* 426) that he made so little success of it at first. The journals he kept during the New York years corroborate this on every page. What was memorable enough to note down had little to do with "the quaintest way of making a living in the world." His interior self, that "decent person in private life," had a separate existence that was far more vibrant and thriving than his professional one. Stevens' apprenticeship as a poet is found here: in the books he read, the exhibitions he saw, the plays and musical performances he enjoyed, the very seasonal changes that never failed to fascinate him. His personal habits, too, played a role as his mature personality emerged and became in large part fixed. His isolation, for example, fostered his peculiar introspection and absorption in the printed word. One senses that Stevens' closest companion from the time he arrived in New York until the letters to Elsie began and even beyond was the journal itself, which received all his most intense impressions, theories, and opinions. In addition, the joy he had derived from the country around Reading was now found in long walks outside New York City as well as visits to the more familiar terrain back home. He was also moving in an important way toward formulating his own theological convictions. In all these spheres, Stevens' poetic life was being shaped, and his zeal was in no way curbed by the strains of his chosen career.

When Stevens chided himself for knowing only "a half-dozen men & no women" after his first few years in New York, he was in fact acknowledging his own preference. From the time he arrived at the age of twenty until his marriage when he was almost thirty, his life remained largely private. Like Hawthorne after leaving Bowdoin, he had a penchant for retirement. Hawthorne recalled his twelve years of isolation in Salem: "I had always a natural tendency . . . toward seclusion; and this I now indulged to the utmost, so that, for months together, I scarcely held human intercourse outside my own family."[1] Stevens had not even family, though he was attending law classes and later practicing law. The great isolation of Hawthorne, Dickinson, Robinson, and Stevens suggests a peculiar disposition of many American writers: their self-consciousness, their distrust of the world beyond an immediate circle, and, above all, the great inward probing that their art variously discloses. Even after his marriage, Stevens cherished his solitude; his daughter recalls that during her childhood "we held off from each other—one might say that my father lived alone" (*SP,* 4). The pattern of self-removal had begun as early as his first year at Harvard, when he chose to remain there alone instead of returning to Reading for the holidays.

When he first arrived in New York, he was far from secure in his new resolutions for the future. But he could at least congratulate himself on self-reliance. No doubt feeling the lack of companionship he had recently enjoyed at Harvard, he now begrudged those years of conviviality: "But Harvard feeds subjectivity, encourages an all consuming flame & that, in my mind, is an evil in so impersonal a world. Personality must be kept secret before the world. Between lovers and the like personality is well-enough; so with poets & old men etc. & conquerors & lambs etc.; but, for young men etc. it is most decidedly a well-enough to be left alone" (*SP,* 82). Only twenty, Stevens had already seen the world as impersonal and open personality as evil. With an air of newly found wisdom, he touted "self-dependence" as "the greatest thing in the world for a young man" (*SP,* 82). Six months later, the experience of witnessing the birth of a new century was shared only with his journal as he sat alone in his room.

"It is brutal to myself to live alone" (*SP,* 81), he also noted in his journal shortly after arriving in New York, and there is no doubt that Stevens occasionally tasted the gall of his isolation. "The very animal in me cries out for a lair. I want to see somebody, hear somebody speak to me, look at somebody, speak to somebody in turn. I want companions" (*SP,* 128), he wrote a few years later.

---

1. Mark Van Doren, *Nathaniel Hawthorne* (New York, 1949), 24.

Stevens was not a recluse; he saw old Harvard classmates from time to time, enjoyed the company of various friends like Russell Loines, Arthur Clous, Charles Dana, and Walter Butler for an evening's recreation or a weekend hike. His brief flirtation with Sybil Gage had occurred in the summer of 1902 while he was visiting the Peckhams. After 1904 he returned to Reading frequently to see Elsie. But the young man did not often seek out company; his toleration of others was limited. "I detest 'company' and do not fear any protest of selfishness for saying so" (*SP*, 163), he wrote in 1906. Earlier in the same year he had described one of his walks: "I loathed every man I met, and wanted to get away, as if I were some wild beast. People look at one so intimately, so stupidly" (*SP*, 158). Stevens was awkward in social exchanges, handled small talk with difficulty, and was offended by uninvited familiarity.

Stevens' aloofness, even to the point of snobbish disdain, is one of his least attractive traits, and it was present to some degree throughout his life. The preference for his own inner life frequently made him appear more scornful than he was, however. It was shyness more than misanthropy that set him apart. At the same time, his removal from others extracted a hard personal price, accounting as much as anything, I suspect, for his inability to take hold successfully of his law practice. To his fiancée he wrote of his impatience with his associates and clients: "What I mean is that these hideous people here in the house (it is not polite to say so) and the intolerable people that come and go all day at the office—they make up the far country and occupy me so much that I forget that I am not one of them and *never* will be" (*L*, 131). A sentence from another letter, apparently destroyed, was rescued by Elsie: "I do not get on well with my equals, not at all with my superiors. Ergo, I have no friends."[2]

Nor did marriage awaken in Stevens the desire for a wider circle of friends, and Elsie, unaccustomed to long days in the empty apartment on Twenty-first Street, grew restless. Before their move to Hartford in 1916, it became her custom during the summer to return for extended visits to Reading and later to resorts in Vinemont, Pennsylvania, and Woodstock, New York. In 1915, while

---

2. "Excerpts from Letters of Wallace Stevens from 1904—" (Notebook, in Elsie Stevens' hand, in Huntington Library), 43.

she was at Woodstock, Stevens wrote: "I think that it is not only my desire for solitude that suggests vacations to me. It appeals to my pride to be able to send you away. I have not made much progress, as the world goes; but I forget that, when I can feel that you are away in the country."[3]

I have dwelt at some length on Stevens' solitude, both to demonstrate the extent to which it influenced his social, professional, and married life, and to observe its role in the poet's evolution. If isolation was a personal burden at times, it was also a liberation. "I long for Solitude," he had declared to Elsie early in their courtship, "not the solitude of a few rooms, but the solitude of self. I want to know about myself, about my world, about my future when the world is ended" (*L*, 80). Behind this yearning lay not a neurotic egotism but the most scrupulous self-discipline and training. The year 1907, for example, two years before his marriage, represented one of the most discouraging and exasperating of his professional life. He went from Eaton and Lewis to "three months of idleness" to a brief connection with Eustis and Foster. Toward the end of the year, it seemed impossible that he would get "something of consequence" (*SP*, 185). In April, Elsie had proved "more or less unmanageable." Back in the city he was "scornful of the people around me" (*SP*, 180). The journals and letters, however, disclose that during the same twelve months his hours of isolation and "idleness" were spent in a prodigious regimen of reading, which included: *Letters of John Keats;* Boswell's *Life of Johnson; The Note-Books of Matthew Arnold; The Proverbs* (New York American Bible Society); "a volume of lectures on Greek subjects"; J. S. Phillimore's translation of Propertius; Bourget's *Une Idylle Tragique; The Carmina of Catullus;* Sellar's *Roman Poets of the Republic;* Mackail's *Select Epigrams from the Greek Anthology;* at least one Roman history by Gaston Boissier; Metchnikoff's *Nature of Man: Studies in Optimistic Philosophy;* and *Discours de Nicholas Machiavel sur la première décade de Tite Liue.* There are random quotations from Balzac and Rabelais in the journal for that year and transcriptions from the *Nation* and *Journal des Savants.* Although unmentioned in the journal, the following books were also purchased, signed, and

---

3. Wallace Stevens to Elsie Kachel Stevens, August 30, 1915.

dated in 1907: S. H. Butcher, *Harvard Lectures on Greek Subjects;* John Davidson, *Holiday and Other Poems;* George Moore, *The Bending of the Bough;* Sir Walter A. Raleigh, *Shakespeare;* and R. A. M. Stevenson, *Velasquez.* Stevens took the journal with him on his evening visits to the Astor Library, and it became his notebook. His catholic taste embraced the classical and modern; French as well as English; history, literature, biography, and philosophy. In an early letter to Elsie he asked, "Are you really fond of books—paper valleys and far countries, paper gardens, paper men and paper women? They are all I have, except you; and I live with them constantly" (*L*, 80).

The New York stage was a favorite entertainment, and musical comedies especially became a lifelong attraction. He saw Sarah Bernhardt's *Hamlet* in 1900 and felt compelled to defend the production in his journal. Ethel Barrymore as Mme. Trentoni in Clyde Fitch's *Captain Jinks of the Horse Marines* so delighted him that he saw it three times in 1901. Shortly after, he outlined in his journal the plot of "Olivia; A Romantic Comedy," a play he planned to write but never did (*SP,* 98–99).

"Work, concerts, letters from Elsie, books, jaunts around town—these are what I seem to live for" (*SP,* 144). The jaunts frequently took him beyond Manhattan—along the Hudson River and over into the New Jersey countryside. Here Stevens discovered a new landscape, one that differed from the area around Reading, but one in which he took as much pleasure. The long walks were taken year-round, and he took advantage of being able to take a train back to the city at the end of the day. Here, too, Stevens found relief from the stresses of his unsettled urban existence, a reconnection with nature's scenes he had loved as a boy. After he met Elsie in 1904, his visits to Reading allowed him to rediscover the countryside there. Just before their marriage, he wrote Elsie about the contrast between his two worlds:

> There is one fundamental difference that has nothing to do with the difference in the country itself. I am not emotional; but I am aware that I look at the country at home with emotion. The twenty years of life that are the simplest and the best were spent there. It has become a memorable scene. But I do not look at the country here with emotion.

When it is beautiful I know that it is beautiful. When the country at home is beautiful, I don't only know it; I feel it—I rejoice in it, and I am proud. (L, 148)

Perhaps his highest encomium had been expressed a few months earlier. He cherished the memories of rural Berks County: "It is pleasant to think of the sunny villages at home, at intervals along the different roads, by contrast. It is such an enormous relief—yes! enormous!—The truth is, it gets to be a terror here. Failure means such horror—and so many fail. —If only they knew of the orchards and arbors, and abounding fields, and the ease, and the comfort, and the quiet. —One might preach the country as a kind of earthly Paradise."[4]

As the summer at Wily's farm in Berkeley had inspired many of his sonnets and other poems, so the pleasures of his jaunts reawakened his interest in capturing the natural settings he saw. After an outing in 1906 he spoke of his practice of fixing certain scenes by seeking their counterparts in simile (SP, 158). The world of his long walks, unspoiled and unpeopled, found its way into descriptive passages in the journals, as well as the "June Book" poems and other incidental lyrics between 1900 and 1914.

The robust young Stevens set out from the confinement of his various law offices and boardinghouse rooms. "I doubt if there is any keener delight in the world than, after being penned up for a week, to get into the woods on such a day—every pound of flesh vibrates with new strength, every nerve seems to be drinking at some refreshing spring" (SP, 111), he noted just after he turned twenty-three. More than six years later he set out to describe the same pleasure to Elsie: "There is as much delight in the body as in anything in the world and it leaps for use. I should like to snow-shoe around our hills—from Leesport to Adamstown, from Womelsdorf to East Berkeley—long trips made at a jog that would pull the air down and give one life—all day trips, hard, fast; and I could do it very well except for the need of being here" (SP, 204). The New York walks were prodigious—he thought nothing of a twenty- or thirty-mile hike in a single day. Once, in 1902, after waiting for "a friend, who failed to keep his engagement," Stevens struck out on what would be a two-day walk that covered "about

4. Wallace Stevens to Elsie Moll [Kachel], May 17, 1909.

forty miles all in all" (*SP*, 105, 106). About a year and a half later he must have set a personal record: "*Mon luth! Mon luth!* Walked from Undercliff to Fort Montgomery yesterday, just failing of West Point. A good 42 miles. Up at four with the help of an alarm clock" (*SP*, 132). Stevens covered wide territory, but he was fond of pausing to sunbathe or nap in the open air. On occasion he stopped in a local library. Sometimes he accepted a ride in a farmer's wagon and enjoyed picking up local lore. Once he encountered "an encampment of gypsies" (*SP*, 113). There were other adventures: "Killed a fair-sized blacksnake that darted at me in its agonies" (*SP*, 108).

In the country, Stevens found his true home. Absorbed mentally and physically by the ever-changing panorama, he cast aside the cares of his urban routine. One thinks inevitably of the equally ambitious walking tours by Coleridge and the Wordsworths, especially their preparing the *Lyrical Ballads* while hiking through Somerset and Devon. Stevens' pleasures were more solitary, though he was occasionally joined by Dana, Butler, and other friends. His jaunts did not lead immediately to important poems, but the discovery of vistas that combined sweeping prospects and immediate details awoke pleasure not unlike that experienced by his Romantic forebears:

> The fact is I have discovered a solitude—with all the modern conveniences. It is on the Palisades—about opposite Yonkers, reachable by cutting in from the Alpine road at the proper place. Silver ropes of spiders' weaving stretched over the road, showing that my retreat had had no recent visitors. There was no litter of broken bottles or crushed egg-shells on the brown needles—but a little brook tinkled under a ledge into a deep ravine—*deep* en vérité—; two thrushes fidgeted on the logs and in the boughs; stalks of golden rod burned in the shadows like flambeaux in my temple; I thought I heard a robin's strain. Oh! I can fancy myself at my ease there. How often I shall stretch out under those evergreens listening to the showers of wind around me—and to that little tinkling bit of water dripping down among those huge rocks and black crevices! It is really very undisturbed there. (*SP*, 109)

In the summer after completing law school, Stevens joined his mentor and boss W. G. Peckham on a six-week hunting trip to British Columbia. Living in a tent in the wilds of the Canadian Rockies, the two men, accompanied by a guide and cook, hunted grouse, deer, bear, goat, even lions, and fished for trout. Stevens seems more at ease here than in any other place mentioned in his journals, and his daughter recalls that "in the last few weeks before his death he spoke of the trip frequently to me" (*SP,* 117). In the journal he brought along, he poked fun at his companions and himself, and he marveled at the natural splendor surrounding him:

> Further up along the trail I shot a partridge; & near the first trap, be-yond the dead-fall, pumped a bullet into a porcupine's belly (stupid beast). We camped in some tall timber on a foot-hill. The moon cov-ered all the hills with a violet haze & looked through our trees in a strangely distant way. I was awake practically all night. At daybreak, & after I had watched the progress of innumerable stars, Hosey [the guide] started with the teapot in search of water. We were off about six in a great sweat. The slope we ascended seemed interminable & we had barely reached the last [     ] of rocks when Hosey caught sight of a lion. We chased it over the summit but without getting a shot. (*SP,* 124)

The mountainous fields around Reading remained precious also. Of its beauty, as he told Elsie, "I don't only know it; I feel it— I rejoice in it." His friend from boyhood days, Ed Livingood, was available as a hiking companion. On a trip to Reading in the fall of 1900, Stevens listened as his friend read *Paradise Lost* to him. A "sickly Hamlet," Stevens called him, but shared with him a love for literature, the Pennsylvania mountains, and an ever-present bottle of spirits: "We went up to Kuechler's Wednesday afternoon & stayed through the evening. Magnificent moon came up over the hills. Stood in K's yard & apostrophized it. Livy very drunk. Com-ing down the hillsides we would turn to the moon through the trees and hold dialogues with it. Charming night" (*SP,* 87).

After 1904, Elsie frequently joined him on shorter excursions; the courtship sharpened his identity with and devotion to the scenes of his youth. "Yesterday I walked over the hills—down Easter Egg Way and over Oriole Road and up Stone Hill and by Eglantine Hedge. The bell at Spies church clattered as I passed. Looked out over Oley and went round the Lake of the Beautiful Lady and so—home. Elsie was in everything" (*SP,* 168). From one of the letters she later destroyed, Elsie copied a single sentence: "We have turned a whole county into a home and had sunsets for hearth, and evening stars for lamps."[5]

5. "Excerpts from Letters," 10.

"For myself, I live by leaves" (*CP,* 134), says Stevens in "Botanist on Alp (No. 1)," and in "The Rock," leaves are "cure" of self
and world "In the predicate that there is nothing else" (*CP,* 527).
Remade in poetry, the synecdoche of the leaf summarizes the
young Stevens' cherished natural world and widens into the metaphors to which he would return again and again. For the self destined to "the leaves / Of sure obliteration" (*CP,* 69), there remains
a locus of concord with pure reality in "the red ripeness of round
leaves" (*CP,* 453), a reconstruction of that reality as "eternal fo-
liage" fixed upon "essential barrenness" (*CP,* 373), and in the
change of living itself: "In the area between is and was are leaves, /
Leaves burnished in autumnal burnished trees" (*CP,* 474). The
consummation of his love of the earth awaited the arrival of his art,
but throughout his youth, around Reading, along the Hudson, on
the Palisades, or in the snows of British Columbia, Stevens unself-
consciously expressed his devotion. His delight in nature excited
verbal enthusiasm—not for the poems of this period, which are
undistinguished—but for long and evocative passages he preserved
in his journal or shared in letters to Elsie.

Contemplation was, in fact, an inevitable result of his hours
outdoors: "In the early part of the day I saw some very respectable
country which, as usual, set me contemplating" (*SP,* 104). One of
his meditations was directed toward theology. The immanence of
God in nature, his own version of transcendentalism, had been a
discovery at least as early as the 1899 summer in Berkeley. Three
years later, invigorated by a seventeen-mile jaunt in New Jersey, he
reformulated that resolution: "An old argument with me is that the
true religious force in the world is not the church but the world
itself: the mysterious callings of Nature and our responses" (*SP,*
104). In view of the Presbyterian and Lutheran orthodoxy of his
youth, and the transcendentalism of his later teens and early twen-
ties, one might suspect, on the basis of early poems such as "Sunday Morning," "The Death of a Soldier," "A High-Toned Old
Christian Woman," and "Ploughing on Sunday," that Stevens'
third step toward an unqualified atheism was all that remained to
complete his reaction against Christianity. The reality, however,
was more complex. Stevens never embraced an unqualified atheism. He did work out a religious stance during the New York years
that both satisfied his personal disposition and offered a premise on
which the poems like those listed above became possible.

As we have seen, the piety of generations of Stevenses and Zellers, Wallace's thorough training in Christian doctrine, his mother's reading a chapter of the Bible every night to the children, his years in the Christ Church choir, all inculcated in the young Stevens a deep orthodoxy. His journal and letters both published and unpublished reveal that he was a fairly regular churchgoer. As late as 1940, he told Hi Simons, a critic to whom Stevens responded with many answers about his poetry, that "no one believes in the church as an institution more than I do" (*L,* 348). Not to attend a service but to enjoy the solace of meditation, he occasionally visited St. Patrick's Cathedral, as well as Trinity Church and St. John's Chapel. While in Reading in 1905, he took communion, and he recorded in his journal or letters that he attended services on February 28, 1909, August 6 and 20, 1911, August 11, 1912, September 8 and October 31, 1913. He told Elsie in 1907 that "it has always been a particular desire of mine to have you join church; and I am very, very glad to know that you are now on the road" (*L,* 96). Two years later he proposed Lenten exercises for the two of them: "Lent began yesterday and Easter is, therefore, forty days away. We must think specially good things of each other in this season. And we might do some trifling thing. I am going to do without cigars and without cakes or apples etc. at night. Would you, on your part, and for your own comfort, take a brisk walk for an hour each day?—Walking becomes an ecstasy, you will find."[6] Stevens was married in a Lutheran ceremony, and his daughter was baptized in the Episcopal church in 1925. There was no dramatic moment of final renunciation, though, as we shall see, there were doubts and disclaimers. Stevens accepted and participated in the "church as an institution."

It is equally true that his links with formal religion suffered severe strains almost from the time of his arrival in New York and probably even earlier. At the moment of the new century's birth, he noted the great transition with a simple gesture: "I was trying to say a prayer but could not" (*SP,* 95). But in the summer of 1902, Stevens was still adhering to the transcendentalism he had found at Berkeley in his resolution of the debate between fact and ideal. At that time he was "completely satisfied that behind every physical

---

6. Wallace Stevens to Elsie Moll [Kachel], February 25, 1909.

fact there is a divine force." Now, however, there were two Gods, just as there were two Stevenses:

> But today in my walk I thought that after all there is no conflict of forces but rather a contrast. In the cathedral [St. Patrick's] I felt one presence; on the highway I felt another. Two different deities presented themselves; and though I have only cloudy visions of either, yet I now feel the distinction between them. The priest in me worshipped one God at one shrine; the poet another God at another shrine. The priest worshipped Mercy and Love; the poet, Beauty and Might. In the shadows of the trees nothing human mingled with Divinity. As I sat dreaming with the Congregation I felt how the glittering altar worked on my senses stimulating and consoling them; and as I went tramping through the fields and woods I beheld every leaf and blade of grass revealing or rather betokening the Invisible. (*SP,* 104)

Stevens' religious yearnings are based here upon a theology not of reason but of feelings, some evoked in the cathedral, others on the highway. Rational consistency might have forced him to choose between his deities, but he sees "no conflict of forces but rather a contrast." As Santayana had taught him, religion and inductive discourse are separate, the former treating the imagination's domain, where empirical fact is perforce mute. Thus one religious need, paying homage to "Mercy and Love," was satisfied in the church through "the priest in me." Another need, honoring "Beauty and Might," was gratified by "the poet" of nature. Before these moral forces, abstractions of both gentleness and power, Stevens worshipped while conceding that they were "cloudy visions." Leaf and grass revealed part of these forces as simply "the Invisible." This early resolution, founded upon a division of deities corresponding to needs, was the base of Stevens' later religious practice. In the first place, it removed him from formal doctrinal religion, especially Christianity, but left intact parts of the institutional trappings. Second, it could in fact and with "no conflict of forces" accommodate both church and world. Finally, it left to the needs of the imagination the reckonings with the supernatural and its manifestations.

Five years after his visit to St. Patrick's, Elsie was about to be confirmed in the Lutheran church back in Reading. In an obviously troubled letter to Stevens, she spoke of recent objections to her beliefs raised by her friend Alice Tragle, one of the women who had been present when Stevens was introduced to Elsie and whom Stevens himself knew. (That letter is no longer extant.) Stevens replied on March 10, 1907:

> I was more interested than you may believe in what you said about religion. A.T.'s opinions are quite elementary. I have never told you what I believe. There are so many things to think of. I don't *care* whether the churches are all alike or whether they're right or wrong. It is not important. The very fact that they take care of A.T.'s "stupid" people is an exquisite device. It is undoubtedly true that they do not "*influence*" any but the "stupid." But they are beautiful and full of comfort and moral help. One can get a thousand benefits from churches that one cannot get outside of them. They purify a man, they soften Life. *Please* don't listen to A.T., or, at least, don't argue with her. Don't *care* about the Truth. There are other things in Life besides the Truth upon which everybody of any experience agrees, while no two people agree about the Truth. I'd rather see you going to church than know that you were as wise as Plato and Haeckel rolled in one; and I'd rather sing some old chestnut out of the hymn-book with you, surrounded by "stupid" people, than listen to all the wise men in the world.

One wonders how Elsie received his contention that churches "do not '*influence*' any but the 'stupid,'" especially if, as he said, they had never before discussed his religious beliefs. In any case, Stevens swept dogma aside, except for the possible consolation of a life after death. That Stevens himself literally believed in that promise is questionable, though, as we have seen, he told Elsie that he valued his solitude in order to ponder "my future when the world is ended." The lasting value of churches lay in prayers, rituals, hymns, and even sermons, in which he took a special interest. Through the outer forms of faith, an "exquisite device," the heart could be uplifted and the imagination stimulated. As for the rest, "There are other things in Life besides the Truth." The same letter continued:

> I am not in the least religious. The sun clears my spirit, if I may say that, and an occasional sight of the sea, and thinking of blue valleys, and the odor of the earth, and many things. Such things make a god of a man; but a chapel makes a man of him. Churches are human. —I say my prayers every night—not that I need them now, or that they are anything more than a habit, half-unconscious. But in Spain, in Salamanca, there is a pillar in a church (Santayana told me) worn by the

kisses of generations of the devout. One of their kisses are worth all my prayers. Yet the church is a mother for them—and for us. (*L*, 96)

One notes at once the modification of his transcendentalism. No longer did he discover the "Beauty and Might" of the "Invisible" in leaf and grass. Now the transports of nature exalted the human and made a god of the perceiver; even so, the human needed more. In his twenty-eighth year, Stevens found himself reciting "my prayers every night" and defending the virtues of the church.

The issue of Jesus' divinity may have been one of those irrelevant "Truths" he urged Elsie to ignore. He returned to it, however, in 1909, just after he had finished reading a biography of Jesus: "I felt a peculiar emotion in reading about John the Baptist, Bethany, Galilee—and so on, because (the truth is) I had not thought about them much since my days at Sunday-school (when, of course, I didn't think of them at all.)." The biography had aroused enough curiosity that he went to St. John's Chapel in pursuit of the "symbols of that life." In his disappointment he found it no wonder that "the church is so largely a relic." The letter then went on to address the central doctrine of Christianity: "Reading the life of Jesus, too, makes one distinguish the separate idea of God. Before to-day I do not think I have ever realized that God was distinct from Jesus. It enlarges the matter almost beyond comprehension. People doubt the existence of Jesus—at least, they doubt incidents of his life, such as, say, the Ascension into Heaven after his death. But I do not understand that they deny God. I think everyone admits that in some form or other. —The thought makes the world sweeter—even if God be no more than the mystery of Life." Stevens' doctrinal position at this point, still six years before "Sunday Morning," approaches a modified version of Unitarianism, though that sect perhaps would have left unsatisfied his yearning for the "wealth of symbols, of remembrances, that were created and revered in times past" (*L*, 140).

In a letter nine days later he indicated that he had gone on to read the New Testament itself: "And I have a chapter or two to read in that thrilling book—'The New Testament.' That is my latest hobby. Extraordinary things like casting out demons, raising the dead, turning two fishes and five loaves of bread into enough to feed a multitude, and so on. —I know of nothing like them even in

Jules Verne or the Arabian Nights."[7] What is noteworthy in all the correspondence at this time is not his repudiation of an outrageous system of belief, but rather his categorizing it as marvelous. In a letter of May 14, he defined the life of Jesus as "a narration of the most incredible adventures that ever befell a human being" (*SP*, 224). It concerned him not that Christians through the ages had been duped by an impostor, but that they had been stimulated by "extraordinary things" and "incredible adventures."

Stevens' rejection of orthodox Christian faith did not occur as dramatically and absolutely as the letter of May 2, 1909, indicates ("Before to-day I do not think I have ever realized that God was distinct from Jesus"). Almost two years earlier he had thrown out his Bible in "a pile of useless stuff" (*L*, 102). And in 1906 he had attended Christ Church in Reading, but was annoyed by the "idiot eyes, spongy nose, shining cheeks" of a young girl seated near him. "Impossible to be religious in a pew," he had concluded. Even so, his own lassitude left him unsatisfied: "I wish that groves still *were* sacred—or, at least, that something was: that there was still something free from doubt, that day unto day still uttered speech, and night unto night still showed wisdom" (*SP*, 158–59).

By the time Stevens wrote "Sunday Morning" in 1915, he no longer believed in the literal divinity of Christ. That did not, however, lead to disavowal. As he had told Elsie, "Don't *care* about the Truth." Nor did he scorn conventional religious practices. In place of a system of belief, one could possess faith. The source of that faith might be nothing more substantial than an acknowledgment of God as "the mystery of Life," his 1909 definition. It might even be a total fiction, but its human necessity rendered it both trustworthy and praiseworthy. As we have seen, Stevens condoned the outward forms of piety.

His poetry could be bolder, though equally consistent. "Death is absolute and without memorial," he said in a 1918 poem, and "Divinity must live within herself" ("Sunday Morning"). If, like the female protagonist of that poem, he hungered for an "imperishable bliss," it would be realized only in the earth's inexorable rhythms of renewal. Like Plato's archaic charioteer described in "The Noble Rider and the Sound of Words," Christian doctrine

7. Wallace Stevens to Elsie Moll [Kachel], May 11, 1909.

could be reduced to "dear, gorgeous nonsense" (*NA*, 3). But, as Santayana had taught him, the human imagination gave life to all religion, and the imagination now craved fresh religious figures and forms, new fictions to account for "the mystery of Life." Many years later Stevens explained to Henry Church that "the major poetic idea in the world is and always has been the idea of God. One of the visible movements of the modern imagination is the movement away from the idea of God" (*L*, 378). In place of the poetic idea of God, Stevens himself proposed another, human sufficiency within the earth's plenitude. In "Sunday Morning," he posited a future that might succeed Christianity:

> Shall our blood fail? Or shall it come to be
> The blood of paradise? And shall the earth
> Seem all of paradise that we shall know?
> The sky will be much friendlier then than now,
> A part of labor and a part of pain,
> And next in glory to enduring love,
> Not this dividing and indifferent blue. (*CP*, 68)

As early as 1907, Stevens had turned from his transcendental faith in the presence of the "Invisible" permeating the natural world to the discovery that "blue valleys, and the odor of the earth . . . make a god of a man." When the figure of the hero began to evolve, especially after "The Man with the Blue Guitar" in 1937, Stevens' program for a new fiction based upon a Christlike figure both human and superhuman found expression. Unlike Christ, however, that figure was nothing divine, but human in a measure more complete and comprehensive than in any known man:

> They [major men] are
> The fictive man created out of men.
> They are men but artificial men. They are
> Nothing in which it is not possible
> To believe, more than the casual hero, more
> Than Tartuffe as myth, the most Molière,
> The easy projection long prohibited. (*CP*, 335)

That "impossible possible" figure remained an image of the future, and nowhere in his many poetic descriptions does Stevens claim to have found the hero fully. As a result, Stevens' poetic faith, and, I think, his personal faith as well, was finally eschatological, based upon the vague and paradoxical personality of the indefinite future. For the present it was enough to propose the neo-savior and to assume his own role as prophet. "I realize that the definition [of "major men"] is evasive," he told a Cuban correspondent, José Rodríguez-Feo, "but in dealing with fictive figures evasiveness at least supports the fiction" (*L,* 489). Because the object of his faith was inchoate and not incarnate, because it allowed for fictional contours while still waiting its fleshly form, his own faith lingered in shadowy transition. He cast his eye behind and ahead, remaining in his private life as he had found himself in 1905, "tired of the want of faith—the instinct of faith. Self-consciousness convinces me of something, but whether it be something Past, Present or Future I do not know" (*SP,* 158–59).

The efficacy of the mind and its constant reunions with the world were never subjects of doubt for Stevens, and when he began to discover the metaphors to contain that dynamic exchange, he had found his vital subject—and his maturity as a poet was complete. This, far more than the influence of the Imagists, the Symbolists, Oriental art, or the New York poets such as Donald Evans and Walter Arensberg, accounts for Stevens' arrival as a modern poet. The imagination's joyous engagements and rude disengagements with reality, fixed in their changing dramatic settings and appropriate tropes, marked his originality as a poet. He appears to have arrived at that discovery, and the confidence to pursue it in his art, at about the same time that the post-Christian conclusions of "Sunday Morning" were resolved—around 1914–1915.

To re-create the world in fantasy and then to reclaim it in fact had been Stevens' impulse ever since the letters he wrote from Ephrata and Ivyland when he was in his mid-teens. In the following two decades, he reveals over and over that the imagination's life as a personal subject was not a pose he adopted for the sake of writing poems but a constant personal emancipation. We have seen that his inner life fed from many sources: the fields and mountains he traversed, the "paper valleys and far countries, paper gardens, paper men and paper women" (*L,* 80) he found in books, the various cultural opportunities in the city, the love letters he exchanged with Elsie, and what he recorded in the journals.

His 1899 concern with ideal versus fact anticipated, as we have also seen, his absorption in the claims on him by the inner life of imagination and the outer world of the real. In his own circumstances in New York, the conflict frequently took the form of various activities to ease the weight of business cares. A half year after completing law school, for example, he observed in his journal the division between his Sunday, which had included a twenty-five-mile hike and then relaxing at home, and "things as they are" awaiting him on Monday: "But to-night I've been polite to a friend—have guzzled *vin ordinaire* & puffed a Villar y Villar and opened my dusty tobacco-jar—and my nerves, as a consequence, are a bit uneasy; so that the thought of that soft star comes on me most benignly. To-morrow, however, I shall reassume the scrutiny of things as they are" (*SP*, 127). As if to check an inordinate dependency on the "thought of that soft star," he composed a homely aphorism in a letter for Elsie not long after they met: "The young man with his star, or the young woman with her dreams are not as happy as the man with his cow—and the woman with her knitting."[8] For "cow" read contracts and clients, and the epigram suited himself. The pull of both, however, set forth the scope of his future art.

In another single sentence (preserved by Elsie from a letter) the poet declared his aversion to the ordinary: "The plain truth is, no doubt, that I like to be anything but my plain self; and when I write a letter that does not satisfy me—why it seems like showing my plain self, too plainly" (*L*, 109). The letters to Elsie between 1904 and 1909, which frequently took the greater part of an evening to write, are constant demonstrations of that struggle to escape the plain.

> I believe that with a bucket of sand and a wishing lamp I could create a world in half a second that would make this one look like a hunk of mud. (*L*, 80)

> But suppose on a summer day I quoted: "Rest, and a world of leaves, and stealing streams." I should be adding another day to the real one, don't you think? So I might ramble on, only suggesting things, not completing them. I do that too much, and I am afraid that sometimes you must be at a loss for a meaning in my scribbles.[9]

8. "Excerpts from Letters," 6.
9. Wallace Stevens to Elsie Moll [Kachel], April 14, 1907.

And can't you possibly close your eyes and, by imagination, feel that it
is perfectly real—the dark circle of poplars, with the round moon
among them, the air moving, the water falling, and that sweet out-
pouring of liquid sound—fountains and nightingales—fountains and
nightingales—and Sylvie and the brooding shadow that would listen
beside her so intently to fountains and nightingales and to her?—If
only it were possible to escape from what the dreadful Galsworthy
calls Facts—at the moment, no more serious than that neighborly bag-
pipes and a dog singing thereto—. (*SP*, 238)

Perhaps, it is best, too, that one should have only glimpses of reality—
and get the rest from the fairy-tales, from pictures, and music, and
books. (*SP*, 217)

Being in love, separated from the woman he longed to marry, and
forced to communicate by the written word quickened Stevens'
imaginative life and led to a continuing statement of its extraordinary value for him.

What "the dreadful Galsworthy calls Facts" had come to have
associations far less appealing than the ones he had thought about
when he considered the ideal. Facts might consist of drudgery and
frustration in his professional life, or an irrepressible perception of
the commonplace: "One of my maladies is to rub the freshness off
things and then to say, 'So, how commonplace they really are!' But
the freshness was not commonplace" (*SP*, 175). "Facts are like flies
in a room. They buzz and buzz and bother" (*L*, 94), he noted elsewhere. On the other hand, he observed, "the imagination is quite
satisfied with definite objects, if they be lofty and beautiful enough.
It is chiefly in dingy attics that one dreams of violet cities—and so
on" (*SP*, 166).

In these remarks, Stevens plots the issues and responses to
which his future poems would turn again and again. They were the
questions by which he lived his own life, and their urgency was as
great to him as other modes of expression—love poems, elegies,
political poems, personal anecdotes—were to other poets. For Stevens, the persistent and elusive quest for the mind's harmonious
encounter with exterior objects was more than fundamental and
absorbing; it was antecedent to all other human interests.

Through his friendships with Pitts Sanborn, Witter Bynner, Walter
Arensberg, and others he had known at Harvard, Stevens was in-

vited into the New York coterie of poets after he resumed his own writing in 1913–1914. Their encouragement was, in fact, vital. "It was not until ten or fifteen years [after leaving Harvard]," he recalled many years later, "when some friends of mine came down from Cambridge that I became interested again. After that, I began all over." Carl Van Vechten, who met him through Arensberg, found him "full of that esoteric banter which may be described as Harvardian, at least generically, but containing some specific elements which made it original in manner as well as matter." When invited to dinner, however, Stevens answered for himself and his wife: "'We are quiet, mouse-like people, so timid. We would die in the company of eight people.'" Elsie herself did not approve of the drinking, and William Carlos Williams remembers Stevens in these years as "diffident about letting down his hair. Precise when we were sloppy. Drank little." [10]

Stevens was inducted as "part of the gang," but it was a peripheral membership at best. He did make the acquaintance of fellow poets Donald Evans and Mina Loy, in addition to Arensberg, Van Vechten, Williams, and others. More important, Sanborn and Van Vechten immediately began publishing Stevens' poems in a magazine called *Trend*. His work also appeared in *Rogue,* newly founded by Allen and Louise Norton, and in *Others,* the magazine published by Alfred Kreymborg. From Chicago, Harriet Monroe, editor of *Poetry: A Magazine of Verse,* made a place for his poems in a war issue in 1914, followed by "Sunday Morning" in 1915. Stevens' identity as a poet had begun to emerge toward the end of his years in New York, and his literary connections in the city smoothed the way for the publication of his poems.

By the time the poet and his wife left New York in 1916 to take up residence in Hartford, the strategies and counterstrategies that had begun to develop when he left Reading for Harvard in 1897 were pushing toward resolution. His professional life as an attorney, beginning as a director of the Hartford Livestock Company, was at last settled, even if it did not mark a significant promotion, and he

---

10. Stevens quoted in Jerald E. Hatfield, "More About Legend," *Trinity Review,* VIII (May, 1954), 30; Carl Van Vechten, "Rogue Elephant in Porcelain," *Yale University Library Gazette,* XXXVIII (October, 1963), 43, 48; Williams quoted in William Van O'Connor, *The Shaping Spirit: A Study of Wallace Stevens* (Chicago, 1950), 15.

would advance in the company hierarchy. The first *Harmonium* poems were completed between 1913 and 1916, and sponsors like Monroe and Sanborn were soliciting additional work. Stevens was thirty-six years old at the time of the move, his life almost half over. One cannot help speculating whether the long delay had its compensations. To his Irish correspondent Thomas McGreevy many years later he wistfully implied regret: "Of course, I have had a happy and well-kept life. But I have not even begun to touch the spheres within spheres that might have been possible if, instead of devoting the principal amount of my time to making a living, I had devoted it to thought and poetry" (*L*, 669). Stevens was never closer to his voyager Crispin than in these lines from "The Comedian as the Letter C":

> How many poems he denied himself
> In his observant progress, lesser things
> Than the relentless contact he desired;
> How many sea-masks he ignored; what sounds
> He shut out from his tempering ear; what thoughts,
> Like jades affecting the sequestered bride;
> And what descants, he sent to banishment! (*CP*, 34)

If Stevens regretted the decision to postpone poetry for the sake of another profession, he had also benefited, as can be seen only in retrospect. Surely, for him, there was a correspondence between the orderly life and the imagination's idea of order, between the discipline of professional routine and the poet's craft, between private independence and poetic originality. The "happy and well-kept life" was the reality, whatever else it had precluded. He told *Time* in 1955 of the choice he had made at the beginning of his career: "It gives a man character as a poet to have a daily contact with a job. I doubt whether I've lost a thing by leading an exceedingly regular and disciplined life."[11]

The pattern of that ordered, conservative, guarded, long-disciplined, and solitary life was firmly set by 1916. The inner life was what mattered most, and here is a key to Stevens both as poet and as man. Few individuals have so deliberately and elaborately constructed a self that abhorred the trite and the vulgar while conferring such value upon enjoying the recognizably rare. If elitism

11. "The Vice President of Shapes," *Time*, August 15, 1955, p. 12.

is the vice of that personal choice, order, taste, and inner pleasure are its rewards. Had he not compromised with law and business through the New York years, he might never have attained that self-possession. When asked in 1953 to speak at a memorial honoring Dylan Thomas, Stevens refused and, in a letter to Barbara Church, explained why:

> While I did this on the ground that I did not speak well in public and particularly because an *oraison funebre* is not in my line, still I don't think that I should ever have been able to get myself in quite the right mood for such an occasion for Thomas. He was an utterly improvident person. He spent what little money he made without regard to his responsibilities. He remarked that he had done what he wanted to do in this country, that is to say, that he had met so and so and Charlie Chaplin, and had insulted a rich industrialist. Notwithstanding all this, he came constantly like the Sitwells and would have kept on coming as long as there was any money to be picked up. Of course, his death is a tragic misfortune, but, after all, if you are going to pronounce a man's funeral oration you do have to have some respect for him as a man. (*L,* 802)

Although his own personal indulgences were not lavish and his resources were not unlimited, Stevens was able to enjoy his financial success. He characteristically preferred the foreign to the domestic, the old to the recent, an unseen French painting from Paris to one from a New York gallery, a small package of "kee-moon" tea from China, an annual order of fresh fruit from California, a carved Buddha from Ceylon. His chauffeur recalls that "we'd go out looking for strange types of flowers. We went up to Pomfret. . . . He'd spend half of the evening walking around this greenhouse looking for oddball flowers, something that no one didn't have in the gardens some other place." Books, too, were valued for their appearance as well as their contents. The handsome bindings and layouts of his own volumes by the Alcestis Press and the Cummington Press were especially esteemed, and he had his personal copies bound in special leather and slipcased by Gerhard Gerlach, "a pupil of Wiemüller and . . . as good a binder as I know of" (*L,* 419). In an unpublished letter to his art and book dealer in Paris, Stevens defined his criterion for selecting a new painting: "To guide you in choosing pictures by other artists, let me say that I should not mind having a picture by Tal Coat, or any other intelligent painter, regardless of manner, provided it is not ugly. A few really experimental pictures touch one as the pictures, say, of the impressionists touch one because the artist starts out to experiment to the exclusion of everything else. An experimental picture may convey a sense of intellectual rigor or of esthetic vitality that is quite as agreeable as anything else but it must not be ugly." [12]

The exclusion of ugliness was coupled with another value for Stevens. What pleased him most was the immediate beauty of objects, but the beauty was heightened by rarity. Yvor Winters incorrectly accused Stevens of hedonism on the basis of *Harmonium*. Sensuous gratification for its own sake was not the issue for Stevens; more to the point was his ascetic fastidiousness. Food and drink, for example, were all the more pleasurable and satisfying when they came from other countries and climates and were difficult and expensive to procure.

Williams said of Stevens that he "was a man who would never acquire the stigma of a popular appeal. He never stepped down to that. Therefore he earned an undeserved reputation for coldness if not sterility." [13] As we have seen, Stevens could assume the pose of superiority, but his snobbery was coupled with humility. He was never an aggressive self-promoter, either in business or in poetry. Harriet Monroe once claimed she had never encountered a poet more indifferent to the fate of his poems after they had been written. Manning Heard, his business associate and friend, said Stevens never made derogatory comments about other poets or their work. To sound his own horn or to engage in jealous conspiracies against other poets would have violated his sense of inner propriety.

It is in this context, I would propose, that the art and the man converge. Poetry was the supreme expression of the beauty, order, and grace he so yearned for in his own life. The mean and the ordinary could be expunged. Poems could "resist the intelligence almost successfully" (*OP,* 171), but reveal forthrightly a wit, urbanity, and even compassion for the mind's potentialities. They came to disclose an innocent world of parabolic vignettes, a joyous exercise of the mind's comic unpredictabilities, a world ever emerg-

12. Corn quoted in Peter Brazeau, *Parts of a World: Wallace Stevens Remembered* (New York, 1983), 54; Wallace Stevens to Paule Vidal, July 28, 1948.

13. William Carlos Williams, "Wallace Stevens," *Poetry: A Magazine of Verse,* LXXXVII (January, 1956), 235.

ing by subtle apposition, overlapping and even circular progres-
sions. And elegance, always elegance.

Stevens' life after 1916 was no longer a novitiate, either poetically
or professionally. The "whole of *Harmonium*" lay ahead. All that
was wanting was the rhetoric, "*Poesis, poesis,* the literal characters,
the vatic lines" (*CP*, 424), and after the hard years of preparation,
he had begun to find them.

# II ✒ THE CRAFT

# 4 ✍ The Birth of a Modernist

During his years at Harvard, Stevens began to be a poet. With letters, journals, personal books, and manuscripts, one can piece together an outline of his progress. As we have seen, he was by 1916 actively assuming that role, and he quickly made the leap to his particular maturity. In addition to biographical evidence, however, there is another view of Stevens as a poet, and it has to do with the craft of writing itself. From his first verse derived from conventional models to his earliest experiments in modernism, the poet was groping for what he called "an authentic and fluent speech for myself" (*L*, 234). Stevens' style and voice were formed during his long labor toward *Harmonium*. Even after that volume was published, there was a ten-year hiatus. When he took up poetry again around 1933, his methods of composition became fixed.

Harvard conspired in a special way to bring about Stevens' beginnings as a poet. There, he met Russell Loines, the law student who was writing and publishing poetry. As a member of the *Harvard Advocate* staff and then briefly as president, Stevens read the work of his college friends and helped make editorial decisions. The famous sonnet exchange with Santayana occurred during his second year. Perhaps most important of all, Stevens' curriculum introduced him to the poets who were to be his first models:

English 28  (the history and development of English literature in outline)

English 7   (literature from the death of Swift to the publication of the *Lyrical Ballads*)

English 8a  (literature from the publication of the *Lyrical Ballads* to the death of Scott)

English 8b  (literature from the death of Scott to the death of Tennyson)[1]

---

1. Robert Buttel, *Wallace Stevens: The Making of Harmonium* (Princeton, 1967), 251.

Paperbound editions of the Romantics, Victorians, and contemporaries were of course unavailable then, and Stevens gathered an extensive library of clothbound books, inscribed his name and date in most of them, marked them thoroughly, and preserved many of them for the rest of his life. They verify the young man's obviously thoughtful reading of Blake, Wordsworth, Shelley, Keats, Hazlitt, Arnold, FitzGerald, Elizabeth Barrett Browning, Pater, Ruskin, Tennyson, and others. He also delved deeply into Emerson's poetry and prose, as well as the letters of Lowell and his *Fable for Critics*. In his copy of Palgrave's *Golden Treasury of the Best Songs and Lyrical Poems in the English Language,* he underlined and marked vertically in the margin the following note: "They [the English poets from 1800 to 1850] renewed the half-forgotten melody and depth of tone which marked the best Elizabethan writers: —that, lastly, to what was thus inherited they added a richness in language and a variety in metre, a force and fire in narrative, a tenderness and bloom in feeling, an insight into the finer passages of the Soul and the inner meanings of the landscape, a larger sense of Humanity."[2] Stevens' poetry during the Harvard years consists almost entirely of sonnets and quatrains—with the notable exceptions of "Outside the Hospital," "Street Songs," and "Ballade of the Pink Parasol," his most original poems. Stevens published sixteen poems in the *Harvard Advocate* and the *Harvard Monthly;* the class ode ("A Night in May"), published as a keepsake for that occasion in 1900; and a sonnet, which appeared in a New York magazine, *East & West.* The journal, however, includes ten unpublished poems, mostly sonnets; there were almost certainly more, but they were clipped from the pages at some later date and are now lost.

Not surprisingly, the poems constantly echo the work of the Romantics. Keats, most of all, obsessed the young Stevens at Harvard (and would through the New York years as well). The speaker in many of Stevens' sonnets recalls the Keatsian youth who finds himself assaulted by time, age, and a rude summons to duty. Keats's "When I have fears that I may cease to be" is remade in a notebook sonnet by Stevens: "When I think of all the centuries long dead." He re-creates fallen cities, lost kingdoms, and days of

---

2. Francis Turner Palgrave, *The Golden Treasury of the Best Songs and Lyrical Poems in the English Language* (London, 1896), 365.

vanished beauty. The sestet of Stevens' sonnet, however, sets up his youthful resistance to the "tread" of mortality, as if to free himself from the seductive morbidity of Keats's premonition:

> Then my youth leaves me, and the blood
> Leaps in its ardor like a flood.
> Others with hot and angry pride, I cry,
> Others in their thin covered dust may lie
> And give their majesty to some pale bud
> But not—if strength of will abides—not I. (*SP*, 30)

Keats's sonnet had ended: "—then on the shore / Of the wide world I stand alone, and think / Till love and fame to nothingness do sink." For his next sonnet in the notebook, Stevens remade "the shore / Of the wide world" into "this wide and star-kissed plain" and echoed the nightingale's "tender is the night" from the ode:

> The rivers flow on idly in their light
> The world is sleeping, and the golden dower
> Of heaven is silent as a languorous flower
> That spreads its deepness on the tender night.
> The distant cities glimmer pale and bright
> Each like a separate far and flaring bower
> Noiseless and undisturbed in resting power
> Filled with the semblance of a vaster might.
>
> Upon this wide and star-kissed plain, my life
> Is soon to feel the stir and heat of strife.
> Let me look on then for a moment here
> Before the morn wakes up my lust for wrong,
> Let me look on a moment without fear
> With eyes undimmed and youth both pure and strong. (*SP*, 30–31)

With its description of cities in early morning, the sonnet shows a greater debt to Wordsworth's account of London and the Thames at daybreak in "Composed Upon Westminster Bridge." Wordsworth's "river glideth at his own sweet will"; Stevens' "rivers flow on idly in their light." At Westminster Bridge, "the very houses seem asleep," but "the world is sleeping" in Stevens' version. Wordsworth's London wears "The beauty of the morning," and Stevens' "distant cities" are "Noiseless and undisturbed." Finally, both poets delight in the momentary calm before the city returns to life: Wordsworth "never felt, a calm so deep"; Stevens looks on "a moment without fear." In the margin beside "Composed Upon Westminster Bridge," Stevens recorded the memory of his friend Livingood's reciting the poem as they crossed Mount Penn one summer.

Keats's "Bright Star," eternally aloof and "watching, with eternal lids apart," had an influential bearing on the octave of a sonnet published in the *Advocate* in the spring of 1899:

> There shines the morning star! Through the forlorn
> And silent spaces of cold heaven's height
> Pours the bright radiance of his kingly light,
> Swinging in revery before the morn.
> The flush and fall of many tides have worn
> Upon the coasts beneath him, in their flight
> From sea to sea; yet ever on the night
> His clear and splendid visage is upborne. (*SP*, 31)

Stevens' morning star, like Keats's, enjoys a "splendid visage": both gaze down upon "the moving waters at their priestlike task" (Keats) and "The flush and fall of many tides" (Stevens). For the sestet, Stevens may have remembered again "Ode to a Nightingale," with the imperishable bird singing to ancient "emperor and clown," as well as "the sad heart of Ruth." Stevens' morning star peered upon

> Sweet Eden's flowers heavy with the dew;
> And so he led bold Jason on his way
> Sparkling forever in the galley's foam. (*SP*, 32)

The strongest general impression of Keats's language and imagery appears in another sonnet, one Stevens left unpublished in his journal. The poem begins with a confession of a season of "bitter discontent" and long-lasting griefs, relieved at last by "A new and rich repose." The sestet then presents the song of the robin, twin to Keats's "immortal Bird" and to his own remorse overcome:

> It seemed as though upon a mournful world
> A pure-voiced robin had sent forth a ray
> Of long-impending beauty, to allay
> Her wild desire; as though her deep unrest
> Was in a moment's minstrelsy uphurled
> Sweet-startling from her heavy-laden breast. (*SP*, 35)

The synesthesia of the robin's song as a "ray," the oxymoron "Sweet-startling," the robin as ethereally "pure-voiced" while possessing a "heavy-laden breast," and the panacea of "long-impending beauty" are all Keatsian.

"Imitation of Sidney" is another unpublished sonnet from the journal. Stevens had inscribed his copy of Sidney's poems seven months before writing the imitation. Stevens' dedication "To Stella" is followed by an unidentified "(Miss B?)." "Unnumbered thoughts my brain a captive holds," the sonnet begins, and these include pastures by the sea, a tower containing maidens, roses, lovers' nooks, and birds. The poem concludes, "Yet these do all take flight at thought of thee" (*SP*, 50–51). In *Astrophel and Stella,* the speaker catalogs his various diversions and digressions that culminate in his recognition of their presence all the while in Stella herself. "You that do search for every purling spring," which Stevens had marked in his own text, is typical.[3] The speaker as poet addresses those who seek inspiration in "the ribs of old Parnassus," "dictionarie's methode," and imitations of Petrarch. These are, he advises, "wrong wayes" because they lack an "inward tuch." His recourse in the sonnet's final line, like Stevens' concluding "thought of thee," is: "Stella behold, and then begin to endite."

One notes the obvious skill with which Stevens the undergraduate mastered the balanced style and portentous moralizing of his Petrarchan predecessors. As we have seen, Santayana, whose own *Sonnets and Other Verses* Stevens purchased in November, 1899, acknowledged as much by writing his personal response to "Cathedrals are not built along the sea."[4]

Stevens was reading other poets besides the Romantics and Sidney. Buttel's notice of the *Rubáiyát's* influence in a sonnet beginning "Lo, even as I passed beside the booth" is corroborated by Stevens' ownership of that poem in a book that he inscribed in 1898. The unmistakable connection between Stevens' "Vita Mea" ("With fear I trembled in the House of Life") and Dante Gabriel Rossetti is further supported by Stevens' owning *Sonnets of This Century,* an anthology in which nine of the *House of Life* sonnets

3. *The Lyric Poems of Sir Philip Sidney*, ed. Ernest Rhys (London, 1895), 14.
4. In the margin beside "For thee the sun doth daily rise and set," Stevens wrote, "As lovely a sonnet as ever was written" (George Santayana, *Sonnets and Other Verses* [New York, 1896], 48).

are represented. In his essay introducing that anthology, William Sharp singles out Rossetti as "not only one of the great poets of the century, but the one English poet whose sonnet-work can genuinely be weighed in the balance with that of Shakespeare and with that of Wordsworth. No influence is at present more marked than his." Sharp also recommends the sonnet generally as "the best medium, the means apparently prescribed by certain radical laws of melody and harmony, in other words, of nature." Stevens also bought Herrick's *Hesperides & Noble Numbers,* which he dated March 14, 1899.[5] On the previous day Stevens' "Song" was published in the *Advocate,* and its banter and insouciance suggest that he had been reading Herrick before:

> She loves me or loves me not,
>     What care I?—
> The depth of the fields is just as sweet
>     And sweet the sky.
>
> She loves me or loves me not,
>     Is that to die?—
> The green of the woods is just as fair,
>     And fair the sky. (*SP,* 28)

Stevens' imitating the Romantics and Sidney and Herrick was in no way eccentric or original. Russell Loines, for example, composed "Invocation to Autumn"—showing that he, too, had read Keats, in this case "To Autumn." The last stanza of Loines' poem begins:

> Holds not the now maturer earth more dear
>     Thy mellow orchards and thy woodland pride,
> Surveying the fruition of the year
>     Lying along the bounteous country-side?[6]

Stevens' first published poem appeared in a publication of Reading Boys' High School. "Autumn" commemorates loss rather than fruition:

---

5. Buttel, *The Making of Harmonium,* 12; *Sonnets of This Century,* ed. William Sharp (London, 1886), lxxi, xxv; Robert Herrick, *The Hesperides & Noble Numbers,* ed. Alfred Pollard, with preface by A. C. Swinburne (2 vols.; London, 1897).
6. *Russell Hillard Loines, 1874–1922: A Selection from His Letters and Poems with Biographical Sketch and Recollections by His Friends* (New York, 1927), 63.

> Long lines of coral light
> And evening star,
> One shade that leads the night
> On from afar.
>
> And I keep, sorrowing,
> This sunless zone,
> Waiting and resting here,
> In calm above. (*SP*, 16)

Stevens' undergraduate verse is imitative, a discipleship in awe of its masters. Addressing an audience at Harvard in 1936, he said: "When I was here at Harvard, a long time ago, it was a commonplace to say that all the poetry had been written and all the paintings painted" (*OP*, 218).

As we have seen, Stevens kept a journal during his summer at Wily's farm in Berkeley. He recorded impressions, plans, and self-instruction—revealing both his joyful ease in the fields and mountains and his commitment to deliberate poetic observation. The journal also affords the first opportunity to witness Stevens' actually composing poems.

After a long walk on August 1, noting "a number of large birds which were new to me," he jotted down some notes for future sonnets, which included:

> Thought for Sonnet: Oh, what soft wings will close above this place etc. (In the Garden) picture angels, roses, fair world etc. on last day.

> Thought for Sonnet: Birds flying up from dark ground at evening: clover, deep grass, oats etc. to Circle & plunge beneath the golden clouds, in & about them, with golden spray on their wings like dew. Produce an imaginative flutter of color. (*SP*, 51)

Both "Thoughts" were expanded into poems, though the first was to wait almost a decade. The second, describing the circling and plunging birds at evening, inevitably recalls the sinking "flocks of pigeons" with which "Sunday Morning" concludes. That poem was still sixteen years away. More directly, and as a step in the progress toward that poem, part I of the four-part "Street Songs" appeared the following April in the *Advocate* and was subtitled "The Pigeons":

> Over the houses and into the sky
> And into the dazzling light,

Long hosts of fluttering pigeons fly
    Out of the blackened night,
Over the houses and into the sky
    On glistening wings of white.

Over the city and into the blue
    From ledge and tower and dome,
They rise and turn and turn anew,
    And like fresh clouds they roam,
Over the city and into the blue
    And into their airy home. (*SP*, 62)

As prescribed in the journal, the "imaginative flutter of color" became the dominant motif of the spiraling birds, but Stevens transformed the rural setting (clover, grass, oats) into the urban milieu
of the rest of "Street Songs" (city, ledge, tower, dome). The result
remains pedestrian; the impulse to capture an image in a moment
of motion and color would be successful only later.

   The other "Thought for Sonnet" was made into a poem while
Stevens was living in New York City. In a letter to his future wife
he described writing the poem "last week": "Looking over my
diary recently I found the line Oh, what soft wings shall rise above
this place—And so, after ten years, I wrote the rest":

In a Garden

Oh, what soft wings shall rise above this place,
This little garden of spiced bergamot,
Poppy and iris and forget-me-not,
On Doomsday, to the ghostly Throne of space!

The haunting wings, most like the visible trace
Of passing azure in a shadowy spot—
The wings of spirits, native to this plot,
Returning to their intermitted Grace!

And one shall mingle in her cloudy hair
Blossoms of twilight, dark as her dark eyes;
And one to Heaven upon her arm shall bear
Colors of what she was in her first birth:
And all shall carry upward through the skies
Odor and dew of the familiar earth. (*SP*, 210)

The poem almost literally transcribes the imagery outlined in the
journal, including the title, the first line (slightly modified), an-

gels, flowers, and last day. Both "In a Garden" and "The Pigeons" are exercise pieces: the forms, the imagery, the sentiments constructed on "blackened night" versus "dazzling light" and on "haunting wings" versus "familiar earth" are clichés. Stevens' first works as a poet show that he absorbed the fashionable modes of expression and wrote decent imitations of Keats and Wordsworth. With a few exceptions, there is little advance in originality and style between 1899 ("The Pigeons") and early 1909 ("In a Garden").

One other experience during the summer at Wily's, mentioned briefly in the journal, anticipates a poem written shortly after: "The last two afternoons before this I lay in a field near the Hospital and watched the wind in the goldenrod and wild-asters— letting it do my thinking for me" (*SP*, 58). The mention of the hospital is a minor but jarring note in his otherwise serenely bucolic summer. In *Souvenirs and Prophecies*, Holly Stevens speculates that those afternoons may have led to the writing of "Outside the Hospital," a poem Stevens published the following March in the *Advocate*:

> See the blind and the lame at play,
>   There on the summer lawn—
> She with her graceless eyes of clay,
>   Quick as a frightened fawn,
> Running and tripping into his way
>   Whose legs are gone.
>
> How shall she 'scape him, where shall she fly,
>   She who never sees?
> Now he is near her, now she is by—
>   Into his arms she flees.
> Hear her gay laughter, hear her light cry
>   Among the trees.
>
> "Princess, my captive." "Master, my king."
>   "Here is a garland bright."
> "Red roses, I wonder, red with the Spring,
>   Red with a reddish light?"
> "Red roses, my princess, I ran to bring,
>   And be your knight." (*SP*, 58)

Although the poem is juvenile, its diction and rhythm commonplace, its setting is starkly unconventional. Stevens' typical arcadia contains here the clinically actual. As Buttel notes, the "juxtaposi-

tion of the grotesquely real and the gracefully imaginative" introduced "Stevens' central theme," the interplay between "things as
they are" and "things as they are changed" by the imagination.[7]
The patients' fantasy game enables the poem to escape, barely, an
unintended parody of the blind woman as "fawn" and the lame
man as "knight." If the hospital near Berkeley did influence the
choice of setting and perhaps the characters, one observes a process of poetic distillation that did not occur with "In a Garden" or
"The Pigeons." Here, Stevens' casual observation was remade, becoming noticeably bolder.

Three weeks before leaving Harvard, Stevens published the most
original of his undergraduate verse. Altogether removed from the
turgid and decorous sonnets, it looks ahead to the exoticism
and daintiness of poems like "Peter Parasol" or "The Ordinary
Women"—still two decades away. The third stanza of "Ballade of
the Pink Parasol" anticipates in theme and form the later poems of
*Harmonium:*

> Where is the roll of the old calash,
>     And the jog of the light sedan?
> Whence Chloe's diamond brooch would flash
>     And conquer poor peeping man.
> Answer me, where is the painted fan
>     And the candles bright on the wall;
> Where is the coat of yellow and tan—
>     But where is the pink parasol? (*SP*, 66–67)

These lines lead one to speculate how Stevens might have developed in the ensuing years with such bravura as his springboard.
The diction ("old calash"), colors ("yellow," "tan," "pink"), and
imagery ("painted fan," "pink parasol") anticipate the panoply of
many of the *Harmonium* poems. There were, however, no other
poems like "Ballade of the Pink Parasol." Instead, journalism, law
school, and legal affiliations interrupted that progress as he left
Cambridge for New York.

Stevens' journal suggests that working for the New York *Tribune,* studying law, and clerking for Peckham did absorb much of
the energy earlier devoted to writing. It is equally obvious that he
never stopped thinking of himself as a poet. Shortly after his ar-

---

7. Buttel, *The Making of Harmonium,* 29.

rival, for example, Stevens observed, "A city is a splendid place for thinking. I have a sonnet in my head the last line of which is— And hear the bells of Trinity at night" (*SP*, 79). His preference for the sonnet was called into question, though he would continue to write them: "Sonnets have their place . . . but they can also be found tremendously out of place: in real life where things are quick, unaccountable, responsive" (*SP*, 80). He already had presentiments of the contrast between the inherited modalities of the sonnet and the urge to capture the elusive fluctuations around him. His intent is unmistakably modern, but the devices were not yet accessible. A New Year's resolution for 1903 included the plan "to write something every night—be it no more than a line to sing to or a page to read—there's gold there for the digging" (*SP*, 112). A year later he scrawled a short lyric ("Be thou my hood / Bright columbine") in his exhilaration after a forty-two-mile hike through the New York countryside (*SP*, 132–33).

But writing remained dilatory—even as his legal career began precariously. As we have seen, a private practice with Lyman Ward failed, and Stevens moved about from firm to firm in the city. His plan to marry Elsie Kachel, whom he met in 1904, endured a long and troubling postponement as a result. But even during these difficult years, he did not altogether forsake his literary interests: "I dream now of writing golden odes; at all events I'd like to read them" (*SP*, 172), he wistfully recorded in 1907. Only when he joined the New York legal staff of the American Bonding Company of Baltimore in 1908 did Stevens find his professional niche in the world of insurance. In the next year he married Elsie and his life became more settled.

The courtship itself, as much as anything else, stirred Stevens to renewed poetic activity. Under the undisguised influence of *Songs from Vagabondia* by Bliss Carman and Richard Hovey, for example, Stevens sent his future wife three quatrains entitled "From a Vagabond" for Christmas in 1907 and spoke of gathering his own "'Vagabondia' book" (*SP*, 186–87). Carman had preceded Stevens at Harvard by a decade; his popular poems, informed by sentimental optimism, clicking meters, and inevitable rhymes, paraded the free, uncomplicated life of the gypsy. There was little in Carman's poetry to move Stevens beyond his undergraduate work.

In 1908 and 1909, he put together a series of short lyrics for

Elsie in honor of her June birthday.[8] Not since Harvard had Stevens enjoyed such a rush of poetic activity; both collections contained twenty poems. Taken as a whole, the forty lyrics are written in freer meters than were the undergraduate poems: iambic pentameter is all but abandoned; the diction is more colloquial, even prosy in the manner of Carman. But most are still the product of established poetic modes. In the 1909 "June Book," for example, "Noon-Clearing" had sprung from Carman's simple cadence "June comes, and the moon comes," a line Stevens had "hummed . . . for a day" (L, 129) before writing the poem for Elsie. Two months after he finished the collection, his flood of rhymes provoked embarrassment: "In the 'June Book' I made 'breeze' rhyme with 'trees,' and have never forgiven myself. It is a correct rhyme, of course,—but unpardonably 'expected.' Indeed, none of my rhymes are (most likely) true 'instruments of music'" (L, 157).

Its weaknesses notwithstanding, the 1909 "June Book" shows that Stevens was seeking new, expressive voices. With a few exceptions, it is a discernible advance over the 1908 collection. In the same letter regretting his choice of rhymes, he added: "It is astonishing how much poetry I can read with sincere delight. But I didn't see much that was 'new or strange'" (L, 157). He had, in fact, begun experimenting with the effects of novelty and surprise in his own poems. One of them, written for but not included in the second "June Book," anticipates the images of urban decay used later by T. S. Eliot, who was then at Harvard and was discovering Arthur Symons' *Symbolist Movement in Literature.* Stevens' discarded poem began:

> The house fronts flare
> In the blown rain;
> The ghostly street lamps
> Have a pallid glare.
>
> A bent figure beats
> With bitter droop,
> Along the waste
> Of vacant streets. (L, 108)

Stevens himself had been reading Laforgue or Laforgue's imitators when he wrote the last of the "June Book" poems, "Pierrot."[9] The

8. In 1902, Stevens had written a brief, lighthearted love poem (SP, 103) to Sybil Gage. Holly Stevens quotes a love poem to Elsie that he wrote around 1907 (SP, 172).
9. From a letter Stevens wrote sometime in 1907–1908, Elsie preserved these remarks:

persona is predictably a self-ironist whose morbidity and severe self-deprecation were far too somber for the future poet of *Harmonium*. On this occasion, however, he adopted the technique, even to the personification of the indifferent moon:

> I lie dreaming 'neath the moon,
> You lie dreaming under ground;
> I lie singing as I dream,
> You lie dreaming of the sound.
>
> Soon I shall lie dreaming too,
> Close beside you where you are—
> Moon: Behold me while I sing,
> Then, behold our empty star. (*SP*, 234)

Such irony for Stevens was too enervating, and the shocking images of "vacant streets" in modern cities were antithetical to the robust antics of the imagination. Stevens realized from the start that these Symbolist elements, soon to be appropriated in "The Love Song of J. Alfred Prufrock" and "Rhapsody on a Windy Night," would remain the property of others.

He told the critic Bernard Heringman thirty years later that "Verlaine meant a good deal more to me. There were many of his lines that I delighted to repeat" (*L*, 636). The ennui and *tristesse* of Verlaine's *Romances sans paroles*, for example, were another experimental model. In "Ariettes oubliées," Verlaine's surrender to inertia is mirrored in the cancellations of nature:

> Dans l'interminable
> Ennui de la plaine,
> La neige incertaine
> Luit comme du sable.
>
> Le ciel est de cuivre
> Sans lueur aucune,
> On croirait voir vivre
> Et mourir la lune.
>
> (In the ennui unending
> of the flat land

---

"And so when summer came, they went in a boat to [a] quiet island, and on the way, Pierrot pulled out a newspaper and read to Columbine a little news of the stupid world from which he was taking her. But Columbine didn't think it stupid. So Pierrot turned the boat around, and they drifted back to town. Yet even while they were drifting, Columbine thought of the quiet island and she knew that Pierrot was thinking of it too" (*L*, 106).

the vague snow descending
shines like sand.

With no gleam of light
in the copper sky,
one imagines he might
see the moon live and die.) [10]

Stevens adopted a similar pose of weariness in the seventeenth poem of the 1909 "June Book":

I am weary of the plum and of the cherry,
And that buff moon in evening's aquarelle;
I have no heart within to make me merry,
I read of Heaven and, sometimes, fancy Hell. (*SP*, 233)

More encouraging in his development was a new interest in Chinese and Japanese art. In 1908 and 1909, Stevens frequented various Oriental exhibits around town, and, as Buttel has shown, the tapestries, water colors, and prints became an energetic channel into his own work. In May, 1909, he wrote in his journal about some Japanese color prints: "Pale orange, green and crimson, and white, and gold and brown / Deep lapis-lazuli and orange, and opaque green, fawn-color, black and gold" (*SP*, 222). At the time, he was preparing the "June Book." The third poem in the collection, destined to be resurrected in the 1914 "Carnet de Voyage" sequence, was entitled "A Concert of Fishes" and obviously imitates the impression recorded in his journal:

Here the grass grows,
And the wind blows;
And in the stream,
Small fishes gleam:
Blood-red and hue
Of shadowy blue
And amber sheen,
And water-green,
And yellow flash
And diamond ash;
And the grass grows,
And the wind blows. (*SP*, 228)

10. Paul Verlaine, "Ariettes oubliées," Part VIII, in *Selected Poems*, trans. C. F. MacIntyre (Berkeley, 1970), 112–13.

A few weeks later he visited an exhibition of Japanese prints. The catalog was prepared by Arthur Morrison: "Frankly, I would give last winter's hat for a copy of that catalogue" (*SP*, 235). Although the cost then seemed prohibitive, he bought the catalog in August.

Stevens' interest in Oriental art and his attempt to reshape its visual effects into verse led him back to the exotic images and wit of "Ballade of the Pink Parasol." That poem had asked, "Answer me, where is the painted fan / And the candles bright on the wall?" For the ninth poem in the 1909 "June Book," the image was recast. Only the final line lapses into a conventional pose:

> She that winked her sandal fan
> Long ago in gray Japan—
>
> She that heard the bell intone
> Rendezvous by willowed Rhone—
>
> How wide the spectacle of sleep,
> Hands folded, eyes too still to weep! (*SP*, 230)

It is principally through the direct introduction of color, however, rather than such images as the Japanese fan or the small fish, that Stevens sought to create the "new or strange." In this he clearly anticipated the Imagists, though he could not have been aware of T. E. Hulme's coterie then convening for the first time in London. His exercises predate the Imagist experiments in color, such as John Gould Fletcher's "Irradiations," which appeared in *Poetry* in 1913:

> Over the roof-tops race the shadows of clouds:
> Like horses the shadows of clouds charge down the street.
>
> Whirlpools of purple and gold,
> Winds from the mountains of cinnabar,
> Lacquered mandarin moments, palanquins swaying and balancing
> Amid the vermilion pavilions, against the jade balustrades;
> Glint of the glittering wings of dragon-flies in the light:
> Silver filaments, golden flakes, repulse and surrender,
> The sun broidered upon the rain,
> The rain rustling with the sun.[11]

---

11. John Gould Fletcher, "Irradiations," *Poetry: A Magazine of Verse*, III (December, 1913), 85.

Stevens had reproduced several years earlier his own spectacle of rainfall. "Shower," for the 1909 "June Book," would have guaranteed its inclusion in *Des Imagistes,* even though it was written before the organization of the Imagist school and, unpublished, was inaccessible to the eye of Pound:

> Pink and purple
> In water-mist
> And hazy leaves
> Of amethyst;
> Orange and green
> And gray between,
> And dark grass
> In a shimmer
> Of windy rain—
> Then the glimmer—
> And the robin's
> Ballad of the rain. (*SP,* 231)

Each "June Book" is in a sense a long poem. They were composed in sequence and around the general theme of his romance with Elsie, but as with his later long poems, he favored variety in topic and form. The second collection was written at intervals but, toward the end, hastily—again, not unlike his habit and pace of writing long poems years later. He reported to Elsie in April that he was pleased with the speed with which he had gone from the seventh to the fifteenth lyric (*L,* 138–39), and two weeks later, he was almost finished: "Progress with the June Book is a bit delayed, but I am at number nineteen" (*L,* 141). Two days later he boasted, "The June-Book is finished." [12]

Stevens suggested to Elsie the background of one of the lyrics in the 1909 "June Book." He wrote in the evenings, sitting alone in a boardinghouse in Manhattan, the cares of the office thrust aside. Here, he jokingly cast himself as the stereotyped Romantic, groping for the muse's favor: "I read, and then I said, 'I'll write poetry. Young men in attics always write poetry on snowy nights, so—I'll write poetry.' I wrote, 'Only to name again / The leafy rose—' To-to-te-tum, la-la-la. I couldn't do another line—I looked at the ceiling, frowned at the floor, chewed the top of my pen, closed my

---

12. Wallace Stevens to Elsie Moll [Kachel], May 4, 1909.

eyes, looked into myself and found everything covered up" (*L,* 120). It is not without irony that Stevens here mocks the very attitudinizing of arch-Romantic poets, while his poem, upon completion, embraces many of their conventions, including expected rhymes, bland adjectival phrases, and a Keatsian "sweet doom." Ronsard's "Ode à Cassandre" ("Mignonne, allons voir si la rose") may also have been a model for Stevens' poem:

> Only to name again
> The leafy rose—
> So to forget the fading,
> The purple shading,
> Ere it goes.
>
> Only to speak the name
> Of Odor's bloom—
> Rose: The soft sound, contending,
> Falls at its ending
> To sweet doom. (*SP,* 230)

Almost four years after the "June Book" poems and his marriage to Elsie, Stevens suddenly resumed writing and with steadier application than at any time since his undergraduate years. Beginning in 1913 and continuing until the publication of *Harmonium,* a remarkable transformation occurred. The poet began to carve, with mounting confidence, his own place in the emerging panorama of modernism. The advance was not immediately recognizable in his work, but by 1915, Stevens had leapt beyond his earlier experiments. What, we inevitably ask, brought this about? The progress from the undergraduate verses to the second "June Book" was behind him: Symbolist modes had been adopted and most of them discarded; his pre-Imagist ventures, nurtured by his fascination with Oriental art, had proved more rewarding. The appeal of the "new or strange" in poetry was already strong by 1909. Moreover, as we have seen, his personal life, both through marriage and professional advancement, allowed the poet to fix his attention once more upon the vocation that had fired his interests at Harvard and remained unextinguished in the intervening thirteen years. It is noteworthy, I think, that his first concentrated flurries of composition took place in Elsie's summer absences. The rediscovery of temporary solitude, so dear to him and distressing to his wife, was another force of liberation. In 1911, Stevens had apologized to Elsie for the habit: "But personally I find pleasure in too many things not sociable. This is largely the result of many years of isolation and of tastes formed under such conditions. . . . But for all that I see your side of it, too. The society of friends is the sweetest of all pleasures—and the one you enjoy most."[13]

During a week in which he had spent a morning in police court and an afternoon on Long Island examining a new sewer for the American Bonding Company of Baltimore, he also was writing, and with a newly found elation that he described to Elsie on August 7, 1913: "I sit at home o'nights. But I read very little. I have, in fact, been trying to get together a little collection of verses again; and although they are simple to read, when they're done, it's a deuce of a job (for me) to do them. Keep all this a great secret. There is something absurd about all this writing of verses; but the truth is, it elates and satisfies me to do it. It is an all-round exercise quite superior to ordinary reading. So that, you see, my habits are positively lady-like" (*L*, 180). Two years later, his poems began to appear in the magazines *Poetry, Trend,* and *Rogue.* Again in Elsie's absence, he seemed anything but lonely: "The truth is, I do not wish to see anyone but to be alone and quiet, so that I may, if possible, accomplish something. Everything is favorable: that is, there isn't the slightest distraction in town" (*L*, 185). Two weeks later he was still absorbed in the exercise:

> I am quite blue about the flimsy little things I have done in the month or more you have been away. They seem so slight and unimportant, considering the time I have spent on them. Yet I am more interested than ever. I wish that I could give all my time to the thing, instead of a few hours each evening when I am often physically and mentally dull. It takes me so long to get the day out of my mind and to focus myself on what I am eager to do. It takes a great deal of thought to come to the points that concern me—and I am, at best, an erratic and inconsequential thinker. (*L*, 186)

One notes from these first confessions to Elsie several emerging patterns in addition to his preference for solitude. Not only is the composition pleasurable, it is also arduous and secretive. Privacy, relative secrecy, and solitude would remain necessary conditions

---

13. Wallace Stevens to Elsie Kachel Stevens, August 16, 1911.

for his art in the years ahead; only the strenuous exertion, which at this time must have been a process of trial and error, would tax him less.

It is possible that Stevens received little if any encouragement from his wife, though the letters of 1913 and 1915 just cited speak candidly to her of his efforts. Holly Stevens recalls a conflict that must have begun about this time: "While I was growing up my mother did not read my father's poems, and seemed to dislike the fact that his books were published. Questioning her about this after my father's death, she told me that he had published 'her poems'; that he had made public what was, in her mind, very private" (*SP*, 227). In the "Carnet de Voyage" suite, which appeared in the September, 1914, issue of *Trend*, Stevens' eight-poem sequence included five from the 1909 "June Book." A poem from the 1908 collection was published in the same magazine two months later. However much this liberty may have displeased his wife, it demonstrates that in the five years between the second "June Book" and the poems for *Trend*, Stevens had advanced very little as a poet; the progress between the 1908 and 1909 collections for Elsie was dramatically greater. Although his commitment was firmer after 1913, his art required fresh stimuli.

Stevens' secrecy about his work included a natural reticence to put himself forward publicly as a poet or to promote his own work. Only during his undergraduate years had he presented himself as *littérateur*. Some of his friends from Harvard, especially Pitts Sanborn, Witter Bynner, and Walter Arensberg, were helpful now in introducing him to other New York poets and in arranging for his new work to be published. Stevens' confidence in his poems was sufficient to bring him out of his self-imposed anonymity, but not without discomfort and deliberate exertion. Carl Van Vechten recalls Stevens' appearance in 1914 at the editorial office of *Trend*, "blushing and holding forward a tiny piece of paper" as he shyly handed over two poems "written on an absurd half sheet of a woman's note paper in the tiniest handwriting, but they were good poems." Alfred Kreymborg, editor of *Others*, recalls a similar episode from the same time: "So slight was Krimmie [Kreymborg] alongside Wallace that the latter was fond of guiding him across crowded thoroughfares and protecting him against the traffic. On one of these walks, the giant suddenly stuffed a package into his editorial pocket, with the hasty proviso: 'I must ask you not to breathe a word about this. Print it if you like it, send it back if you don't.' It was the manuscript—in the most minute handwriting— of the now famous poem, *Peter Quince At The Clavier*."[14] Even after Knopf had accepted *Harmonium* for publication at Van Vechten's urging, Stevens was writing to Harriet Monroe to keep the news "confidential for the present" (*L*, 228).

As we have seen, he published some of his undergraduate verse pseudonymously. If Carl Zigrosser is right, that reticence now shielded the businessman from public identity with art generally:

> Stevens was rather secretive in manner. He once said to me at the gallery, "Don't tell anybody that I come in here"; and I had the feeling that when he went out of the gallery door, he glanced up and down the avenue to make sure that no one caught him in the act. I suspect that he especially did not want his associates in the insurance business to know that he had a taste for art, even though he later did buy a Portfolio for one of them. It could be that the fear of being considered "bohemian" was genuine at first, but later became a habit and a kind of pose.[15]

The conflict between self-identity as poet and as business executive in 1914 and the years following must have reawakened the more acute anxiety he had endured as an undergraduate when torn between appeasing his practical-minded father and satisfying his own yearnings to be a poet. Now, however, there would be no postponement; he would risk embarrassment, submitting, on tiptoe, his newest arrangements.

Stevens' uncertainty about his verse experiments is further displayed by his giving in to three editorial excisions. He allowed Harriet Monroe to reduce "Sunday Morning" from eight to five stanzas and to reorder four of the five for *Poetry* (he confidently restored the poem to its original form in *Harmonium*). William Carlos Williams, who was reading manuscripts for Kreymborg's *Others* in 1916, proposed rephrasing one line in "The Worms at Heaven's Gate":

> I have changed line two from: "Within our bellies, as a chariot," to the following: "Within our bellies, we her chariot,"
>     I think the second version is much the better for the reason that THE

14. Carl Van Vechten, "Rogue Elephant in Porcelain," *Yale University Library Gazette*, XXXVIII (October, 1963), 41; Alfred Kreymborg, *Troubadour* (New York, 1957), 187.

15. Carl Zigrosser, *My Own Shall Come to Me: A Personal Memoir and Picture Chronicle* (Haarlem, Netherlands, 1971), 84.

WORMS ARE HER CHARIOT and not only seem her chariot. Then again: "bellies" "as a chariot" (plural and singular) sounds badly while "we her chariot" has more of a collective sense and feels more solid. What do you say?

Williams also suggested omitting the last two lines as redundant. His judgment in both cases was sound, and Stevens must have seen it at once: the alterations were permanently adopted. "For Christ's sake yield to me[;] become great and famous," Williams had entreated good-humoredly in conclusion.[16]

Six days earlier Williams, considering Stevens' poem "Eight Significant Landscapes" for *Others,* had suggested flaws in two of the landscapes. The fifth section—"Wrestle with morning-glories, / O, muscles! / It is useless to contend / With falling mountains"— was an inevitable target. Williams allowed, however reluctantly, that one could "wrestle" with flowers, "but all mountains are not falling etc. (the usual bunk)." He was summoning his friend back to the literal, reminding him that the presentation of the untrue was bunk. The lesson was not lost: two sections were omitted, including this one, and the poem was retitled "Six Significant Landscapes."[17]

Stevens' reserve was successfuly challenged by various editors. "Carnet de Voyage," the eight-poem miscellany for *Trend,* was his first offering. In the following two years, new poems appeared in *Rogue, Others, Soil,* and *Poetry.* His works published in these pages mark the birth of Stevens as a modern poet. A. Walton Litz speculates that Pitts Sanborn, editor of *Trend* and Stevens' friend from Harvard days, asked as a personal favor that Stevens break his silence with the "Carnet de Voyage" group. We know that two other poems were published in the same magazine later in 1914 while Van Vechten was acting editor, though they had been solicited by Sanborn. Similarly, Allen and Louise Norton published two poems by their friend in the first number of *Rogue* early in 1915. Norton had written requesting "your poem about radishes," and Stevens sent "Cy Est Pourtraicte, Madame Ste Ursule, et Les Unze Mille Vierges." He personally presented "Peter Quince at the Clavier" to Kreymborg at *Others,* as we have seen. After his second appearance

16. Buttel, *The Making of Harmonium,* 190.
17. *Ibid.,* 144.

in Kreymborg's magazine, Amy Lowell inquired, "Who is Mr. Stevens? Tell me something about him."[18] Publishers of poetry in New York shared a social life with their poets, and Stevens, once introduced to the circle, found them receptive. In short, he began publishing his work in part because his friends asked him to. The practice set a pattern that became lifelong; further, those who solicited his work had a major role in his writing poetry—petitions for "scraps" or "one or two things" set him off.

Stevens also responded to the challenge of poetry contests, especially those sponsored by *Poetry,* during the early years. Whether it was the lure of prize money, the prospect of recognition as a winner, or the summons to competition, the announcement of a forthcoming prize roused the poet repeatedly. Like invitations from editors, contests gave him an excuse to write. His first submission to *Poetry* in 1914, "Phases," was sent in response to the notice of a prize for the best poem or group of poems on war or peace. Stevens did not win, but four of his eleven poems were accepted for the issue. A year later, *Poetry* offered a prize for a one-act poetic play, and this time Stevens was successful. "Three Travelers Watch a Sunrise" won $100 and was published in *Poetry* the following July. The fourteen "Pecksniffiana" poems, including the popular "Anecdote of the Jar" and "Ploughing on Sunday," were selected for the Helen Haire Levinson Prize for 1920, a $200 award presented annually since 1914 and earlier claimed by Carl Sandburg, Vachel Lindsay, Edgar Lee Masters, and others. Another group of poems under the title "Sur Ma Guzzla Gracile" was accepted by Monroe's *Poetry,* and four of the twelve brief lyrics received honorable mention in the 1922 awards. Curiously, "The Snow Man," the most distinguished of those poems, was overlooked in favor of "Another Weeping Woman," "Tea at the Palaz of Hoon," "On the Manner of Addressing Clouds," and "Hibiscus on the Sleeping Shores." Finally, the first draft of "The Comedian as the Letter C" was prepared to round out the collection for *Harmonium,* but also in response to the Blindman Prize offered by the Poetry Society of South Carolina. However, Stevens' poem "From the Journal of Crispin" was edged out by Grace Hazard Conkling's work, in the

18. A. Walton Litz, *Introspective Voyager: The Poetic Development of Wallace Stevens* (New York, 1972), 9; Van Vechten, "Rogue Elephant in Porcelain," 41; Allen Norton to Wallace Stevens, 1915; S. Foster Damon, *Amy Lowell: A Chronicle* (Boston, 1935), 316.

estimation of Amy Lowell, the judge. Stevens, nonetheless, had explained to Monroe while he wrote the poem, "But what's the use of offering prizes if people don't make an effort to capture them" (*L,* 224).[19]

For a poet so long delayed in coming to the writing of poems and, having arrived, so radical in his experiments, the encouragement of editors and the challenge of competition were major incentives in his emergence before *Harmonium.* He discovered that his work was admired, solicited, and acclaimed.

Part of the consolidation that took place in Stevens' poetry by 1915 was the revision of the Wordsworthian style that had characterized his first sonnets. He did not abandon the Pateresque world of beauty presented sensuously and sometimes preciously, though it was occasionally conditioned now by a mild irony, as in "Le Monocle de Mon Oncle." Stevens' recurring inclination toward the elevated rhetoric of the "grand pronunciamento" (*CP,* 43) was most successfully refashioned and refined in "Sunday Morning," though even that poem is not exempt from preciosity. Another poem written about 1915 and not published, "For an Old Woman in a Wig," is smudged with erasures in its incomplete draft. It is, as Litz suggests, "a curious and revealing pendant to 'Sunday Morning.'"[20] The poem demonstrates how troublesome the cultivation of Stevens' grand style could be.

The poem strains for a Dantesque prophecy of a redefined inferno and paradise. Except for the incongruous title, there is none of the wit and irony on which his other experiments were prospering. Rather, the vatic voice of Miltonic diction, Latinate phrases piled in apposition, and, above all, jangling rhymes in loyalty to Dante's terza rima (mumble/tumble, begotten/forgotten, resemblance/remembrance) render the exercise lifeless:

> Is death in hell more death than death in heaven?
> And is there never in that noon a turning—
> One step descending one of all the seven
>
> Implacable buttresses of sunlight, burning

---

19. Theodore Weiss reports that Stevens offered him this advice in March, 1951: "Moreover, he continued instructing me, I must never compete for prizes, awards, fellowships. 'Let them come to you'" ("Lunching with Hoon," *American Poetry Review,* VII [September/October, 1978], 43).
20. Litz, *Introspective Voyager,* 52.

In the great air? There must be spirits riven
From out contentment by too conscious yearning.

There must be spirits willing to be driven
To that immeasurable blackness, or . .
To those old landscapes, endlessly regiven,

Whence, hell, and heaven itself, were both begotten. (*PEM,* 13)

He apparently showed a draft of the poem to Williams, who, surprisingly, rather liked the last part.[21] "Sunday Morning," whether
written before or after "For an Old Woman in a Wig," rescues the
voice toward which the poem is straining. The first line, for example, rang true in "Sunday Morning": "Is there no change of
death in paradise?" (*CP,* 69). The tercets, already adopted for parts
of "Carnet de Voyage" and "Phases," would become a favorite
form once the impediment of rhyme was overcome. The poem
shows that in 1915–16, Stevens' evolution was not constant even as
he persisted in developing what might be called his rabbinical
idiom, which would triumph in poems like "Credences of Summer" and "To an Old Philosopher in Rome." The tendency to
overwrite in this idiom was successfully purged only after he
allowed himself the prolonged description of Crispin's travels and
adventures. The bloated style of "The Comedian as the Letter C"
could be regarded as self-parody, ridiculing all styles from Elizabethan drama to Romantic sonnets. Some lines in "From the Journal of Crispin," which were removed from the published poem,
pile scorn upon the very form that had so entranced Stevens:

They say they still scratch sonnets in the south,
The bards of Capricorn. Medicaments
Against the weather. Useful laxatives.
Petrarch is the academy of youth
In Yucatan.[22]

Both "Sunday Morning" and "For an Old Woman in a Wig"
also show that Stevens' poetics, in whatever style it was set, would
begin by discarding the creeds of Christianity, a conclusion his earlier work had already begun to assert. The pallidness of the church

21. Buttel, *The Making of Harmonium,* 216.
22. Louis L. Martz, "'From the Journal of Crispin': An Early Version of 'The Comedian
as the Letter C,'" in Frank Doggett and Robert Buttel (eds.), *Wallace Stevens: A Celebration*
(Princeton, 1980), 33.

beside the spectacle of the natural world was a contrast Stevens had drawn in "Cathedrals are not built along the sea" and "The Beggar," part II of "Street Songs." He took up the theme again in 1914, when he prepared a series of eleven poems for the war issue of *Poetry*. The "Phases" sequence shows a new preoccupation, the value of death for mortal man. In the first poem he belittles the "heaven, / Full of Raphael's costumes." In the final poem he recognizes war's claim upon the human heart, along with envy, hate, fear, malice, and ambition. This "commune" can be expelled by looking not toward heaven but inward:

> Who shall impart,
>
> To that strange commune, strength enough
> To drive the laggard phantoms out?
> Who shall dispel for it the doubt
> Of its own strength? Let Heaven snuff
>
> The tapers round her futile throne.
> Close tight the prophets' coffin-clamp.
> Peer inward, with the spirit's lamp,
> Look deep, and let the truth be known.[23]

Heaven's throne rendered "futile," Stevens could proceed to the writing of "Sunday Morning" and, at the same time, prepare his poetic claims for the values of the self ("Peer inward") voluptuously alive in the physical world.

In the same month that four of the "Phases" poems appeared in *Poetry,* Stevens published two poems in Van Vechten's issue of *Trend*. The first was entitled "From a Junk":

> A great fish plunges in the dark,
> Its fins of rutted silver; sides,
> Belabored with a foamy light;
> And back, brilliant with scaly salt.
> It glistens in the flapping wind,
> Burns there and glistens wide and wide
> Under the five-horned stars of night,
> In wind and wave . . . It is the moon. (*SP*, 260)

Stevens' independent movement toward Imagism, which began with the 1909 "June Book," had carried him to what is an unmistak-

---

23. Litz, *Introspective Voyager,* 305, 308.

able Imagist poem. In T. E. Hulme's "Autumn," for example, the
moon was found to "lean over a hedge / Like a red-faced farmer,"
and Stevens may have seen this poem, which was reproduced in
Pound's *Ripostes* in 1912.[24] Other Imagist poems were published in
*Poetry* and elsewhere by 1914. It is equally likely, however, that
"From a Junk" is the inevitable consequence of Stevens' earlier experiments like "A Concert of Fishes" and "Shower." Although
Imagist techniques would continue to appeal to him, especially in
"Thirteen Ways of Looking at a Blackbird," he came at once to a
conclusion he later preserved in one of his "Adagia": "Not all objects are equal. The vice of imagism was that it did not recognize
this" (*OP*, 161). "Fins of rutted silver" might surprise and even ex-
cite the reader of the poem, but it was limited. That stunning moon
could assume its true human value only in a context devoid of, inferior to, or resisting its dazzle. Stevens turned to other kinds of
poetic narrative that, once introduced, were not abandoned. Opposing values intervened constantly, as Stevens well knew, when the
mind took possession of the world. Imagination and reality con-
tended in the universal and lifelong duel, and the claims of each,
dramatized in countering images, characters, and tropes, provided
the frame that he embraced at once in 1913 and 1914.

If the "Phases" poems showed Stevens' rejection of the hieratic,
and "From a Junk" hinted at the value of the physical world on its
own terms, then the imagination's demands upon that world, described in a poetic narrative where objects were hierarchical rather
than equal (as the Imagists would have it), were in evidence at the
same time:

> I have lived so long with the rhetoricians
> That when I see a pine tree
> Broken by lightning
> Or hear a crapulous crow
> In dead boughs,
> In April
> These are too ready
> To despise me
> It is for this the good lord
> Gave the rooster his lustre

    24. *Ripostes of Ezra Pound, whereto are appended the complete poetical works of T. E. Hulme
with prefatory note* (London, 1912), 60.

And made sprats pink
Who can doubt that Confucius
Thought well of streets
In the spring-time
It is for this the rhetoricians
Wear long black equali
When they are abroad [25]

Stevens had arrived at a *modus operandi* to which he returned again and again in *Harmonium*. Here it formulates a debate between rhetoricians and Confucius, with the speaker caught between them; a clash between the black equali and pink sprats beside lustred roosters; a transition between winter's death and April's revival. Ultimately, the poem is a repudiation of life governed by rational rules and self-consciousness in favor of the unplotted delight in color and reviving life. The fish in this poem has a value greater than mere presentation in an Imagist mode. Rendered all the dearer by the rhetoricians' favoring their funereal black, the vitality of spring's colors prevails. More than thirty years later, in "Bouquet of Roses in Sunlight," Stevens was still recommending the personal and direct apprehension of roses "So far beyond the rhetorician's touch" (*CP,* 431). This 1914 poem was not published by Stevens and is unpunctuated in manuscript; perhaps the poet considered it incomplete. But the mark of the maturing Stevens is here nonetheless. In a way different from the "Phases" poems or "From a Junk," there is an indulgence in exotic and unfamiliar diction (crapulous, sprats, equali), a playful internal rhyming ("the rooster his lustre"), and the slight self-mockery of the speaker who may or may not have liberated himself from the rhetoricians' spell. The poem remains a minor piece, but as evidence of an advance toward the best poems of *Harmonium,* it is a singular accomplishment. "Disillusionment of Ten O'Clock" and "Cy Est Pourtraicte, Madame Ste Ursule, et Les Unze Mille Vierges" would follow a few months later.

    In arriving at a voice sui generis, emancipated from the *grands maîtres* who had hovered over the poet since his youth, Stevens had to discard his own poetic rhetoricians with whom he had lived so long. From Keats and Wordsworth to Verlaine and Laforgue and

25. Litz, *Introspective Voyager,* 30.

finally to Carman and other contemporary poetasters, Stevens could now leap beyond them toward a style peculiarly his. His own experience and personal observations, together with an increasing confidence in the play of his mind freed from derivation and convention, made him bolder with each poem.

It is not certain that Stevens attended the influential Armory Show in 1913 that introduced Post-Impressionists, Fauves, and Cubists to America on a large scale, though his daughter is under the impression that he did.[26] Many years later Stevens recalled Arensberg's excitement: "I don't suppose there is anyone to whom the Armory Show of 1913 meant more than it meant to him" (L, 821). Stevens' study of Japanese color prints and the "June Book" exercises, with their stark catalogs of color, attest to his fervent interest in the correlations between the visual and the verbal. Picasso, Matisse, Braque, Duchamp, and the others demonstrated that dislocating juxtapositions of color and geometric planes could also expose startling new insights. In 1915, Stevens met Duchamp, who was using Arensberg's apartment as a studio, and he described to Elsie his interest in the strange canvases: "After dinner, we went up to the Arensberg's apartment and looked at some of Duchamp's things. I made very little out of them. But naturally, without sophistication in that direction, and with only a very rudimentary feeling about art, I expect little of myself" (L, 185). But the poet's eye was becoming educated. Buttel is surely correct in recognizing the similarity between "Nude Descending a Staircase" and these lines from "Floral Decorations for Bananas":

> Pile the bananas on planks.
> The women will be all shanks
> And bangles and slatted eyes. (CP, 54)[27]

The sensibility that Stevens must have seen as closely allied to his own was that of Matisse. For both painter and poet, the pleasures of living were derived from the thickly colored world awash in sunlight. "Matisse at Vence and a great deal more than that" was how Stevens described his "chapel of breath" (CP, 529) replacing St. Armorer's Church in the poem. The opening lines of "Sunday

26. Buttel, The Making of Harmonium, 82.
27. Ibid., 164.

Morning"—the woman and her "Coffee and orange in a sunny chair, / And the green freedom of a cockatoo" (*CP*, 66)—have reminded many readers of the French painter. The two were contemporaries; they came to their work as artists relatively late and after the study of law. Stevens and Matisse were temperamentally reserved and conservative, but in their art they shared a love for what the epigraph (from Mario Rossi) to "Evening without Angels" called "the great interests of man: air and light, the joy of having a body, the voluptuousness of looking" (*CP*, 136).

The poems of *Harmonium* frequently reveal characteristics of the new art: a single object in multiple and sometimes distorted perspectives, stark contrasts of color wherein pigment or tint supersedes the object to which it is attached, surreal representations framed within the quotidian world, insertions or superimpositions of the exotic, gaudy, bizarre, and Oriental.

In 1919, Stevens wrote to Harriet Monroe with what was for him a rare request: the withdrawal of a poem that had been submitted and accepted for publication. "Peter Parasol" was scheduled to appear in *Poetry* as one of the "Pecksniffiana" group, but Stevens was sufficiently dissatisfied with it to substitute "The Weeping Burgher" and to justify the revocation: "Not to provoke, but to stifle, discussion, my reasons are that the element of pastiche present in Aux Taureaux ["Peter Parasol"] will not be apparent and the poem will go off on its substance and not on its style" (*L*, 214). (Monroe, however, published both poems.) The cultivation of style and pastiche over substance, a poem's bravura over its beseechings, marks another new preoccupation.

Although Stevens in the "June Book" poems had broken away from rigid iambic pentameters, few of those poems could be said to demonstrate the technique of free verse: they are typically iambic dimeters, trimeters, and tetrameters. The defense of measure and rhythm remained for Stevens a commonplace, but his acceptance of a new range of musical effects, nowhere better shown than in the prosodic alterations among the several parts of "Peter Quince at the Clavier," was liberating. As Stevens' eye became sharper and more precise, his ear entertained cadences less clicking and clotting. The number of stresses per line was never again mechanically predetermined, though his poetic pace was spontaneously iambic and he finally found most congenial the line of ten to twelve syllables. When Ferdinand Reyher wrote in 1921 complaining of the popularity of free verse, Stevens responded:

> The fact is that not withstanding the large amount of poetry that is written over here at the moment there is practically no aesthetic theory back of it. Why do you scorn free verse? Isn't it the only kind of verse now being written which has any aesthetic impulse back of it? Of course, there are miles and miles of it that do not come off. People don't understand the emotional purpose of rhythm any more than they understood the emotional purpose of measure. I am not exclusively for free verse. But I am for it. However, all this kind of thing I should rather talk about than write about.[28]

Stevens' reference to the emotional purpose of rhythm and measure hints, I think, at the theory that meter should be liberated from the form that insisted on numbering syllables and stresses by some predetermined metronome. The musical cadences should be emotional, that is, spontaneous, impulsive, and shrewdly self-effacing. The ideal mode for Stevens was not, finally, free verse, in which even the emotional purpose of rhythm was subverted. At the same time, however, the emancipating effect of free verse was an advance, and he was "for it."

The "June Book" poems had not quite managed to break free of the monotonous iamb, though a few of them give evidence of Stevens' trying. The second poem in the 1909 collection and "Depression before Spring," published exactly nine years later, both present images of imminent spring and the desired call of birds. The earlier poem is relentlessly iambic, interrupted only in the final line:

> If only birds of sudden white,
> Or opal, gold or iris hue,
> Came upward through the columned light
> Of morning's ocean-breathing blue;
>
> If only songs disturbed our sleep,
> Descending from that wakeful breeze,
> And no great murmur of the deep
> Sighed in our summer-sounding trees! (*SP*, 228)

---

28. Wallace Stevens to Ferdinand Reyher, May 13, 1921 (photocopy).

"Depression before Spring," on the other hand, might be designated free verse, but the emotional strategy of its cadence is no less plotted:

> The cóck cróws
> But nó queén ríses.
>
> The háir of my blónde
> Is daźzling,
> As the spíttle of cóws
> Threáding the wínd.
>
> Hó! Hó!
>
> But kí-kí-rí-kí
> Brings nó rou-coú,
> Nó rou-coú-coú.
>
> But nó queén cómes
> In slípper greén. (*CP*, 63)

The poem takes itself far less seriously than does the earlier piece, indulging in the second stanza in a lyrical parody and then laughing at it immediately afterward. But the poem is more than mockery; its yearning for the "rou-cou" of the absent queen is as genuine as the plaintive call for the "birds of sudden white" in the earlier poem. The nonsense sounds of the birds become a rhythmic duel between the harshly staccato velars ("ki-ki-ri-ki") and the elongated vowels of the absent queen ("no rou-cou, / No rou-cou-cou"). The softer and more soothing dovelike cooing prevails by rhythmic and phonetic force alone. The "No rou-cou-cou" converges with the "no queen comes" by rhythmic and alliterative parallel, just as "Brings no" and "But no" meet in similar balance. The full internal rhyme of "queen" and "green" establishes a final harmonious resolution. The sibilants of the queen who "rises" and "comes" in "slipper green" contests throughout the poem with the velars of the crowing cock and his "ki-ki-ri-ki." Although literally absent from the poem, the queen, by the sounds, rhythms, and rhymes associated with her, is fully present and even triumphant.

The dramatic difference between the two poems has to do with the poet's boldness and confidence. In "Depression before Spring" he has let himself go, putting his trust entirely in the play among sounds and stresses rather than glib content. Stevens' clearest apology for freedom of style and commentary on his own prosody come in a letter to Norman Holmes Pearson almost twenty years later, apparently in response to another inquiry about form: "There is such complete freedom now-a-days in respect to technique that I am rather inclined to disregard form so long as I am free and can express myself freely. I don't know of anything, respecting form, that makes much difference. The essential thing in form is to be free in whatever form is used. A free form does not assure freedom. As a form, it is just one more form. So that it comes to this, I suppose, that I believe in freedom regardless of form" (*L,* 323). He told Edwin Honig in 1955, "Now I never worried about the line. I've always been interested in the whole thing, the whole poem." [29]

Of all Stevens' poet-friends in New York, none leaves a firmer mark than Donald Evans (1884–1921), a poet all but forgotten today. A direct descendant of William Penn, Evans was on the editorial staff of the New York *Times* and was later general manager of the *Daily Garment News*. He founded the publishing house Claire-Marie Press and printed the work of Allen and Louise Norton, Gertrude Stein's *Tender Buttons,* and his own *Sonnets from the Patagonian.* Evans took his own life, exhausted by a separation from his wife and a difficult career. Stevens learned of the suicide shortly afterward and wrote to Reyher that the news was "appalling, devastating." He called Evans "one of the great ironists, one of the pure littérateurs." [30] A few weeks later he sent obituaries to Van Vechten along with newspaper clippings that referred to some of Evans' last work.

William Carlos Williams himself noted some of the similarities between Evans' poems and Stevens':

> Maybe that young lamented poet—what was his name?—who disappeared just prior to the final breaking through of the "modern". What was his name? He was an important figure. Donald something. You may know of him. If he and Stevens knew each other at that time I suspect that Stevens was strongly influenced—or admired him a lot. It

29. Edwin Honig, "Meeting Wallace Stevens," *Wallace Stevens Newsletter,* I (April, 1970), 12.
30. Wallace Stevens to Ferdinand Reyher, June 1, 1921 (photocopy).

is a pure guess on my part. Not Donald Evans—but something like
that. He wrote:

> In what room shall it be tonight,
> darling? (looking up at the
> illuminated nightbound hotel) In
> every room, my sweet.

I think this has a lot of the early Stevens in it.[31]

Williams referred to Evans' "Dinner at the Hotel De La Tigresse
Verte."

Exactly when Stevens and Evans met is uncertain, but Evans'
1914 collection *Sonnets from the Patagonian* appeared at the very time
Stevens resumed his own writing. According to Yvor Winters, the
two poets once projected a collaborative volume: "[Stevens] and
Donald Evans had once planned to write a volume of one-line
poems, but had begun almost at once to quarrel about where the
poems would go on the page and so had never written the poems."
Evans' typical pose in the poems—the fastidious but disaffected
dandy who scoffs at life's infidelities—anticipates a stance that
Eliot would discover through Laforgue.[32] Evans' poems, however,
never quite succeed in breaking through the idiom of the *fin de
siècle:* for all his irony, there are also sentimentality and simple self-
pity. Unlike Stevens, he had not moved beyond Petrarchan sonnets, facile adjectival phrases, and blurry abstractions. But his
occasional glints of irony disclose another mode altogether: one
allowing for mockery and debunking, even of the very excesses of
his verse.

"Her Smile" presents melodramatically an unidentified woman
who smiles grimly through a night of terrors, La Gioconda as
*femme fatale.* The poem extends the same tone through the sestet
until the unexpected final line:

31. William Carlos Williams to William Van O'Connor, August 22, 1949 (photocopy),
in Huntington Library.
32. Winters quoted in Glen MacLeod, *Wallace Stevens and Company: The "Harmonium"
Years, 1913–1923* (Ann Arbor, 1983), 66. Van Vechten commented on Evans during the
time he was preparing the 1914 volume: "In fact my most intense remembrance of him at
this period is connected with absinthe, raw eggs, and coffee, with an occasional bowl of raw
beef blood, which he ordered at Jake's on Sixth Avenue. He was content to survive for weeks
at a time on such food and stimulants, alternating them as occasion demanded" ("The Origin of the Sonnets from the Patagonian," annotated and with an introduction by Bruce
Kellner, *Hartwick Review*, III (Spring, 1967), 53.

The cold hours ebbed, and still she held her throne;
   Across the sky the lightning made mad play.
And then the scarlet screams stood forth revealed.
She turned her back, and grasped a monotone;
   It answered all; she lived again that day
She triumphed in the tragic turnip field.[33]

The same ironic contrast between the exalted sanctity of the pious virgin making her religious offering with a bouquet of radishes is far more skillfully realized by Stevens in "Cy Est Pourtraicte, Madame Ste Ursule, et Les Unze Mille Vierges." In 1916, Stevens sent the poem to *Rogue,* where many of Evans' own poems also appeared.

Kenneth Fields has called Evans' "En Monocle" his "finest poem," and Buttel has noted the indebtedness of "Le Monocle de Mon Oncle" to "the title and the general irony" of the sonnet. Stevens heard Evans recite the poem several years after its publication at a party given by the poet Lola Ridge; Williams and Marianne Moore also attended. Kreymborg preferred "En Monocle" to the poem Stevens read that evening—"he drew forth a paper that looked like a poem but sounded like a tête-a-tête with himself." And he suggests the stir that Evans' rendition must have made: "Toward the close of the party, Donald Evans leaned forward a little and with a low, suave accent, intoned the precise and beautifully modelled phrases of a sonnet—the form in which no American ever surpassed him. It was clearly a self-portrait."[34]

Born with a monocle he stares at life,
   And sends his soul on pensive promenades;
   He pays a high price for discarded gods,
And then regilds them to renew their strife.
His calm moustache points to the ironies,
   And a fawn-coloured laugh sucks in the night,
   Full of the riant mists that turn to white
In brief lost battles with banalities.

Masters are makeshifts and a path to tread
   For blue pumps that are ardent for the air;

---

33. Donald Evans, *Sonnets from the Patagonian* (New York, 1914), 39.

34. Kenneth Fields, "Past Masters: Walter Conrad Arensberg and Donald Evans," *Southern Review,* n.s., VI (1970), 336; Buttel, *The Making of Harmonium,* 92; Kreymborg, *Troubadour,* 260–61.

Features are fixtures when the face is fled,
  And we are left the husks of tarnished hair;
But he is one who lusts uncomforted
  To kiss the naked phrase quite unaware.[35]

Evans' aging subject, like Stevens' speaker in "Le Monocle de Mon Oncle," views the world through his scholarly eyepiece, aware that his very aloofness removes him from the vigorous passions of life. His "lost battles with banalities" anticipates Stevens' *oncle:*

Like a dull scholar, I behold, in love,
An ancient aspect touching a new mind.
It comes, it blooms, it bears its fruit and dies.
This trivial trope reveals a way of truth.
Our bloom is gone. We are the fruit thereof. (*CP*, 16)

That lost bloom, too, is decried in Evans' poem: "Features are fixtures when the face is fled, / And we are left the husks of tarnished hair." Evans' figure buys back the "discarded gods" and then "regilds" them. Stevens acknowledges more adamantly: "The honey of heaven may or may not come, / But that of earth both comes and goes at once." He prefers instead a more earthly "damsel heightened by eternal bloom" (*CP*, 15). Evans pointed Stevens toward insouciance, irreverence, and self-mockery. Once directed, Stevens quickly surpassed his New York friend, whose irony rarely transcends other and simpler emotional indulgences.

Walter Conrad Arensberg was a closer friend: he, too, was a native of Pennsylvania, and Stevens had known him at Harvard, where they had taken two courses together.[36] Arensberg's *Harvard Monthly* had published Stevens' sonnets while Stevens was editing the *Advocate.* And in New York City, Arensberg introduced Stevens to the literary coterie there. They exchanged poems and commented on each other's work. On June 4, 1914, Stevens signed and dated a copy of Arensberg's new volume, *Poems.* The collection has none of Evans' irony and shows little evidence that Arensberg was influenced by Imagism. As Buttel has noted, a quatrain called "The Masterpiece" may have commanded Stevens' notice, however. Its conclusion was one Stevens was to appropriate often:

35. Evans, *Sonnets from the Patagonian,* 17.
36. MacLeod, *Wallace Stevens and Company,* 20.

> I think ere any early poet awed
> Men with a haunted image of Mankind,
> They buried in a grave gone out of mind
> The supreme poet who imagined God.[37]

A direct association, first noted by Hi Simons, connects Arensberg's "Voyage à L'Infini" and "Sunday Morning." Published in *Others* in September, 1915, Arensberg's poem and its French title seem indebted to Mallarmé. The poem's conclusion describes a swan's image of itself reflected in water. As in the first stanza of "Sunday Morning," there is a visionary procession:

> And breast to breast it is confused.
> O visionary wedding! O stateliness of the procession!
> It is accompanied by the image of itself
> Alone.
>
> At night
> The lake is a wide silence,
> Without imagination.[38]

"Voyage à L'Infini" and "Sunday Morning" were written almost simultaneously. Arensberg and Stevens, arm in arm, were consciously absorbing the delicate, even precious, imagery of Symbolist voluptuousness.

The early friendship with William Carlos Williams led in a different direction. Williams had carried Imagist premises farther than had any other poet. Stevens, building his own poetics upon the need for decreating the imagination's distortions as part of the process of valid perception, found Williams' poems salutary in their devotion to objectivity. He was sufficiently taken by the older poet's dedication to "the thing itself" to reproduce the four lines of Williams' "El Hombre" in his own "Nuances of a Theme by Williams" (1918). For him, however, the direct presentation of phenomena for their own sake was as objectionable as Imagism had been. Williams' disparaging the imagination for its "associational or sentimental value" was too extreme for Stevens, and Williams himself acknowledged, "Here I clash with Wallace Stevens." Stevens' reservations about the direction of Williams' experiments

37. W. C. Arensberg, *Poems* (Boston, 1914), 77; Buttel, *The Making of Harmonium*, 98.
38. Hi Simons, "Wallace Stevens and Mallarmé," *Modern Philology*, XLIII (May, 1946), 258; Walter Arensberg, "Voyage à L'Infini," *Others*, I (September, 1915), 53.

were outlined in a letter to the poet after the 1917 publication of *Al Que Quiere,* a letter reproduced in Williams' "Prologue to Kora in Hell." Stevens disliked the "casual character" of Williams' poems, their whimsical and fragmentary quality: "My idea is that in order to carry a thing to the extreme necessity to convey it one has to stick to it. . . . Given a fixed point of view, realistic, imagistic or what you will, everything adjusts itself to that point of view; the process of adjustment is a world in flux, as it should be for a poet. But to fidget with points of view leads always to new beginnings and incessant new beginnings lead to sterility." Stevens' opinion was unchanged in 1953 when he wrote that Williams "rejects the idea that meaning has the slightest value and describes a poem as a structure of little blocks" (*L,* 803). Stevens was resolved to push beyond Williams' objectivism, though it had been instructive, as had Evans' use of irony, at a crucial point in his development. The differences between "these two unlikely sons of Emerson and Whitman," as Paul Mariani has noted, set the terms for the "struggle to determine the nature of reality and the imagination and the direction American poetry was to take in the 20th Century."[39]

Stevens' surest guide to his developing style was his own instinct, which went back to "Ballade of the Pink Parasol" and the second "June Book." By 1913 and 1914, he had also found a theme that began to open before him: the mind's spontaneous fictions contending with its inherited dogmas. He began to exploit the relentless tension between the power to revise the world metaphorically and the need to reclaim and repossess it purely. The mind's processes became the poet's patterns. Stevens used the Imagists and ironists, those who worked in free verse, the Cubists and the Fauves, all to educate his sensibility as he pushed ahead with his own experiments. He also saw the limitations of these various models, and none became a complete exemplar. *Harmonium* is, in fact, the bringing together of opposing styles, sometimes for the purposes of irony. If Stevens cultivated his Wordsworthian grand style in such poems as "Sunday Morning" and "To the One of Fictive Music," he also indulged in exercises of irony, mockery, exoticism, dazzle, extravagance, surprise, whim, and humor. If the

39. William Carlos Williams, "Prologue to Kora in Hell," *Selected Essays of William Carlos Williams* (New York, 1954), 11, 12; Paul Mariani, "Williams on Stevens: Storming the Edifice," *Poetry Society of America Bulletin,* LXX (Winter, 1980), 19.

grand style tended toward expression in blank verse, for the vernacular performances, like "Depression before Spring," he preferred the mischief of more irregular measures. In the prophetic mode, the voice was one of instruction and admonition; in the ironic mode, which resisted easy concessions to paraphrasable "meaning," he relied on the poem's effect, which was often wry, witty, and opaque. These came to fruition around 1915 and, though modified in certain ways, continued in his work for the next forty years. The very convergence of the portentous and the playful, sometimes ironic, set Stevens apart as a poet and fixed him securely on the path to modernism.

Once assured that his own instincts and conscious choices were moving him forward as a poet, he found another source to guarantee his progress: the direct observation of his own experience, the play of his eye upon a disparate and changing world. Landscapes beyond and within his ordinary range became his field of play.

In the summer of 1915 when Stevens wrote to his wife that he was back at work on his "flimsy little things," he also described a visit to the New York Botanical Gardens "where I spent several hours in studying the most charming things. I was able to impress on myself that larkspur comes from China. Was there ever anything more Chinese when you stop to think of it?" (L, 184). Stevens' continuing interest in the Orient was now being fed by direct observation rather than the Astor Library. The first poem of "Six Significant Landscapes," published the following spring in *Others,* shows the results of the visit:

> An old man sits
> In the shadow of a pine tree
> In China.
> He sees larkspur,
> Blue and white,
> At the edge of the shadow,
> Move in the wind.
> His beard moves in the wind.
> The pine tree moves in the wind.
> Thus water flows
> Over weeds. (*CP,* 73)

The natural movement of water and wind contrasts in the sixth landscape with the "Rationalists, wearing square hats," who, like the rhetoricians of his earlier poem, miss the larkspur of life as they "confine themselves / To right-angled triangles" (*CP,* 75).

Shortly after moving to Hartford in 1916, Stevens was commissioned to make various business trips on behalf of his new employer, the Hartford Accident and Indemnity Company. New locations reveal further the role of direct observation in his work. Most of these trips led him to Florida, frequently in the company of Judge Arthur Powell of Atlanta, though he occasionally traveled to Minnesota as well as Texas, Oklahoma, and Nebraska. Stevens represented the home office in casualty claims and he must have been especially resourceful in these enterprises: he would continue such trips for the next twenty years. In the various cities, Stevens took advantage of long walks before or after the day's work, and his letters to Elsie indicate his fascination with the people and the landscapes beyond those he was most familiar with. The vistas from the train were rural and urban, with children and adults at work and play, and he saw vegetation he had known only from books. He especially savored the escape from chilly New England during winter and spring. The trips stirred his creativity and introduced geographical contexts, especially of the South, which appear throughout the poems of *Harmonium.* Here again, personal observation provided both stimulus and setting.

One of Stevens' first sequences was based upon the impressions he garnered during his travels. "Primordia," the nine poems published in *Soil* in January, 1917, had the subdivisions "In the Northwest" and "In the South." He had visited both areas of the country on business trips in the spring of 1916, and he returned to St. Paul for several days in June and once again in October. Of the four poems prompted by the trips to Minnesota, none was preserved in *Harmonium;* they are little more than Imagist exercises. The fourth poem shows Stevens' experiment with nonsense sounds ("La, la, la, la, la, la, la, la, / Dee, dum, diddle, dee, dee, diddle, dee, da") at the end of a few surreal lines about horses and trees (*OP,* 8). Such sounds of course would become commonplace in Stevens' later work. He went to Florida almost immediately afterward, and the discovery of early spring in the South astonished him: "I have had the most amazing trip. Dogwood, apple-blossoms, cherry and peach blossoms, irises in the gardens, laurel in the woods. The country is full of bare-foot boys, girls in white, boys in white trousers and straw hats. I am perspiring as I write! But I am tired and sickeningly dirty and am going right up-stairs to bathe my weary hide and to sleep over the beautiful things I have seen" (*L*, 191). The trip, described after he arrived in Atlanta, almost certainly had taken Stevens through North and South Carolina, to which Crispin in "The Comedian as the Letter C" would be dispatched five years later. The irises on which he remarked to Elsie and the general prominence of pines in the region were drawn into the seventh of the "Primordia" poems, later reproduced in *Harmonium* as "In the Carolinas":

> The lilacs wither in the Carolinas.
> Already the butteflies flutter above the cabins.
> Already the new-born children interpret love
> In the voices of mothers.
>
> Timeless mother,
> How is it that your aspic nipples
> For once vent honey?
>
> *The pine-tree sweetens my body*
> *The white iris beautifies me.* (*CP*, 4–5)

The same trip to Florida in 1916 may well have provided the germ of a poem he did not publish for another six years. In Miami at Easter, Stevens wrote to Elsie:

> Easter greetings, as the old song runs. There will be a stiff parade on Fifth-Avenue to-day. Here, people have been going by on bicycles to-ward the beach. It is difficult to believe in the absolute midsummer of the place . . Miami is a small place. My hotel is opposite the Royal Palm Park. There is a church on the corner. In the quiet air of the neighborhood the voices of the choir are as audible as they used to be at Reading. Unfortunately there is nothing more inane than an Easter carol. It is a religious perversion of the activity of Spring in our blood. Why a man who wants to roll around on the grass should be asked to dress as magnificently as possible and listen to a choir is inexplicable except from the flaggelant [*sic*] point of view. (*L*, 192–93)

The parade, the flagellant, and the palms—the last noted in his previous letter ("You soon grow accustomed to the palms")—all reappear in "A High-Toned Old Christian Woman," the title itself coming from a description by Judge Powell.[40]

Another trip in the fall included additional stops in Omaha,

---

40. Peter Brazeau, *Parts of a World: Wallace Stevens Remembered* (New York, 1983), 100.

Kansas City, and Oklahoma City. Oklahoma he particularly looked forward to: "Oklahoma City is, goodness knows, still farther away: a land of mustangs, Indians etc. I am glad to have a Sunday there" (*L*, 198). "Earthy Anecdote" and "Life Is Motion," published together in 1919, caught the hoopla of that state, and we know from manuscript evidence that "The Jack-Rabbit" was originally considered as the second part of a longer poem in which "Earthy Anecdote" was the first part. All three poems likely resulted from this trip.

It is commonly assumed that the popular "Anecdote of the Jar" followed his long trip through Chattanooga, Knoxville, Elizabethton, Johnson City, and Nashville in the spring of 1918. Stevens apparently returned to Nashville in January, 1919 (*L*, 210), and the poem, first published in October, 1919, may have been completed after that visit.

A visit to Washington, D.C., about the same time led to the composition of "Anecdote of Canna." Stevens explained to Hi Simons its source: "The beds of the terraces around the Capitol were filled with canna. The place became a place in which the President (the 'mighty man') was the man walking round and everything became huge, mighty, etc. X is the President" (*L*, 465). These remarks tell us something about the poem's origin, though the uninformed reader is not likely to share Stevens' identifying "X" as Woodrow Wilson or even "his capitol" as the one in Washington:

> Huge are the canna in the dreams of
> X, the mighty thought, the mighty man.
> They fill the terrace of his capitol. (*CP*, 55)

He went back to Florida on business early in 1919. Three of the fourteen prize-winning "Pecksniffiana" poems he gathered for *Poetry* in October of that year were the result—"The Place of the Solitaires," "Fabliau of Florida," and "Homunculus et La Belle Etoile." Writing to Ronald Lane Latimer many years later, Stevens insisted on the importance of his poems' actual settings: "While, of course, my imagination is a most important factor, nevertheless I wonder whether, if you were to suggest any particular poem, I could not find an actual background for you. I have been going to Florida for twenty years, and all of the Florida poems have actual backgrounds. The real world seen by an imaginative man may very well

seem like an imaginative construction" (*L*, 289). "The Place of the
Solitaires" does not refer specifically to the state, but the "restless
iteration" of thought finds a counterpart in the "perpetual undula-
tion" of mid-sea and beaches (*CP*, 60). His own turns on the Miami
beaches yielded an exquisite pleasure he described to Elsie: "At
Miami, on a bright, sunny day in mid-winter, the climate must be
as fine as any in the world. The wind whips the water, the strange
birds: pelicans and so on, fly about, there are strange trees to see"
(*L*, 211). Another "Pecksniffiana" poem, "Fabliau of Florida,"
which was submitted to *Poetry* the following summer, was inspired by the beaches:

> Barque of phosphor
> On the palmy beach
>
> Move outward into heaven,
> Into the alabasters
> And night blues.
>
> Foam and cloud are one.
> Sultry moon-monsters
> Are dissolving.
>
> Fill your black hull
> With white moonlight.
>
> There will never be an end
> To this droning of the surf. (*CP*, 23)

For "Homunculus et La Belle Etoile," the location is identified directly in the environs of Miami:

> In the sea, Biscayne, there prinks
> The young emerald, evening star,
> Good light for drunkards, poets, widows,
> And ladies soon to be married. (*CP*, 25)

Stevens later recalled that the poem had actually been written in
Miami (*L*, 305).

Writing in 1922 from Long Key, Florida, Stevens announced to
Elsie the successful conclusion of the case that had been going on
since 1916. He incorrectly forecast that future trips south would
have to be "at my own expense." But with Judge Powell and some
of his friends, he was enjoying a respite on Long Key, a small island
north of Key West. His delight in the January setting was ecstatic:

"The place is a paradise—midsummer weather, the sky brilliantly clear and intensely blue, the sea blue and green beyond what you have ever seen. What a fool I should be not to come down here when I can give the results already achieved in return and still have a little fun out of it" (*L,* 225). He had apostrophized Biscayne in "Homunculus et La Belle Etoile," and the apostrophe expands in "O Florida, Venereal Soil," a poem published seven months after he visited Key West and Long Key. The state is personified as the seductive "Donna, donna, dark," as voluptuous as the paradise he had described to Elsie:

> Swiftly in the nights,
> In the porches of Key West,
> Behind the bougainvilleas,
> After the guitar is asleep,
> Lasciviously as the wind,
> You come tormenting,
> Insatiable. (*CP,* 47–48)

The journey in 1922 had begun in Georgia, where Stevens again met Powell. It is possible that their train passed through the town of Tallapoosa. Peter Brazeau reports that the two of them were often "zigzagging from Miami to Atlanta on claims."[41] "Stars at Tallapoosa," one of Stevens' richest pageants of the images of winter, was published five months later in *Broom.*

Whether Stevens rejoined Powell and his friends a year later for business or pleasure or both is not clear, but he returned to Long Key and Key West, and then was briefly in Havana. His delight in Florida's benign winter was as acute as it had been before: "Last night I lay in bed for several hours listening to the wind: it sounded like a downpour of rain, but outside was the balmiest and clearest moonlight and when I woke this morning the palm at my door was red in the sunlight" (*L,* 234). The poem he published later in the year in *Harmonium,* "Two Figures in Dense Violet Night," draws on the same images:

> Be the voice of night and Florida in my ear.
> Use dusky words and dusky images.
> Darken your speech.
> · · · · · · ·

41. *Ibid.,* 97.

> Say, puerile, that the buzzards crouch on the ridge-pole
> And sleep with one eye watching the stars fall
> Below Key West.
>
> Say that the palms are clear in a total blue,
> Are clear and are obscure; that it is night;
> That the moon shines. (*CP*, 86)

Reminiscent of the red palm outside Stevens' door, "Nomad Exquisite" pictures a "big-finned palm" on "blessed mornings," and its speaker acknowledges himself "flinging / Forms, flames, and the flakes of flames" (*CP*, 95).

Stevens' wonder at the balmy climate, the wind and the droning of the sea, and the birds and trees made Florida over into a personal paradise. The rhapsodic outbursts in the letters to his wife record the direct impressions and the sources of the trope. Surrendering to the place where "Sultry moon-monsters / Are dissolving," he invariably cast his Florida as female—seductress, mistress, "a wanton / Abundantly beautiful, eager, / Fecund" (*CP*, 26). Florida was the woman of perpetual motion, mysteriously alive in the moonlit, starlit, watery, and wind-driven night, surrounding the beholder in luxuriant beauty.

From Key West, Stevens sailed to Havana for a weekend visit after leaving Florida in 1923. The sight of bananas reappeared in "Floral Decorations for Bananas," a poem that was published before *Harmonium* the following April. The unadorned fruit—"Blunt yellow in such a room!"—required the lush and rank foliation of the tropics:

> And deck the bananas in leaves
> Plucked from the Carib trees.
> Fibrous and dangling down,
> Oozing cantankerous gum
> Out of their purple maws,
> Darting out of their purple craws
> Their musky and tingling tongues. (*CP*, 54)

"Academic Discourse in Havana" also derived from the visit to Cuba in February; it appeared in *Broom* the following November. Omitted from *Harmonium,* it was perhaps composed too late for inclusion, but it was collected in *Ideas of Order* (1935). The poem was also occasioned by a request from "a man running a bookshop in Cambridge." As Stevens later explained, the man "planned to issue a collection of poems by various poets. Nothing came of this. DISCOURSE was to have been my contribution to that project" (*L*, 335). Some of the poem's details mirror the weekend in Havana: "Canaries in the morning, orchestras / In the afternoon, balloons at night," and the "old casino in a park" with swans nearby (*CP*, 142).

In July, 1922, Van Vechten offered to assist Stevens in arranging for the publication of a first volume. His response was reluctant: "I feel frightfully uncertain about a book" (*L*, 228). Furthermore, in his earlier letter to Williams, he wrote: "Personally I have a distaste for miscellany. It is one of the reasons I do not bother about a book myself."[42] Van Vechten was persistent, however, and persuaded Alfred A. Knopf, his own publisher, to consider the venture. For all his diffidence and deference as a poet, Stevens must have been aware of the long strides the ephebe had made in the preceding decade.

His commitment to the world of business remained, and after the move to Hartford, he began to see the possibilities for advancement. In the two years following the publication of the "Pecksniffiana" poems, for example, his writing was curbed; no poems were published in 1920, and until "Sur Ma Guzzla Gracile" appeared in *Poetry* in October, only four short pieces were published in 1921. The following year he told Gilbert Seldes, editor of the *Dial*, that "I am not likely to be able to send you anything more before the beginning of April. My spasms are not chronic" (*L*, 226). Even Harriet Monroe, to whom the poet had shown such obsequiousness in 1915, was told to wait in 1922: "When I get back from the South I expect to do some short poems and then to start again on a rather longish one; so that sooner or later I shall have something for Poetry, to which I send what I like most. But it takes time and, besides, I have no desire to write a great deal. I know that people judge one by volume. However, having elected to regard poetry as a form of retreat, the judgment of people is neither here nor there" (*L*, 230). The writing of poetry, as much as it refreshed and stimulated him and as important as it was to his own thinking, remained a "form of retreat." The self-conscious

42. Williams, "Prologue to Kora in Hell," 12.

effacement in the first volume is openly labeled in his proposed title, one Knopf shrewdly discouraged: *The Grand Poem: Preliminary Minutiae.* While putting together the collection, Stevens wrote to Monroe, reflecting on his work, his habit of composition, and his resolve for the future:

> The book will amount to nothing, except that it may teach me something. I wish that I could put everything else aside and amuse myself on a large scale for a while. One never gets anywhere in writing or thinking or observing unless one can do long stretches of time. Often I have to let go, in the most insignificant poem, which scarcely serves to remind me of it, the most skyey of skyey sheets. And often when I have a real fury for indulgence I must stint myself. Of course, we must all do the same thing. . . . Only the reading of these outmoded and debilitated poems does make me wish rather desperately to keep on dabbling and to be as obscure as possible until I have perfected an authentic and fluent speech for myself. (*L*, 231)

*Harmonium* was published September 7, 1923.

# 5   After *Harmonium*

Another extended hiatus in Stevens' activity as a poet occurred after *Harmonium's* appearance, and it puzzled and even exasperated his friends. From 1923 until the publication of "The Brave Man" and "A Fading of the Sun" in 1933, Stevens wrote and published only a handful of poems. When a second edition of *Harmonium* was issued in 1931, he deleted three and added fourteen poems, re-marking in a letter to R. P. Blackmur, though, that "none of it was really new."[1] Just as the interval of thirteen years (1900–1913) separated the undergraduate verse from the early *Harmonium* poems, so now ten years elapsed during which Stevens wrote only occasionally and published even less.

One of the poems added in the second edition of *Harmonium*, "Sea Surface Full of Clouds," was new. In October, 1923, Stevens and his wife sailed aboard the Panama Pacific liner *Kroonland* from New York, to Cuba, through the Panama Canal, and north past the Gulf of Tehuantepec, to California. Elsie's 800-word memoir, which Stevens may have consulted when he wrote the poem, is entitled "Sea Voyage" and contains many details that appear in the poem—vantage points, vicissitudes of weather, seascapes, and even the dress of fellow passengers. The stimulus of this rare vacation with his wife was sufficient to rouse the poet from his dormancy, but it was a singular effort. Written just before the appearance of his first volume, it properly belongs to the earlier period of his work.

Stevens had written Monroe disconsolately of his "outmoded and debilitated poems" and of the need for "an authentic and fluent speech for myself." Moreover, the financial failure of the book may have reinforced this impression. He told her that "my royalties for

1. Wallace Stevens to R. P. Blackmur, October 18, 1930, in A. Walton Litz, *Introspective Voyager: The Poetic Development of Wallace Stevens* (New York, 1972), 166.

the first half of 1924 amounted to $6.70" (*L*, 243). Most impor-
tant, Stevens was bent upon advancing in the Hartford Accident
and Indemnity Company. In 1937 he wrote candidly to Latimer: "I
deliberately gave up writing poetry because, much as I loved it,
there were too many other things I wanted not to make an effort to
have them. . . . But I didn't like the idea of being bedeviled all the
time about money and I didn't for a moment like the idea of poverty, so I went to work like anybody else and kept at it for a good
many years" (*L*, 320). In 1924, his daughter Holly was born and,
responding to Williams' inquiries the following year, he acknowledged, "I have read very little and written not at all. The baby has
kept us both incredibly busy" (*L*, 245). Even Ezra Pound, who had
his eye on more than one American poet during these years, asked
Williams in 1927 to try once more to prod Stevens. "I am humble
before Pound's request," answered Stevens, but he pleaded again
the all-absorbing routine of office and home life.[2] "The extreme
irregularity of my life makes poetry out of the question, for the
present, except for momentary violences" (*L*, 249), he explained
to Marianne Moore in the same year. Stevens' daughter speculates
that a noisy two-family house on Farmington Avenue in Hartford,
where Stevens and his family were living, further dampened his
desire to write. As late as August, 1932, though he had published a
few new poems such as "The Sun This March" and "Autumn Refrain," he wrote to Harriet Monroe, "Whatever else I do, I do not
write poetry nowadays" (*L*, 262). "Autumn Refrain" itself had
come as a result of Blackmur's request in 1931 for a poem to accompany his essay "Examples of Wallace Stevens" in *Hound and
Horn*. Stevens had seen Blackmur's comments in the essay on "The
Emperor of Ice-Cream" and liked the effort well enough to permit
a momentary lapse from his vow of silence.

For all his complaints about the demands of business and family,
Stevens mysteriously turned away from the activity for which he

2. "A Letter," *Antaeus*, XXXVI (Winter, 1980), 146. Ellen Williams has summarized
Pound's attitude toward Stevens: "Possibly it was the strong cerebral element in Wallace Stevens' early poems that kept Pound dubious about him. Nowhere in his voluminous correspondence to Harriet Monroe does he make a remark about Stevens or about his work. In
the year 'Sunday Morning' was published, Pound on August 30, 1916, made his usual can-
vass of candidates for the Levinson Prize without noticing Stevens' poem amid the 'overwhelming amount of rubbish' he found in the magazine" (*Harriet Monroe and the Poetry Renaissance: The First Ten Years of "Poetry," 1912–22* [Urbana, 1977], 166).

had been longing since his Harvard days. What accounts for the abrupt reversal? Had *Harmonium* in some way embarrassed or discouraged him? Although many reviewers praised the collection, a few judged it harshly and questioned the poet's ability to progress beyond it. Did his Hartford business associates berate their colleague's hobby? Did his wife press harder her apparent disapproval? Or had Stevens reached a point in his development that left him uncertain about the future direction of his work? Had the writing of his longest poem, "The Comedian as the Letter C," left him with the sense that it was an overwrought *tour de force* in spite of its parody? Was Crispin's surcease, "Concluding fadedly" (*CP*, 46), no more than a disguise for his own? The evidence to resolve these questions remains incomplete, but neither is there cause to believe that Stevens intended this respite to be permanent.

One should not overlook the marked reluctance on Stevens' part to put himself forward publicly as a poet, even from the Harvard years when he had signed his sonnets R. Jerries, John Morris 2nd, and Hillary Harness. Writing poems and eventually publishing them were essential to Stevens, but a part of him recoiled from the public image of the poet, an image in his own mind incompatible with his business suit and affidavits. *Harmonium* had created a minor stir. Stevens may have preferred to shore up his identity as businessman and family man before indulging again in poetry. The conflict that had begun a quarter century earlier, with his father's opposition to his poetic ambitions, would be resolved to his own satisfaction only about ten years after the publication of his first volume.

In a notable letter on March 13, 1933, Stevens confided to Morton Dauwen Zabel at *Poetry* that he was writing again after a decade's silence: "For some reason I have had a good many requests for poems recently. I have complied with a few of these. The truth is that I am not willing to use unpublished manuscript; moreover I do not much like the new things I write. Writing again after a discontinuance seems to take one back to the beginning rather than to the point of discontinuance" (*L*, 265). In about 1930 he had apparently begun collecting notes for titles and phrases, eventually entering them in a notebook called *From Pieces of Paper*. Two years later he had purchased a house on Westerly Terrace that guaranteed his privacy and was to be his permanent home in Hartford. His business endeavors were clearly going well, and in 1934 he was named a vice-president. The pleas from Monroe, Williams, Pound, Moore, and others were not in vain, and it is noteworthy that the requests he mentioned casually to Zabel aided in his renewed concentration.

Conrad Aiken reports his own role in the new poems of the 1930s:

> In 1933 or 1934 I suggested to J.M. Dent, via Richard Church, that they should bring out HARMONIUM in their poetry series, and I was asked to write Stevens about this, or rather, to ask him for a new book—in their perverse way, they didn't want a book ten years old. Stevens in due course replied that he didn't have anything, he hadn't been writing. End of correspondence. In 1936 I first met him at Ted Spencer's, after he had given a reading in Sanders Theatre. When we were introduced, he at once said that he regarded me as the godfather of all his recent work, and that it was my request for a book for Dent that had started him off again.[3]

It was, in fact, the invitation from Dent that led Stevens to write "Owl's Clover," though that long poem had been written after the poems for *Ideas of Order* (1935).

A larger factor in the renewal of Stevens' poetry was his correspondence beginning in 1933 with Ronald Lane Latimer. To this day, Latimer remains the most enigmatic of those individuals who figure prominently in Stevens' career. Only twenty-three and a complete stranger to Stevens, he approached the poet for contributions to his new magazine in 1933, and Stevens was immediately responsive and increasingly friendly thereafter. Latimer's letters are polite, but never familiar; through them and his various publishing ventures, he gradually became a new sponsor at the very time Stevens was disposed to start anew. Latimer replaced Harriet Monroe as the sympathetic critic and editor who prodded the recalcitrant poet with the proper balance of delicate flattery and encouragement. Charles Robertson, a classmate and a friend, discusses Latimer's elusive identity:

---

3. Conrad Aiken to [?], 1960, Letter 218, in *Selected Letters of Conrad Aiken,* ed. Joseph Killorin (New Haven, 1978), 305. Aiken's original letter to Stevens, proposing the project for Dent, is in the University of Massachusetts Library, Amherst, and is dated, not "1933 or 1934," but January 5, 1935.

His original name, James Leippert, stayed with him through public schools in Kingston, New York, where he was born, and Columbia College, where he was graduated with the class of 1934. During the next year, which saw the start of the Alcestis Press, he took the name of Mark Jason, then Martin Jay. Not long after that he started calling himself J. Ronald Lane Latimer. The Ronald came from Ronald Firbank, one of his favorite writers, the Lane from John Lane, the English publisher whose career he would have liked to emulate. Besides being fairly unusual, Latimer simply caught his fancy at the time. The J was soon dropped, although Jay had been his nickname and remained so among his friends. After about another year, he went into court and made the change legal. There was no need to hide his identity or anything sinister about the changes.[4]

For his own part, Stevens encouraged Latimer in his publishing operations, offered business advice, and forfeited the royalties on *Ideas of Order* to aid him financially. Latimer was full of questions about the poems and was the first of several people to whom Stevens wrote many letters offering explanations of his work. Stevens told Hi Simons in 1940 that "I owe a very great deal to him [Latimer]. I don't mean to say because he published some of my things, but because he started me up to doing them" (*L,* 359). Latimer offered to publish both individual poems and a collection, and "The Idea of Order at Key West" and seven other poems appeared in the first number of Latimer's *Alcestis* in October, 1934. "The Idea of Order at Key West," among the first new poems of the 1930s, was, like the earlier Florida poems, the result of return visits to Key West. Stevens was, in fact, at the Key West Colonial Hotel in February, 1934. One of the major poems of the *oeuvre,* it must have been recognized immediately by the poet as superior to the other Florida poems. Clearly, Stevens' powers as a poet were undiminished.

As early as 1932 or 1933, Stevens read the newly completed "Mud Master" to Judge Powell while they were in Key West: "He had just finished it," Powell recalled, "and was trying it out on me,

4. Charles Robertson, "Communications," *Wallace Stevens Journal,* I (Summer, 1977), 81. The Alumni Federation of Columbia University adds the following information: "This is in response to your inquiry about James Leippert who received a Bachelor of Arts degree from Columbia College in October 1933. Mr. Leippert who was born on October 27, 1909, changed his name to Ronald Lane Latimer in 1935. I am sorry to say we have no further information to give you" (Marion Moscato to George S. Lensing, July 10, 1979, in the possession of the recipient).

as the dog. He was specially pleased with the word 'pickanines' in the third verse." In 1934 Stevens arrived in Tampa three days ahead of Judge Powell, who recovered the manuscript of "The Pleasures of Merely Circulating" from Stevens' hotel room. A year later, when Stevens was writing with great speed to prepare *Ideas of Order,* he was again in Florida with Powell: "In February, 1935, we were at Key West again; and his poem 'Mozart 1935' . . . was forming in his mind. In the second and third lines, for sound effect, he uses the phrases, 'hoo-hoo-hoo,' 'shoo-shoo,' and 'ric-a-nic.' I now have in my possession a scrap of brown paper, a piece of a heavy envelope, with this written on it in his handwriting: 'ses hurlemente, / 'ses chucuotments, ses ricaments.' / 'Its hoo-hoo-hoo, / 'its shoo-shoo-shoo, its ric-a-nic.'"[5]

When Latimer proposed in 1934 that his Alcestis Press publish a volume, Stevens greeted the idea warmly: "I cannot imagine anything that I should like more" (*L,* 271). Gathering poems for *Ideas of Order* led in turn to the writing of new ones. He declined, for example, Latimer's appeal for an introduction to Ernest Dowson's poems, writing in December: "It might be a very good thing, therefore, if I were to concentrate during the next month or two on poetry, and forego the Dowson." Perhaps with such poems as "Autumn Refrain" and the just completed "Like Decorations in a Nigger Cemetery" in mind, he added in the same letter, "Since it is the tone of the whole that is important, I might want to work on the thing, adding, say, 10 or 15 pages, in order to give a little gaiety and brightness. My mind is not ordinarily as lamentable as some of these poems suggest" (*L,* 273).

As he had bantered with Elsie over the composition of the "June Books" twenty-five years earlier, he re-created a twitting self-caricature for Latimer. It is, however, the jest of a newly confident poet, for one of Stevens' most fruitful periods of composition was under way: "I sit down every evening after dinner, and, after a little music, put my forefinger in the middle of my forehead and struggle with my imagination. The results have really been quite shocking. The other night I took it into my head to describe a deathbed farewell under the new regime ["Waving Adieu, Adieu, Adieu"]. And I am bound to say that I liked the result immensely for the moment.

5. Peter A. Brazeau, "'My Dear Old Boy': The Wallace Stevens–Arthur Powell Friendship," *Antaeus,* XXXVI (Winter, 1980), 156, 157.

So you see what happens when one tries to pump up floods of color" (*L*, 273).

We know that Stevens' process of writing poems at this time was not always so simple. A month earlier, when he had sent the fifty short poems of "Like Decorations in a Nigger Cemetery" to Zabel at *Poetry,* he disclosed a new method of composition: "If you do not like these, do not hesitate to say so. It is very difficult for me to find the time to write poetry, and most of these have been written on the way to and from the office" (*L*, 272). The epigrammatic quality of "Like Decorations" (most of the poems are in tercets or quatrains) hints at brisk improvisation: in March he told Latimer that "spontaneity and fluidity" were among the effects he sought (*L*, 276). Walking to and from his office that autumn reminded Stevens of Whitman: "In the far South the sun of autumn is pass- ing / Like Walt Whitman walking along a ruddy shore" (*CP*, 150). Much of the poem's imagery, however, derives from the view from Terry Road, Asylum Avenue, or the setting of Elizabeth Park and its large pond, all on Stevens' way to work. In late October he promised the poem to *Poetry* and he submitted it on December 6, so it was likely written in November:

> It was when the trees were leafless first in November
> And their blackness became apparent, that one first
> Knew the eccentric to be the base of design. (*CP*, 151)

(The month is named again in section XXXIV.) The dominant motif of "Like Decorations" is the spoliation of the year in late au- tumn and its metaphorical counterpart in the decreations of the imagination within the self. Accordingly, the poem scans the locus of its source in Hartford: "rouged fruits in early snow" (XV); "A teeming millpond . . . / Gray grasses rolling windily away / And bristling thorn-trees spinning on the bank" (XXXI); "chrysanthe- mums' astringent fragrance" (XLI). "Like Decorations in a Nigger Cemetery" signals a sharp contrast to the exoticism of the south- ern Florida and Cuban poems, even though the title and one line ("The hen-cock crows at midnight and lays no egg") came from Judge Powell's colorful speech.[6]

Between November 28, 1934, when he responded favorably to

6. *Ibid.*, 154.

Latimer's proposal for a new volume, and March 26, 1935, when he reported that he had turned the manuscript over to a stenographer, Stevens wrote with astonishing speed. Almost half of the thirty-three poems in *Ideas of Order* were composed then, though he spent part of February in Key West on business. In the middle of that outburst, Stevens submitted to Latimer a discovery: "One of the essential conditions to the writing of poetry is impetus. That is a reason for thinking that to be a poet at all one ought to be a poet constantly. It was a great loss to poetry when people began to think that the professional poet was an outlaw or an exile. Writing poetry is a conscious activity. While poems may very well occur, they had very much better be caused" (*L,* 274).

In the March 26 letter Stevens also mentioned the invitation from Richard Church of J. M. Dent that Aiken had promoted. From London, Church had encouraged him "to write a long poem for a series of long poems which his firm is publishing." Here again it was a request that prompted a new project. He later told Knopf that Church has asked for something of "approximately seven hundred lines."[7] The writing of "Owl's Clover," one of his least successful poems, was to occupy Stevens intermittently for more than a year. No other poem proved as troublesome. In this case, the impetus that had carried him through *Ideas of Order* was wanting.

"Owl's Clover" was also the result of a personal accusation. Writing a review of *Ideas of Order* for the *New Masses,* a young poet-critic named Stanley Burnshaw attacked Stevens on several grounds, but finally for his irrelevance in the social turmoil of the mid-1930s. *Harmonium,* for example, "is remembered for its curious humor, its brightness, words and phrases that one rolls on the tongue. It is the kind of verse that people concerned with the murderous world collapse can hardly swallow today except in tiny doses." The second volume, according to Burnshaw, was even worse: "Stevens can no longer write. His harmonious cosmos is suddenly screeching with confusion." A member of a class "menaced by the clashes between capital and labor," Stevens was seen "in the throes of struggle for philosophical adjustment."[8] Burn-

---

7. Wallace Stevens to Alfred A. Knopf, March 23, 1936, in possession of Alfred A. Knopf, Inc., New York.

8. Stanley Burnshaw, "Turmoil in the Middle Ground," *New Masses,* XVII (October 1, 1935), 42.

shaw, Stevens told Latimer, "lament[s] in a way that would have given Job a fever" (*L,* 286). Prompted by Burnshaw, Stevens struggled to sustain a disapproval of collective materialism in favor of the individual imagination. When he told Simons, for example, that "The Statue at the World's End" ("Mr. Burnshaw and the Statue") was concerned with "*adaptation to change*" (*L,* 366), that change was not envisaged as political revolution, but, ironically, every life in every epoch lived "incessantly in change" (*OP,* 50). In short, Stevens adapts Burnshaw's cant to his own ends. Political cliché is remade, though often without sufficient focus over so prolonged and forced an exercise, into the poet's personal and poetic values.

In addition to the Burnshaw review, Stevens looked back to a poem of his own, one that had just appeared in the *Southern Review,* "The Old Woman and the Statue." (This poem eventually became the first of the five parts of "Owl's Clover.") As he explained to Latimer, the image of the statue, "about which I am doing a great deal of writing now-a-days" (*L,* 290), was being reassigned to "Mr. Burnshaw and the Statue." The parallelism of the two titles, the use of the statue as a major image in both, and the longer form (the former in five parts, the latter in seven), must have led Stevens to think of them at once as companion poems. He also saw that, putting the two together, he had 179 lines of the 700-line poem Dent was requesting. Three weeks after completing "Mr. Burnshaw and the Statue," Stevens wrote to Latimer: "I intend to do a set of six or seven STATUES; you have now seen two of them. That is the group that I intend to submit to Dent, provided Mr. Church has the patience to wait for the group" (*L,* 296).

Latimer's encouragement pushed Stevens through the long writing of "Owl's Clover," but, in comparison with his work on "The Comedian as the Letter C," for example, progress was slow. "I have no idea when I shall write the balance, except that I like to spend my evenings at this time of year doing this sort of thing" (*L,* 296), he told Latimer in November, 1935. Two and a half months later, he was still justifying his inability to complete it: "I am sure that my manuscript will not be ready for some months, but I shall bear in mind your wish to have it as early as possible. I never like to use anything until I have got well away from it and until its effect on me is pretty much what its effect would be likely to be on any reader" (*L,* 308). Stevens submitted the complete poem to Latimer on May 16, 1936, and it was published as a separate volume.[9] It was extensively revised and shortened (from 861 to 607 lines) for *The Man with the Blue Guitar and Other Poems* and of course excluded altogether from the *Collected Poems*.

The way Stevens composed the two Alcestis Press volumes established his pattern for the next twenty years: flurries of easy and rapid writing followed by protracted periods when business interests prevailed. In his last published letter to Latimer, on June 28, 1938, he defended this practice:

> My own objection is that I do not feel that I have yet said what I have to say. The few things that I have already done have merely been preliminary. I cannot believe that I have done anything of real importance. The truth is, of course, that I never may, because there are so many things that take up my time and to which I am bound to give my best. Thinking about poetry is, with me, an affair of weekends and holidays, a matter of walking to and from the office. This makes it difficult to progress rapidly and certainly. Besides, I very much like the idea of something ahead; I don't care to make exhaustive effort to reach it, to see what it is. (*L,* 333)

In 1938, Latimer gave up his press and left the United States. Stevens had earlier made inquiries at the Hartford Accident and Indemnity Company about a possible job for him, but nothing came of it. Stevens later reported that his former editor had "turned Buddhist, and is a monk or priest in one of the temples of Tokio. Latimer is an extraordinary person who lives in an extraordinary world" (*L,* 391).

Alfred Knopf remained Stevens' commercial publisher and reissued *Ideas of Order* in a trade edition in 1936 with three new poems. Knopf himself never exercised the direct influence that Latimer had, but the New York publisher's steady support of Stevens through the succeeding volumes nourished a cordial relationship that was tested only briefly during an unsuccessful effort to publish Stevens in England.[10]

---

9. Holly Stevens notes that "the book was not published by the Dent firm; no correspondence relating to that possibility has been found by Mr. Church or the editor" (*L,* 311). This is corroborated in a letter from Peter Shellard, director of J. M. Dent & Sons Ltd., to George S. Lensing, August 13, 1976, in possession of the recipient.

10. See George S. Lensing, "Wallace Stevens in England," in Frank Doggett and Robert Buttel (eds.), *Wallace Stevens: A Celebration* (Princeton, 1980), 130–48.

It was Knopf's practice to write Stevens at various intervals to suggest a new volume; such a proposal invariably led to several months of intensified organizing and writing. For example, when Knopf suggested the volume that was to become *The Auroras of Autumn,* Stevens wrote Barbara Church about his reaction: "Last week was a week of some importance for me because Knopf sent me a letter about another book. I promised to send him a manuscript by the end of the year. This will keep me busy" (*L,* 639). On such occasions, Stevens worked toward a larger balance and cohesion in the selection, arrangement, and even writing of individual poems. Just as he had written to Latimer in 1934 about his desire to come up with "a little gaiety and brightness" to counter the "lamentable" tone of some of the poems he was then including in *Ideas of Order,* Stevens consistently strove for organic unity in his collections. When Latimer tried to interest Stevens in a third volume for the Alcestis Press in 1938, Stevens spoke further of that architectonic quality: "I have one or two things in mind about which it would be possible to organize a book. But I am a little careful about committing myself to any of these ideas." Although he did not dismiss Latimer's suggestion, he asked for time: "The force of a book is dependent on the force of the idea about which it is organized, and ideas of real force don't occur to one every day. Besides, I want my poetry to grow out of something more important than my inkwell" (*L,* 329).

Whatever unity Stevens discovered as he moved on in the preparation of a volume, he found a new momentum as the poems rapidly appeared. While organizing *Transport to Summer* in 1946, for example, he was suddenly able to comply bountifully with some of the endless requests he received from magazine editors. To Theodore Weiss of the *Quarterly Review of Literature* he sent a dozen poems, saying, "No doubt, this is more than you want or even thought of. But you could make a choice." [11] In a second letter a week later, he explained that he was working on a new volume for Knopf, and the twelve poems appeared in the same order in *Transport to Summer* (1947).

After *Ideas of Order,* requests for poems increased, and, though Stevens might plead for time, he was extraordinarily generous in

11. Wallace Stevens to Theodore Weiss, June 25, 1946, in possession of the recipient.

trying to satisfy them, no matter how obscure or financially fragile the magazine. Stevens never engaged the services of a literary agent. Near the end of his life he told Renato Poggioli, his Italian translator: "I have never collected reviews even in English: have never had a clipping service and have never tried to make a literary business out of poetry." [12] When Hi Simons was preparing a bibliography of Stevens' published work in 1938, the poet explained how he submitted his poems: "I always contributed because somebody asked me to do so, and never by way of sending things round. This is just the opposite of the common experience" (*L,* 336). That practice continued. For example, an Englishman, Clifford Collins, had written Stevens in 1948 requesting new poems—one longer work and a few shorter ones as well—for a pamphlet to be published in London. Stevens spoke to Norman Holmes Pearson about his assignment: "Some time ago I promised some people in England a group of poems about September 1st. I am at work on these now. They want one long one of, say, one hundred lines or more. If I can finish that one this week, I shall take a chance on the others and probably accept your invitation" (*L,* 604–605). The longer poem was "The Bouquet," which contains 108 lines in tercets. He mailed the poems to Collins on August 8, and they arrived almost precisely on the prescribed date. There is, however, no evidence that Collins ever published the five poems intended for the *Critic Miscellany* series. In December, in fact, Stevens complained to McGreevy that the poems had not been returned to him (*L,* 625). Again, in 1952, Margaret Marshall extended a special invitation: a complete page of poems by him for the *Nation.* She needed about 100 lines of poetry, and the poems could be long or short, she explained. [13] He responded with seven short poems, "An Old Man Asleep," "The Irish Cliffs of Moher," "The Plain Sense of Things," "One of the Inhabitants of the West," "Lebensweisheitspielerei," "The Hermitage at the Center," and "The Green Plant." The choice, he said in his cover letter, was in close accord with her instructions: "It was easier for me to do a group of short poems than a long one, and here they are. There are 115 lines, to which there must be added lines for titles and title

12. Wallace Stevens to Renato Poggioli, February 26, 1954.
13. Margaret Marshall to Wallace Stevens, August 18, 1952.

spaces, so that this is a little more than you asked for" (*L,* 764). Although the procedure in these instances seems almost mechanical, the fact remains that Stevens did some of his best work as the result of invitation, restriction, and deadline.

More rarely, but with increasing frequency toward the end of his life, invitations to read his poems furnished another stimulus. In December, 1946, for example, he wrote to Rodríguez-Feo that he was to deliver a lecture sponsored by the Morris Gray Fund at Harvard: "On this occasion I am only thinking about my subject, not reading about it. I am not going to quote anybody. Taking a new and rather quackish subject and developing it without the support of others is not quite the easiest thing in the world to do. If, however, I get nowhere with it, I can always abandon it and do something else. It is curious how a subject once chosen grows like a beanstalk until it seems as if there had never been anything else in the world" (*L,* 544). He ended up with a lecture, "The Realm of Resemblance," and two new poems, "Someone Puts a Pineapple Together" and "Of Ideal Time and Choice." "An Ordinary Evening in New Haven" was written after Louis Martz asked him to address the Connecticut Academy of Arts and Sciences, and Stevens recited the poem in 1949 at the academy's thousandth meeting. In addition, he wrote "Description without Place" for the Phi Beta Kappa exercises at Harvard in 1945 and "The Sail of Ulysses" for the same ceremony at Columbia in 1954.

Except for the various war poems that Stevens wrote throughout his career, he did not often produce occasional verse. "To an Old Philosopher in Rome" was written while his mentor Santayana was dying at the Little Company of Mary nursing home. The friendship with Henry Church, a wealthy editor and sponsor of the arts, began in 1939 and continued until Church died eight years later. "The Owl in the Sarcophagus," which does not specifically name him, "was written in the frame of mind following Mr. Church's death" (*L,* 566).

During the last twenty years of his career, Stevens' business routine continued to determine the time he could allot to poetry. Many poems were written during the evening hours, but the poet habitually retired early, around 9:00 or 10:00 P.M. Furthermore, he liked to read and listen to music during the hours before bed. Weekends, too, provided a chance to write and, frequently under pressure to make good on promises to magazine editors or to complete a forthcoming volume, he made use of them. "I'm glad I'm mainly a weekend poet," he told Theodore Weiss in 1945. "Otherwise I would write too much." He was "compelled to compose his poetry on Sunday afternoon walks," he told Signe Culbertson in 1955.[14] Preparing the manuscript for *Harmonium* for Van Vechten had taken longer than he expected—it was, for a poor typist, "an awful job to typewrite" (*L,* 232). His stenographer at the office (Marguerite Flynn for many years) received his drafts when he arrived in the morning and, as time allowed, prepared a clean typescript. Partly for this reason, Stevens tended to favor writing in the mornings. Moreover, he was an early riser, and the walk through Elizabeth Park provided additional time to organize and make notes, as he had done when he wrote "Like Decorations in a Nigger Cemetery."

Just after completing "An Ordinary Evening in New Haven" in 1949, he commented on his writing schedule in two letters, both dated July 13. To McGreevy, he said: "I shall have to go on with these short poems perhaps to the end of August [Stevens was working on *The Auroras of Autumn*] since it is not possible for me to write more than a very few of them a month. I have a little time each morning before I come to the office" (*L,* 640). In his letter to Samuel French Morse, he wrote about a manuscript of "The Man with the Blue Guitar" that he had donated to the University of Buffalo: "About the manuscript at the Lockwood Memorial Library: that ought to have gone into the wastebasket because I have no real manuscripts in the sense in which people speak of manuscripts. Most of the poems that I have written, at least in recent years, have been written in the morning on my way to the office. I make notes and try to fix things in my mind and then when I arrive at the office arrange these things and, finally, when I am at home in the evening I write the thing out. The result is hardly a manuscript" (*L,* 641). And in 1951, he outlined a similar program. John Sweeney, director of the Lamont Library poetry room at Harvard, had asked for worksheets to display at an exhibition of Stevens' books. Stevens replied: "I have no worksheets. My custom is to make notes, then to transcribe them and, finally, to have the poem typed here at the office whenever my stenographer has a little leisure. As soon as the thing has been typed, I throw everything else away so as not to be bothered with it" (*L*, 713).

How much of the transcribing and revising actually took place during business hours is a matter of speculation. Stevens mentioned in one letter that he did not own an *Oxford English Dictionary,* and one of his business associates, Charles O'Dowd, recalls Stevens' frequent use of the unabridged *Webster's* in the firm's law library. At least two persons from the company occasionally went to the Connecticut State Library at Stevens' request to check words in the *OED*. Stevens' habit of composing on his way to work was witnessed by several people. The image of "fat Jocundus" in full stride is unique, as Brendan Gill has recorded: "Once, my sister, glancing out of a window, saw Stevens going by her house. As she watched, he slowed down, came to a stop, rocked in place for a moment or two, took a step backward, hesitated, then strode confidently forward—left, right, left, right—on his way to work. It was obvious to her that Stevens had gone back over a phrase, dropped an unsatisfactory word, inserted a superior one, and proceeded to the next line of the poem he was making."[15]

Stevens' walks brought the immediacy of the season and day to his keenest attention. Holly Stevens remembers the general scene: "But the street was terraced, that is, divided into two roads running parallel along a hillside, with the green strip between the roads planted with cherry trees that bloomed profusely in season. And on Terry Road there was a whole field of daffodils to pass on spring days, on the way to my school, or to Dad's office, or to Elizabeth Park, a portion of which ran along Asylum Avenue where Terry Road came into it." A dictionary and a stenographer waited at his office; revisions and final touches could be completed at his desk or at home. "But I don't revise much," he told the New York *Times* when the *Collected Poems* was published. "Anything I've finally gotten out, I'd be reluctant to change. A change resulting from no more than forced labor is not the right thing for poetry."[16]

15. Peter A. Brazeau, "Poet in Grey Business Suit: Glimpses of Stevens at the Office," *Wallace Stevens Journal,* I (Spring, 1977), 30; Brazeau, *Parts of a World,* 48, 68; Brendan Gill, *Here at the New Yorker* (New York, 1975), 57.
16. Holly Stevens, "Bits of Remembered Time," *Southern Review,* n.s., VII (1971), 653;

His dislike of "forced labor" notwithstanding, some poems proved more troublesome. We have seen his failure to arrive at a satisfactory draft of "For an Old Woman in a Wig" around 1915 and his working for six months on "Owl's Clover" in 1935 and 1936. Samuel French Morse reproduces stanzas omitted from "Le Monocle de Mon Oncle" (*OP*, 19), "The Man with the Blue Guitar" (*OP*, 72–73), and "Examination of the Hero in a time of War" (*OP*, 83–84). After Stevens read "The Sail of Ulysses" at Columbia in 1954, he said: "Perhaps I shan't throw it away. But I shall certainly never use it in its present form nor allow anyone to see a copy of it" (*L*, 834). He then condensed the poem from 176 lines to 24 and retitled it "Presence of an External Master of Knowledge" before it was published in the *Times Literary Supplement*.

Stevens also quietly withdrew a few poems from the canon. "The Silver Plough Boy," "Exposition of the Contents of a Cab," and "Architecture" were omitted from the second edition of *Harmonium*. He removed "Life on a Battleship" from the *Collected Poems* and "The Woman That Had More Babies Than That" that had been in *Parts of a World*. A satisfactory draft of a poem may have come without great fuss, but the poet was not indifferent to its success, and he could excise one if it came to displease him.

Few of Stevens' poems were rejected by the editors of magazines, but on those occasions he took the setback seriously enough to reexamine the poem carefully. Such apparently was the case with "A Pastoral Nun." He sent the poem to Randall Jarrell at the *Nation* in 1946, adding some revisions a few days later: "In the last line of the sixth verse *he* should be *it*. The line will then read "'Contending against a rider it does not know.'"[17] Jarrell rejected the poem, and when it appeared in *Transport to Summer* the following spring, it had been reduced to five tercets, and the line cited in his letter was eliminated altogether. When "From the Journal of Crispin" failed to take the Blindman Prize in 1922, he held it back from Harriet Monroe, who wanted it for *Poetry*. In his extensive revisions, he omitted large parts of its four sections and added a final two sections for its first publication in *Harmonium*.

In a few instances, there are extant manuscript variations of lines

---

Lewis Nichols, "Talk with Mr. Stevens," *New York Times Book Review*, October 3, 1954, p. 31.

17. Wallace Stevens to Randall Jarrell, July 17, 1946.

or groups of lines, in spite of the poet's routinely disposing of them. A small cache was donated to Yale by a fellow tenant in the Stevenses' first home in Hartford: "Once in a while my Mother would grab a few pages from the trash can that were obviously Mr. Stevens' work—that is the source of the enclosed material." The collection includes "From the Journal of Crispin" and a few autograph and typescript versions of shorter poems. We know about William Carlos Williams' minor role in the editing of "The Worms at Heaven's Gate" for *Others* in 1916, and his deleting the final two lines as "a sentimental catch at the end." Those lines are now disclosed: "O, stallions, like a pitiless charioteer . . / *She will forget us in the crystalline.*"[18] Stevens' rhapsodic indulgence, evidenced in other poems from this period, is here unrestrained.

"Sonatina to Hans Christian," a poem that was added to the second edition of *Harmonium,* shows a more thoroughgoing review—this time at the poet's own urging. The poem poses the possibility that a duck, presumably like Hans Christian Andersen's ugly duckling, might have a mother either "Regretful that she bore her" or "Barren, and longing for her." The duck's origin is sadly unresolved. The poem concludes (ll. 9–16):

*Earlier version*

What of the dove,
Or lark, or any bird one sees?
What of the very trees,
And intonations of the trees?

What of the light
That lights and dims the stars?
Do you know, Hans Christian,
Now that you know the night?[19]

*Final version*

What of the dove,
Or thrush, or any singing mysteries?
What of the trees
And intonations of the trees?

---

18. Louis L. Martz, "Manuscripts of Wallace Stevens," *Yale University Library Gazette,* LIV (October, 1979), 52 (quoting Reverend John Curry Gay), 66.
    19. *Ibid.,* 65.

What of the night
That lights and dims the stars?
Do you know, Hans Christian,
Now that you see the night? (*CP,* 110)

The process is one of apotheosis as the duckling moves through dove, thrush, trees and their intonations, and finally to night. But the later and more exalted figures are also orphans in a world whose begetters are either hostile or barren. The poem simply surrenders the dilemma of universal solitude to Hans Christian's vision of darkness. In his revisions, Stevens achieves both precision and starkness. The second mother, originally "Full of first longing for her [the duckling]," is remade as "Barren, and longing for her"—thus sharpening the meaning and deepening the poignancy. Line 10—originally "Or lark, or any bird one sees?"—is rewritten "Or thrush, or any singing mysteries?" The bird is *not* to be "any bird," but now one enlarged to "singing mysteries" and "intonations of the trees" (l. 12). Such birds are not common ducklings ("any duck in any brook") or even doves, but angelic. Originally it was "light / That lights and dims the stars" (ll. 13–14). But the redundancy ("the light / That lights") is overt, and the substitution of "night" enhances the cosmic mystery of the cumulative panorama. The reader is left with Hans Christian's vision of terror in that night (the sharper "see" of line 16 instead of the more abstract "know"). Not recasting the poem, but tidying it up, Stevens made his changes confidently. The majority of his poems apparently underwent similar revisions with a minimum of alteration.

Autographs in pencil of two later poems, "The Old Lutheran Bells at Home" and "Questions Are Remarks," are preserved among Stevens' papers at the Huntington Library. In each case, Stevens wrote alternate conclusions on the reverse of the leaves. "The Old Lutheran Bells at Home" ends with the tercet:

Each truth is a sect though no bells ring for it.
And the bells belong to the sextons, after all,
As they jangle and dangle and kick their feet. (*CP,* 462)

For the final line, however, he considered the following: "As they teeter and totter in the caterwaul"; "As the sextons jangle & dangle & kick their feet"; and "As they teeter & totter in the belfry [walls?]." The wobbling motion is obviously foremost in Stevens'

conception—he twice experiments with "teeter & totter." The caterwaul may have seemed too shrill for church bells, though the
sound of the uncommon word had its own appeal; it also offered
an effective rhyme with "after all" in the preceding line. The second alternate is of course closest to the final choice. Replacing
"sextons" with "they" introduces an obviously intended ambiguity. "They" could refer to "bells" and "sextons" in the previous
line. The "feet" seem more appropriate to the sextons, but the
"jangle" closer to the bells.[20]

"Questions Are Remarks" was written at the same time and
submitted simultaneously with "The Old Lutheran Bells at Home"
and four other poems to *Botteghe Oscure.* The poem in its final version ends:

> His [young Peter's] question is complete because it contains
> His utmost statement. It is his own array,
> His own pageant and procession and display.
>
> As far as nothingness permits . . . Hear Him.
> He does not say, "Mother, my mother, who are you,"
> The way the drowsy, infant, old men do. (*CP,* 462–63)

The final tercet again gave Stevens pause. As the manuscript in the
Huntington Library reveals, he wrote variations on the reverse
side:

> As far as nothingness permits. He thinks
> Without alleging but he alleges too
> The potencies he thinks his mother knows.
>
>                    Hear him
> He does not say Mother who are you. Adult
> Babblers declare themselves by such lost words
>
> As far as nothingness permits. He speaks
> But he does not say "Mother, who are you?" The adult
> Babblers declare themselves by their lost words
>                                   Adult
> Babblers declare themselves by such lost words.
>            confound

20. When the poem was being translated into Italian, Stevens gave instructions that the
pronoun "they" should agree with "bells"; the language itself disallowed the ambiguity.
Wallace Stevens to Princess Bassiano, July 26, 1949.

The first alternate is the weakest: line 2 is confusing and the poem would end with a limp abstraction ("potencies"). The other tercets are closer to the final choice. His adherence to "adult babblers" in both is consistent with "adult enfantillages" earlier in the poem. But the image has changed altogether with the line he finally chose, "The way the drowsy, infant, old men do." The caesuras retard the pace, and the shift from "babblers" to "drowsy, infant, old men" extends the connotations of senility and imminent death; Peter's grandparents' perceptions are unpurified. The periphrastic slackness of the drafts is excised in the final selection.

Stevens here struggles with the problem of concluding both poems. The ideas and even the images are already worked out; it is phraseology that troubles him. But the movement from the obvious mediocrity of the alternates to the final versions reveals the sure hand of the artist advancing through trial and error to the most forceful result. Although there may have been earlier drafts of both poems, one nonetheless notes how few other alterations there are between the drafts and the published poems. Erasures are evident in the autograph copies, but their number is small.

The evidence suggests that Stevens did not struggle inordinately in the process of writing, and his frequent references to the impetus that carried him along indicate that the rhythm of composition was relatively unbroken. After another visit to Key West in 1940—this time he went by air—Florida was still a potent influence: "Since coming back, I must have written a good many things. The truth is that I am at one of those stages at which it is hard to get away from one's thoughts. The difficulty with such a stage is that there is so much push that one is not willing to stop to make things perfect, the desire is to get them down as they come." In an early draft of his essay "A Collect of Philosophy," he even acknowledged: "The poet, in moments of exceptional concentration sometimes experiences an automatism in which the poem writes itself. It seems as if the imagination realized its intention, however obscure its intention may have been, with an instantaneous directness." More typically, something other than automatism directed the poet. "What I do is mostly instinctive," he told Latimer, who was requesting commentaries on his poems. "I mean by this that I go by feeling, and, generally speaking, I rather think that explanations of feeling, or of the results of feeling, are likely to be a little unreal." Frank Doggett, drawing on the essays, has outlined Stevens' psychology of composition: "Stevens' lifelong interest in the unconscious and the fortuitous as sources of inceptions, especially those of poems, in no sense obviates his dependence on the work of the intelligence in the making of poems. When his subject enters the center of consciousness, then the poet is the maker; he mediates the idea and shaping of his poem as carefully as a philosopher the logic of his thought."[21]

Stevens preserved a holograph in pencil of "Esthétique du Mal," written on legal-size note pads, which is now at the Huntington Library. Examining the apparent erasures in the poem, I found the most extensive changes in parts I, II, and XV, where corrections were made in eight lines, eight lines, and six lines, respectively. There appear to be none at all in parts III, VII, VIII, IX, X, XII, XIII, and XIV. The evidence points to the fact that the long poem came to Stevens without great effort, though it is not possible to gauge the time and concentration he invested. Edwin Honig once asked Stevens about the varying lengths of the parts in "Esthétique du Mal." "'The reason for that,' he said in his deep, unchanging voice, 'is that I was writing on a pad of paper, and the contents of each sheet became a separate stanza. Some had more lines than others—I didn't bother to count them up.' I couldn't tell from his voice or facial expression if he was pulling my leg or not." Almost certainly he was not: in the manuscript, each section occupies a single page of the pad, with from one to four unused lines at the bottom of the pages.[22]

Stevens' practice of composing several shorter poems in sequence suggests the same disposition that led to the writing of his longer poems. When he informed Barbara Church late in his career that he had just sent off six short poems to a magazine at Harvard, he added: "As usual, I now want to go on under the impulse of ideas that occurred to me but which I did not use, and I do in fact intend to go on" (*L*, 685). As he told Margaret Marshall, sev-

21. Wallace Stevens to Henry Church, April 17, 1940; Peter A. Brazeau, "Three Manuscript Endings for 'A Collect of Philosophy,'" in Doggett and Buttel (eds.), *Wallace Stevens*, 51; Wallace Stevens to Ronald Lane Latimer, September 25, 1935, in Box 1, folder 16, Ronald Lane Latimer Papers, University of Chicago Library; Frank Doggett, *Wallace Stevens: The Making of the Poem* (Baltimore, 1980), 22–23.
22. Edwin Honig, "Meeting Wallace Stevens," *Wallace Stevens Newsletter*, I (April, 1970), 12.

eral shorter poems had been easier than a single long one, but he frequently favored the long poem, a preference he also expressed to Barbara Church (*L*, 648). In 1907, Stevens had purchased an edition of Keats's letters. Beside these remarks he drew a marginal line: "I have heard Hunt say, and I may be asked—*why endeavor after a long Poem?* To which I should answer, Do not the Lovers of Poetry like to have a little Region to wander in, where they may pick and choose, and in which the images are so numerous that many are forgotten and found new in a second Reading: which may be food for a Week's stroll in the Summer?"[23] The "little Region to wander in" was congenial to the poet as well as the reader, and Stevens welcomed the freedom and range of longer meditations. He confessed to McGreevy: "I should try to write a number of shorter things for people to whom I have made promises. As a matter of fact, a short poem is more difficult to write than a long one because a long poem requires an impetus of its own" (*L*, 640).

Each of Stevens' volumes contains long poems, and most were written with far greater ease than was "Owl's Clover." As he was writing "The Comedian as the Letter C" in 1922 he boasted to Monroe: "I find that this prolonged attention to a single subject has the same result that prolonged attention to a senora has according to the authorities. All manner of favors drop from it" (*L*, 230). Stevens' attitude toward the long poem, the fact that it progressed "pretty much as one talks" (*L*, 648), suggests that he did not have precisely organized plans or outlines before him as he wrote and that the tone of improvisation and spontaneity was not mere affectation. "I almost always dislike anything that I do that doesn't fly in the window" (*L*, 505), he wrote to one correspondent in 1945.

The longer poems typically build upon a series of dramatic vignettes that serve as informal poetic parables. They are often playful, even childlike, delighting in novel and sometimes eccentric metaphorical expression. Many times they defy easy critical summary or paraphrase. The progress of Stevens' long poems is discursive; their structure is casual. They resist the tight interlocking of closely argued ideas. As Marie Borroff has said:

> The most important of the long poems, "Notes toward a Supreme Fiction," "The Auroras of Autumn," and "An Ordinary Evening in New

23. Keats to Benjamin Bailey, October 8, 1817, in Sidney Colvin (ed.), *Letters of John Keats to his Family and Friends* (London, 1891), 34.

Haven," lack the architectonic unity, the linear movement toward cul-
mination and resolution or systems of complementary relationships
among parts, of "When Lilacs Last in the Dooryard Bloomed," "The
Tower," *Four Quartets,* or even "The Waste Land"—though each has its
own emotional climate, its dramatic succession of moods and modes,
its risings and fallings off of intensity, its thematic repetitions. In a
sense, each is a collection of shorter poems, a set of variations rather
than a symphonic movement. When Stevens does develop a single fictional concept at length, as in "Examination of the Hero in Time of
War," "Chocorua to Its Neighbor," and "The Owl in the Sarcophagus," he is not at his most compelling. Something in him did not love
the building of massive monolithic structures.[24]

Before they were married, Elsie sent Stevens a poem, and his
comments unwittingly describe his own future method of composition, particularly the longer works: "From one of the many
possible figures—regard the mind as a motionless sea, as it is so
often. Let one round wave surge through it mystically—one mys-
tical mental scene—one image. Then see it in abundant undula-
tion, incessant motion—unbroken succession of scenes, say. —I
indulge in heavenly psychology—I lie back and drown in the del-
uge. The mind rolls as the sea rolls" (*L,* 118–19). Almost thirty
years later he rephrased the power of the mind's "unbroken succession of scenes" in terms of his own poetry: "I am thinking of using
images that are never fully defined. We constantly use such images:
any state of mind is in effect such an image. This is part of the
rapidity of thought" (*L,* 319).

Often in his prose Stevens gives unrehearsed evidence of this
very disposition of mind that adapted itself so naturally to the
making of poems. His first letter to Thomas McGreevy, for example, notes McGreevy's eagerness as a poet to receive a response
to his work. "It is the same satisfaction, if I may try to put my fin-
ger on it, that one gets from a sudden sense of kindness in an extremely unkind world. It is one of those things about poets that is
usually misunderstood, but it is something that it is important to
understand. And while I don't profess to understand it, nevertheless I do have a feeling about it. It is one of the vital characteristics
or areas" (*L,* 586). Here, his mind has taken hold of a central idea

---

24. Marie Borroff, *Language and the Poet: Verbal Artistry in Frost, Stevens and Moore* (Chicago, 1979), 76–77.

and performed a series of feints around it. This habit of thought and expression became endemic. It is one reason, I think, that his essays by and large lack precision and organization. In his eloquent definition of religious decreation in the essay "Two or Three Ideas," for example, he speaks of what remains after the deities have been dismissed: "There was always in every man the increasingly human self, which instead of remaining the observer, the non-participant, the delinquent, became constantly more and more all there was or so it seemed; and whether it was so or merely seemed so still left it for him to resolve life and the world in his own terms." Again the poet declares preemptively and climactically a conclusion—man is independent of the gods—but retreats slightly to concede that it seemed so and then to balance both possibilities ("whether it was so or merely seemed so") and finally to reassert the original conclusion that life has to be resolved on man's own terms (*OP,* 207).

Denis Donoghue has noted this fluidity of thought in Stevens' work: "Stevens loved to declare a theme, and then go walking around it as if it were a cathedral or a blackbird; he loved the process of thinking, not the thought that presses for a conclusion." The results are not surreal; Stevens' metaphors and parables are based in the phenomenal world, but the "pools of thought" out of which images and episodes evolve, the inveterate disposition to make conjunctions and extend appositions, and the penchant for fablelike and half-private symbolism, all derive from a poetic expansiveness that allowed for the mind's caprice. Marie Borroff sees the same "restlessness of mind" as accounting for Stevens' inventive, versatile, unpredictable diction.[25] Even the titles of many of his poems speak of notes, nuances, variations, extracts, repetitions, thirteen ways, decorations, asides, versions and prologues.

Stevens himself did not view his longer poems as necessarily inviolate. After completing "35 or 40 short pieces" (*L,* 316) of "The Man with the Blue Guitar," he sent only twelve to *Poetry* in 1937, and these (II, IX, XV, XVII, XVIII, XXIV, XXVII, XXVIII, XXIX, XXX, XXXI, XXXIII) appear to have been selected randomly. At the same time, he chose cantos V and XXVI for Julian Symons' *Twentieth Century Verse* in England. A similar dissection

25. Denis Donoghue, "The Snow Man," *New York Review of Books,* March 3, 1977, p. 22; Borroff, *Language and the Poet,* 73.

occurred for the first publication of "An Ordinary Evening in
New Haven." The poem's thirty-one sections were reduced to
eleven and reordered for *Transactions of the Connecticut Academy of
Arts and Sciences.* For an anthology Nicholas Moore was assem-
bling in 1943 for the Fortune Press in England, Stevens, because he
still controlled the copyright to the poem, suggested that Moore
select whatever parts of "Notes toward a Supreme Fiction" that
suited his purpose. In 1945 he authorized five parts of the same
poem and six sections from "The Man with the Blue Guitar" for
a Stevens issue of *Voices.* At Knopf's suggestion Stevens chose
eighty-six of his poems in 1950 for a proposed but never published
*Selected Poems.* He included "Esthétique du Mal" (sections III, VII,
VIII, XIII, and XIV); from "Notes toward a Supreme Fiction," "It
Must Be Abstract" (I, VII, and X), "It Must Change" (IV, V, VII,
and VIII), and "It Must Give Pleasure" (II, IV, VII, IX, and X);
"The Auroras of Autumn" (VIII and IX); "Things of August" (II,
III, and VII).[26] Stevens' willingness to publish parts of his long
poems separately and independently is testimony to his attitude
toward the order of his work. The poems clearly display unity and
progress of thought, but the organization remains loose, developed often by fits and starts, "part of the rapidity of thought."

Stevens' letters make it possible to chart with some precision
how long it took him to write some of the better-known longer
poems; personal circumstances during the period of composition
can be filled in as well. Invariably the poems were written easily—
sometimes with astonishing speed, sometimes unhurriedly. But if
the idea for a poem did not evolve readily, the poet threw it over.

"The Man with the Blue Guitar," for example, was begun in the
winter of 1936–37. Stevens told Latimer on March 17 that he had
completed "something like 35 or 40 short pieces, of which about
25 seem to be coming through" (*L,* 316). Five days later he sent
twelve sections to *Poetry.* After the volume with the same title was
published, Stevens reflected on the relation between the order of
writing and the poem's final text. "My impression is that these are
printed in the order in which they were written without rearrangement. There were a few that were scrapped. I kept them in their
original order for my own purposes, because one really leads into

26. The manuscript of the proposed volume is in the Huntington Library.

another, even when the relationship is only one of contrast" (*L,* 359). Even here, the progression from one section to the next is not rigorously logical; it is founded upon the associational and impressionistic linkings forged by a mind at play.

His next long poem, "Notes toward a Supreme Fiction," was begun five years later, also in the winter. He told Henry Church on January 28 of his decision to write the poem for publication by the Cummington Press. Katherine Frazier, the director of the press, had written Stevens on December 19, proposing to issue a small volume of his work. Located in Cummington, Massachusetts, the press produced special editions for small markets and eventually published three volumes by Stevens, in the manner of Latimer's Alcestis Press during the 1930s. "As yet I have not written a word of it," he said. "I don't expect to have any difficulty. This is the best time of the year for me: this and spring and early summer" (*L,* 401). There was an initial false start, as he explained to Church after he completed the poem: "At first I attempted to follow a scheme, and the first poem bore the caption REFACIMENTO. . . . But I very soon found that, if I stuck closely to a development, I should lose all of the qualities that I really wanted to get into the thing, and that I was likely to produce something that did not come off in any sense, not even as poetry" (*L,* 431). The distribution of parts and stanzas in "Notes toward a Supreme Fiction" was to be much more symmetrical than was usually the case with Stevens and this also proved restrictive. Stevens was not troubled for long with the problem, however. Although it is not known exactly when he began, by early spring the greater part of the poem was completed, and on May 14, he informed the Cummington Press of the general organization and progress of the poem:

> There will be 30 poems, each of seven verses, each verse of three lines. In short, there will be 21 lines of poetry on each page.
>
> These thirty poems are divided into three sections, each of which constitutes a group of ten. There will be a group title, but the separate poems will not have separate titles; thus, there will have to be a page or two between each of the groups.
>
> The title of the book will be NOTES TOWARD A SUPREME FICTION. Each of the three groups will develop, or at least have some relation to, a particular note: thus the first note is . . .
> IT MUST BE ABSTRACT
> The second note is

IT MUST CHANGE
Both of these sections are completed and I am now at work on the
third section, the title of which is . . .
IT MUST GIVE PLEASURE. (*L*, 406)

Despite the poem's symmetrical arrangement, Stevens always
thought of it as incomplete. He was probably referring to his progress up to May 14 when he wrote to Gilbert Montague a year later
that the poem "was written during March and April of 1942" (*L*,
443). On May 19, Stevens informed Katherine Frazier that "I am
now approaching the end of NOTES etc., and have, in fact, only one
more poem to do, although I am thinking of doing a few lines as a
sort of epilogue." Again, he defined his momentum: "Until I have
done them, I don't want to look back at anything that I have done. I
shall send you shortly a copy of one of the poems, but not until I
have completed the whole thing, because it bothers me to look
back" (*L*, 407). On June 1, Stevens sent the completed manuscript
to Cummington, though a couple of weeks later he added a dedication to Henry Church. "Notes toward a Supreme Fiction," for
all its neatness of structure, continued to suggest to the poet possibilities for expansion. He told Knopf in 1945 that he still expected
to double its length (*L*, 502), and as late as 1954 he repeated to
Robert Pack his plan for more sections, especially one entitled "It
Must Be Human." But he added as an afterthought, "I think that it
would be wrong not to leave well enough alone" (*L*, 864).

"Esthétique du Mal" came about after John Crowe Ransom's invitation that Stevens submit a poem to the *Kenyon Review*. Stevens
began the poem after June 17, 1944, on which day he wrote that "it
might be interesting to try to do an esthetique du mal" (*L*, 468).
And on July 28, he sent the complete poem to Ransom.

Requests for his work continued to spark Stevens' interest.
Having agreed to do the 1945 Phi Beta Kappa poem at Harvard, he
started "Description without Place" in April: "Although this is the
second or third subject that I have had in mind," he told Henry
Church, "unless it develops quickly and easily as I go along, I may
change it. It seems to me to be an interesting idea: that is to say, the
idea that we live in the description of a place and not in the place
itself, and in every vital sense we do" (*L*, 494). He mentioned to
Allen Tate that he was "at work" on the poem on May 2, but it was
completed in time for the June exercises.

Stevens described to McGreevy the writing of "An Ordinary

Evening in New Haven" in 1949 shortly after its completion. Again, the cumulative effect of the poem's evolution is emphasized:

> Very early last spring things began to pile up. My letters became more or less of a web. In particular, the amount of reading to be done that accumulated became just too much. I decided to step out from under the whole thing for a while. Then, about the same time, perhaps as part of the pleasure of this relaxation, I became interested in doing a poem, which, like most long poems, is merely a collection of short ones, and they went on and on. . . . I seem to need a lot of leisure and space around me now and then. (L, 640)

He later told Louis Martz, who had proposed the poem, "'So I just fixed on this idea of a poem about a walk in New Haven, but then branching out.' He said it really got so far away from the base that New Haven hardly appears in it, 'It's only the title, really, but,' he said, 'that's the way things happen with me. I start with a concrete thing, and it tends to become so generalized that it isn't any longer a local place. I think that puzzles some people.'"[27] Begun in early March, the poem was still unfinished when he wrote Bernard Heringman on May 3. His plan of action was "to keep studying the subject and working on it until I am quite through with it" (L, 637). The poem appears to have been completed by July, when he wrote to McGreevy, but he did not read it before the Connecticut Academy of Arts and Sciences until November 4.

The long poems seem, in a sense, to have written themselves. As Stevens said about "An Ordinary Evening in New Haven," it was "like most long poems . . . a collection of short ones, and they went on and on." He expected to progress fluidly, and he so relied on the poem's natural unfolding that he did not look back until the work was completed. Stevens' longer poems began with a general idea that he sought in advance; once the larger theme was in place, all the evidence suggests that the writing was unlabored and rapid. The poems appear to be unrehearsed improvisations that correspond loosely to the set theme, but that allow for deviation and variation.

Stevens' poems generally emerged from his eavesdropping upon his mind's leisurely discourse. A poem found its occasion in ordi-

---

27. Martz quoted in Brazeau, *Parts of a World*, 175.

nary things, as he told Barbara Church: "At the moment what I
have in mind is a group of things which mean a great deal more
than they sound like meaning: for instance, airing the house in the
morning; the colors of sunlight on the side of the house; people in
their familiar aspects" (*L,* 643). Within a year he described "the
houses of New England" as they "catch the first sun" in "A Discovery of Thought" (*OP,* 95). Shortly after, "Could it be that
yellow patch, the side / Of a house, that makes one think the
house is laughing?" appeared in "Long and Sluggish Lines"(*CP,*
522). More often than not, however, the sources of Stevens' poetry
are difficult to trace. In the letter to Barbara Church, he added:
"Often when I am writing poetry I have in mind an image of reading a page of a large book: I mean the large page of a book. What I
read is what I like. . . . At least what one ought to find is normal
life, insight into the commonplace, reconciliation with every-day
reality. The things that it makes me happy to do are things of this
sort" (*L,* 642–43). One sees poems spring from letters, books,
and paintings, and the epigraphs are frequent hints of how that
transformation occurred. And he used *Schemata* and *From Pieces of
Paper,* notebooks where he kept lists for titles and phrases.

One of Stevens' major poems derived from something he read.
When Ransom requested a poem for the *Kenyon Review,* he sent
along a copy of the spring issue. There was an essay by Ransom
himself, which was entitled "Artists, Soldiers, Positivists." In it,
Ransom quoted a letter from an unnamed soldier at the front:
"What *are* we after in poetry? Or, more exactly, what are we at-
tempting to rout? The commandos of contemporary literature are
having little to do with Eliot and even poets of charming distem-
per like Wallace Stevens (for whom we all developed considerable
passion). . . . Men like Karl Shapiro (his "Anxiety," in *Chimera* recently, is notable), John Berryman, Delmore Schwartz transcend
the aesthetic of poetry, thank God! I find the poetry in *Kenyon Review* lamentable in many ways because it is cut off from pain. It is
intellectual and it is fine, but it never reveals muscle and nerve."
Ransom in his own remarks rallied to justify that aesthetic as
something separate from public issues: "Art is addicted to peace.
Its contribution is not very large if measured by its plea for the
military or revolutionary cause, or in general the moral and/or sci-
entific causes which are the Positives of human life." At the same

time, art is an expression of "valuable ideals" and a paradigm of "rational human process."[28] We have seen the result of Stanley Burnshaw's review a decade earlier; here again, Stevens was roused to respond in verse.

Stevens had defined his position as early as the "Lettres d'un Soldat" series in 1918. In 1939 he had responded to an inquiry in the *Partisan Review* about the responsibilities of writers in war: "A war is a military state of affairs, not a literary one. Conceding that the propagandists don't agree, does it matter that they don't agree? The role of the writer in war remains the fundamental role of the writer intensified and concentrated."[29] Part of that concentration included a necessary resistance to the brutal fact of war as it preyed upon the human consciousness. In a brief prose memorandum for *Parts of a World* he wrote: "The poetry of a work of the imagination constantly illustrates the fundamental and endless struggle with fact. . . . But in war, the desire to move in the direction of fact as we want it to be and to move quickly is overwhelming" (*PEM*, 206). The poet cannot skirt the heinous facts of war, but neither does he indulge them for realism's sake. Rather, it is relief and survival in human terms ("fact as we want it to be") that give efficacy to his art. And in 1944 he took Ransom's notion of the positive aesthetic and the soldier's comments "about the relation between poetry and what he calls pain. Whatever he may mean . . . it is the kind of idea that it is difficult to shake off" (*L*, 468). The result was "Esthétique du Mal."

A few poems came about as the result of breaks in the poet's routine. Parts of *Harmonium* and *Ideas of Order* were prompted, as we have seen, by Stevens' business trips and vacations. In July, 1939, the Stevens family spent a few weeks at Christmas Cove, Maine. Elsie sent a postcard to her mother: "This is the view of the Atlantic ocean from our rooms in Holly Inn. The water between the islands along the 'rock bound' coast of Maine, as far as we can see from here—and farther—is called the Thread of Life—the islands are mostly rocks that are very white in the sunlight and the brilliantly green spruce trees seem to grow right out of them.

28. John Crowe Ransom, "Artists, Soldiers, Positivists," *Kenyon Review*, VI (Spring, 1944), 276, 278–79.
    29. Wallace Stevens, "The Situation in American Writing," *Partisan Review*, VI (Summer, 1939), 40.

Many birds here: gulls, terns, kingfishers and we saw some herons on an island the other day when we passed in a boat."[30] "Variations on a Summer Day" is Stevens' own record of the vacation. The poem names nearby places—Monhegan, Pemaquid, Damariscotta. And Elsie's brief observations are shared by Stevens. "Everywhere spruce trees bury spruce trees," he says in part XII, and the islands are described in XV:

> The last island and its inhabitant,
> The two alike, distinguish blues,
> Until the difference between air
> And sea exists by grace alone,
> In objects, as white this, white that.

The brilliant configurations of the rocks account also for the metamorphosis: "The rocks of the cliffs are the heads of dogs / That turn into fishes and leap / Into the sea" (III). The gulls Elsie saw appear in the poem's first line, and her boat trip may have inspired the simile that concludes section X:

> To change nature, not merely to change ideas,
> To escape from the body, so to feel
> Those feelings that the body balks,
> The feelings of the natures round us here:
> As a boat feels when it cuts blue water. (*CP*, 232–36)

"Variations on a Summer Day" is a series of short impressions, twenty in all, founded upon the poet's whimsical responses to the Maine setting.

An altogether different kind of experience led to the writing of "A Fish-Scale Sunrise." In 1933, Stevens joined James and Margaret Powers for a social evening in New York City. Powers had been his assistant in Hartford for two years and had gone into private practice. The friendship between the two men was an especially warm one. The evening was long and even boisterous, as Margaret Powers told Peter Brazeau:

> Jim and Wallace had been together all afternoon, and I met them about six or so. And then we started out. We went to a couple of speakeasies, then the place where we got the singer to play "La Paloma." That's

---

30. Elsie Stevens to Mrs. Lehman W. Moll, July, 1939, in Huntington Library.

where we had our dinner. When we got through there, it was eleven-thirty or twelve, and we went on to the Waldorf Roof, which had just opened, and did the dancing. First time he had ever danced, so we danced. He was doggone good; he had a wonderful sense of rhythm. He seemed to enjoy it thoroughly, and that was a new experience for him. . . . He insisted on having the pickled herring in cream. That's from Reading [Pa.] German, I suppose. We tried it, but he loved them. . . . It was an impetuous evening. I think we just meant to meet and have cocktails, but we went on and on and on. . . . I think he felt quite close to Jim and me that evening.

The poem, describing the next morning's anticlimax, begins:

> Melodious skeletons, for all last night's music
> Today is today and the dancing is done.
>
> Dew lies on the instruments of straw that you were playing,
> The ruts in your empty road are red.
>
> You Jim and Margaret and you singer of La Paloma,
> The cocks are crowing and crowing loud. (*CP*, 160–61)

There is a hint of a hangover in the line "The mind is smaller than the eye," but Stevens remembered the evening without remorse: "Now that the Katzenjammer is over, we did have a good time, didn't we?"[31]

There were good times at the Powerses' vacation home in Cornwall, Connecticut. Margaret recalled that Stevens would "always bring up . . . real croissants [from] a place in Hartford, great batches of those, and brioches. . . . He loved Cornwall."[32] The return to Hartford after one visit—"We drove home from Cornwall to Hartford, late"—provided the setting for Stevens' late poem of cosmic volatility: the poet in motion and the "visible transformations" of earth and sky in their own "going round." The poem is "Reality Is an Activity of the Most August Imagination" (*OP*, 110).

When *Transport to Summer* came out, Naaman Corn, a chauffeur for Hartford Accident and Indemnity Company, discovered from one of the officers that he had been named in "Certain Phenomena of Sound," a poem published five years earlier:

---

31. Margaret Powers quoted in Brazeau, *Parts of a World*, 90; Wallace Stevens to James A. Powers, July 18, 1933 (copy).
32. Brazeau, *Parts of a World*, 92.

So you're home again, Redwood Roamer, and ready
To feast . . . Slice the mango, Naaman, and dress it

With white wine, sugar and lime juice. Then bring it,
After we've drunk the Moselle, to the thickest shade

Of the garden. We must prepare to hear the Roamer's
Story. (*CP*, 286)

Corn recalls the private association of "Redwood Roamer," one
Stevens must have expected to remain forever unidentified: "That's
the one about the Redwood Roamer. That was a man by the name
of Addison Posey. He was one of the vice-presidents here, but he
went back to California. You know the redwoods grow in California. Then he used to roam up and down Albany Avenue, coming
to work. Mr. Stevens used to come into the office that way, too,
and he would run into Mr. Posey."[33]

The scenes nearest home, the daily walk to the office, the garden
behind the house, were Stevens' most immediate world, the one in
"Like Decorations in a Nigger Cemetery." A walk through Elizabeth Park in 1948 took him past "a group of nuns [who] came
there each morning to paint water colors especially of the water
lilies" (*L*, 610). "Inside our queer chapeaux, we seem, on this
bank, / To be part of a tissue, a clearness of the air" (*OP*, 92), he
wrote in "Nuns Painting Water-Lilies."

Stevens speaks most formally about the sources of poetry, including his own, in "The Irrational Element in Poetry." An impression, then only a few days old, was recalled for his audience
late in 1936: "A day or two before Thanksgiving we had a light fall
of snow in Hartford. It melted a little by day and then froze again
at night, forming a thin, bright crust over the grass. At the same
time, the moon was almost full. I awoke once several hours before
daylight and as I lay in bed I heard the steps of a cat running over
the snow under my window almost inaudibly. The faintness and
strangeness of the sound made on me one of those impressions
which one so often seizes as pretexts for poetry" (*OP*, 217). Apparently, Stevens had not yet exploited that pretext for poetry, but in
the poem he began a few weeks later, "The Man with the Blue
Guitar," he transformed the impression. The cats contrast with the

33. *Ibid.*, 53.

exuberant motions and sounds ("ai-yi-yi") of the man who "held the world upon his nose":

> Sombre as fir-trees, liquid cats
> Moved in the grass without a sound.
> They did not know the grass went round. (*CP,* 178)

The mischief of a rabbit caught his anxious eye in the spring of 1937. He described it to Latimer: "One side of my bed there is nothing but windows; when I lie in bed I can see nothing but trees. But there has been a rabbit digging out bulbs: instead of lying in bed in the mornings listening to everything that is going on, I spend the time worrying about the rabbit and wondering what particular thing he is having for breakfast" (*L,* 321). In the fall, *Poetry* published "A Rabbit as King of the Ghosts."

Holly Stevens recalls another scene near home:

> Just beyond the bridge which spanned the Hog on Albany Avenue was a vast stretch of barren land that people used as a dump. It was full of tin cans, old bottles, rags, crates, and miscellaneous junk. It was a mess and an eyesore, but it glittered here and there on days when the sun shone.
> On this lot a man, seemingly coming from nowhere, built his home. . . . Since my father walked to work, and used either Albany Avenue or Asylum Avenue, he passed the lot frequently. I remember Dad saying that the occupant was a White Russian. We spent hours imagining things about him, and making up stories.[34]

"The Man on the Dump" appeared in the *Southern Review* in 1938: "One sits and beats an old tin can, lard pail. / One beats and beats for that which one believes" (*CP,* 202).

Stevens addresses the sun ("Master Soleil") directly in "Of Hartford in a Purple Light," the light that illumined his own paths and perspectives:

> Look, Master,
> See the river, the railroad, the cathedral . . .
>
> When male light falls on the naked back
> Of the town, the river, the railroad were clear. (*CP,* 227)

34. Holly Stevens, "Bits of Remembered Time," 652.

He also remembered Reading and Berks County, the rivers and mountains of Pennsylvania he had explored throughout his youth. Shortly before his marriage, he described to Elsie his memory of the town: "To lose it entirely would be like losing everything— because the thought of it is always with me. There are fugitive moods when it seems quite gone. Afterwards, it comes back as vividly as ever." After the move to Hartford, Stevens rarely visited Reading, but the memory of the unspoiled pastoral world remained a ripe field for the poet—in a way that New York and Hartford could never duplicate. He delighted especially in the Indian, Dutch, and German names—the Swatara, a river northwest of Reading, is mentioned in "The Countryman," "Metaphor as Degeneration," and "Our Stars Come from Ireland"; the Schuylkill River is identified in "A Completely New Set of Objects" and "Our Stars Come from Ireland." In connection with the former work, Samuel French Morse notes "the annual festival on the Schuylkill River 'down which paraded canoes and boats lighted at night with candled Chinese lanterns.'"[35] The Tulpehocken, which empties into the Schuylkill just north of Reading, is named in "Extraordinary References." The town a few miles to the southwest where Stevens had spent the summer of 1895 is evoked in "Memorandum":

> The katy-dids at Ephrata return
> But this time at another place.
> It is the same sound, the same season,
> But it is not Ephrata. (*OP*, 89)

The harvested hayfields in the valley of Oley in eastern Pennsylvania, "A land too ripe for enigmas" (*CP*, 374), appear in "Credences of Summer," and Stevens identified the area for Charles Tomlinson: "An accord with realities is the nature of things there" (*L*, 719). Another accord, that of a late-summer evening near Mount Neversink, is re-created in "Late Hymn from the Myrrh-Mountain."

For his genealogist, Lila James Roney, Stevens recalled the Per-

---

35. Wallace Stevens to Elsie Moll [Kachel], May 13, 1909; Samuel French Morse, *Wallace Stevens: Poetry as Life* (New York, 1970), 205.

kiomen: "Neshaminy is a little place seven or eight miles from Doylestown. To the west of it lies the country through which the Perkiomen Creek runs. This creek, when I was a boy, was famous for its bass. It almost amounts to a genealogical fact that all his life long my father used to fish in Perkiomen for bass, and this can only men [sic] that he did it as a boy."[36] "Thinking of a Relation between the Images of Metaphors" also describes the creek:

> The wood-doves are singing along the Perkiomen.
> The bass lie deep, still afraid of the Indians.
>
> In the one ear of the fisherman, who is all
> One ear, the wood-doves are singing a single song.
>
> The bass keep looking ahead, upstream, in one
> Direction, shrinking from the spit and splash
>
> Of waterish spears. (*CP*, 356)

Stevens' memories of Reading were intensified in the 1940s and early 1950s when the family genealogy became a consuming interest. The poet invested thousands of dollars in the enterprise, employed the services of professional genealogists, visited cemeteries throughout the state, and became an active member of the St. Nicholas Society, a Dutch genealogical organization. He attended the society's dinners in New York for more than ten years, and once he read his poem "Tradition," later retitled "Recitation after Dinner" (*OP*, 86). He published privately in 1943 a collection of photographs, *Stevens Family Portraits,* with a brief commentary.

The poem that most closely reproduces the world he discovered through his hobby is "Extraordinary References," which begins:

> The mother ties the hair-ribbons of the child
> And she has peace. *My Jacomyntje!*
> *Your great-grandfather was an Indian fighter.*
>
> The cool sun of the Tulpehocken refers
> To its barbed, barbarous rising and has peace.
> These earlier dissipations of the blood
>
> And brain, as the extraordinary references
> Of ordinary people, places; things,
> Compose us in a kind of eulogy. (*CP*, 369)

---

36. Wallace Stevens to Lila James Roney, November 2, 1942.

The "extraordinary references / Of ordinary people" led him to another distant ancestor, his great-great-great-grandmother, Blandina Janse van Woggelum Stevens, who is named in "Analysis of a Theme." Stevens had begun imagining her life: "These men, Abraham, John, Abraham, Benjamin, etc., were a curiously self-contained pietistic lot. Doesn't it seem to you as you think of them that their wives were far more interesting people? . . . And then too Blandina must have had a certain pride in her family, which had been in the country the greater part of a century when she married Abraham." [37]

"The Bed of Old John Zeller" and "Dutch Graves in Bucks County" are the best known of what might be called Stevens' genealogical poems. John Zeller, who is also named in "Two Versions of the Same Poem," was Stevens' maternal great-grandfather; he was buried in Amityville, Pennsylvania. In September, 1944, the Reverend Howard A. Althouse sent Stevens a description of the grave, and "The Bed of Old John Zeller" was ready for *Accent* shortly thereafter. In "Burghers of Petty Death," Stevens wrote:

> These two by the stone wall
> Are a slight part of death.
> The grass is still green. (*CP*, 362)

Thomas Lombardi argues persuasively that the poem was written after Stevens' visit to the cemetery in January, 1945, when he saw where John and Catherine Zeller were buried. To an acquaintance in Amityville he wrote: "All the graves in the yard were like objects that had ceased to be part of time." [38]

All the poems that can be traced to Stevens' interest in genealogy share certain characteristics in addition to their "extraordinary references." They never reproduce genealogical data in systematic outlines or as obscure and private allusions. Rather, they focus in some way upon the distant past; through the poet's evocation, history will be brought closer. In "Dutch Graves in Bucks County," for example, the elegiac tone pits the soldiers of the then current war against the "semblables" of his ancestors who marched under

37. Wallace Stevens to Lila James Roney, December 3, 1942.
38. Thomas F. Lombardi, "Wallace Stevens and the Haunts of Unimportant Ghosts," *Wallace Stevens Journal*, VII (Spring, 1983), 50–51; Wallace Stevens to John Z. Harner, June 15, 1953.

"the old flag of Holland" (*CP*, 290). Names such as Jacomyntje and Blandina, instead of requiring annotation, evoke an exotic, faraway time and place; the names seem almost imaginary. The poems are also associated geographically with Stevens' own past. After the deaths of his parents in 1911 and 1912, Stevens had gradually become a stranger to his brothers and sisters. With John's death in 1940 and Elizabeth's in 1943, the immediate family was gone. Mary Katharine had died in 1919 and Garrett, Jr., in 1937. It was then that Stevens' preoccupation with genealogy became most acute.

Peter Hanchak, his grandson, was born in 1947; now, instead of ancestors, there was a new descendant. "Peter the voyant," as Stevens defined him in "Questions Are Remarks," was "aetat. 2" when Stevens wrote the poem in the summer of 1949 (*L*, 642). The boy addresses his question about the sun, "'Mother, what is that,'" without metaphorical encumbrances, making him "the expert," unlike the "drowsy, infant, old men" (*CP*, 462–63). Barbara Church later remembered the poet's speaking of his grandson as "the voyant."[39]

In the end, there is no accounting for a poet's particular genius. Because no poet stands in isolation, it is possible to examine some of the movements and individual figures that worked as Stevens' sources, sponsors, and critics. In addition, the journals and letters are rich in information about how he exercised his craft; his personal library indexes part of his mind's growth; there are the recollections of those who knew him well or only casually. A year before his death, he wrote of the compulsion to continue making poems: "I have been trying to do a few poems. Just as one experiences the world in terms of one's age and physical condition, so one experiences poetry, I am afraid, in the same terms. The feelings, the great source of poetry, become largely the feeling of + desire to sit under the trees on a bench in the park. Still, I have managed a few: poems. Curious—the satisfaction of this sort of thing, as if one had fulfilled one's self and, in a general sort of way, done something important—important to one's self" (*L*, 842).

---

39. Barbara Church quoted in Peter Brazeau, "The Irish Connection: Wallace Stevens and Thomas McGreevy," *Southern Review*, n.s., XVII (1981), 539.

Eight years earlier, Stevens wrote his great celebration of the imagination, "Credences of Summer." The victories of the imagination, dearly purchased and always fleeting, are defined as one of life's great assuagements, "Man's mind grown venerable in the unreal."[40] The satisfactions described in the poem are much like Stevens' own as a poet nearing the end and surveying his work. In the larger view, the poet's lifetime of poems and the mind's joyous engagements with the world were the same thing. Both proclaimed a capture—in the words of the poem, "This hard prize, / Fully made, fully apparent, fully found" (*CP,* 376).

40. See George S. Lensing, "'Credences of Summer': Wallace Stevens' Secular Mysticism," *Wallace Stevens Journal,* I (Spring, 1977), 3–9.

# 6 ✐ *Schemata*

In this notebook by Wallace Stevens, three pages contain forty-one items arranged by roman numerals. Below the word *Schemata* on the first page, *Memorias Antiguas* is canceled out. The pages are holographs in pencil. There are extensive erasures on pages 1 and 2, which made way for new entries in the same spaces. In addition, thirty entries are marked through with a single horizontal line, though each remains legible. The eleven items remaining uncanceled (II, IV, VI, VII, IX, XI, XIII, XVII, XXV, XXX, XXXI) were then recopied, renumbered consecutively, and typewritten, also under the title *Schemata*. The text here reproduces the original forty-one entries of *Schemata*. Stevens' later adaptations of twenty entries are indicated by my notes in the column to the right.

*Page 1*

I   Twenty quail flying in
     moonlight.

II   A vivid fruit in vivid
      atmosphere

"A perfect fruit in perfect
   atmosphere"—"New England
   Verses," pt. XVI, l. 1 (*CP*, 106)

III   Riding the shadow of basalt.

IV   Wear only your golden masks
      tonight.

"Wear the breeches of a mask"—
   "The Revolutionists Stop for
   Orangeade," l. 13 (*CP*, 103)

V   This is the emotion of love
     made visible

VI   Land of pine and marble

Subtitle pt. XII, "New England
   Verses" (*CP*, 106)

VII   Good worm . .

VIII   The grand simplifications

"Life on a Battleship," pt. II, l. 4
   (*OP*, 78)

158

IX    Diamond on the slipper of
      her naked ghost

X     Flight of red pigeons                "A red bird flies across the golden
                                           floor"—"Le Monocle de Mon
                                           Oncle," pt. II, l. 1 (*CP*, 13).
                                           "A blue pigeon it is, that circles
                                           the blue sky, / On sidelong
                                           wing, around and round and
                                           round. / A white pigeon it is,
                                           that flutters to the ground, /
                                           Grown tired of flight"—
                                           "Le Monocle de Mon Oncle,"
                                           pt. XII, ll. 1–4 (*CP*, 17).

XI    Is it a goat or a cock you
      chase now, skeleton death?

XII   Cry of the simple man

XIII  The old marble is gray in
      the rain

*Page 2*

XIV   The mother, the one
      unknown

XV    The purple dress in autumn    "New England Verses," pt. XV,
                                     l. 1 (*CP*, 106)

XVI   Experiments on Adam

XVII  A weaving of the slow
      shadow-wheel

XVIII  Soupe aux perles             Subtitle pt. III, "New England
                                    Verses" (*CP*, 104)

XIX   Serenade in Guatemala         "Only it requires a skill in the
                                    varying of the serenade that
                                    occasionally makes one feel like
                                    a Guatemalan when one par-
                                    ticularly wants to feel like an
                                    Italian" (*L*, 230).

XX    For speaking in the fatal
      solitudes

XXI   Hymn from a water-melon       Title (*CP*, 88)
      pavilion

XXII   Wetted by the dew of his
own land

XXIII   Holly, kingfisher, grapes
and cosmos

XXIV   Churches as crystals

XXV   The hairy saints of the
north

XXVI   Funereal magnolias

XXVII   The idea of a colony

"New England Verses," pt. XII, ll.
1–2 (*CP*, 106)

"Two at Norfolk," l. 13 (*CP*, 111)

Subtitle pt. IV, "The Comedian as
the Letter C" (*CP*, 36)

*Page 3*

XXVIII   A young man fond of
his grandmother

"It is the grandfather he liked"—
"The Lack of Repose," l. 11
(*CP*, 303)

XXIX   Polo ponies practicing

XXX   Mrs. Burfanti's cakes[1]

XXXI   Time on time's revenges

XXXII   Mr. Goldsmith's desire
to live it out in Guadalajara

XXXIII   Saturday night at the
chiropodists

XXXIV   The man who could
not sell even nectarines

XXXV   Poetry supreme fiction

Title (*OP*, 37)

Title (*OP*, 27)

"Poetry is the supreme fiction,
madame"—"A High-Toned Old
Christian Woman," l. 1 (*CP*, 59)

XXXVI   Sexual promenades

"Smacking their muzzy bellies in
parade"—"A High-Toned Old
Christian Woman," l. 16 (*CP*, 59)

XXXVII   Woman with umbrella

"It is not so with women. / I wish
they were all fair / And walked
in fine clothes, / With parasols,
in the afternoon air"—"Peter
Parasol," ll. 11–14 (*OP*, 20)

1. In the typewritten version of *Schemata*, this became "Mrs. Burbank's cakes," the only
notable difference between the two texts.

| | |
|---|---|
| XXXVIII   Of the world simple | |
| XXXIX   How the constable carried the bed-pot across the public square | Title rephrased, "How the Constable Carried the Pot Across the Public Square" (*Measure* [April, 1923]). Title rephrased, "The Public Square" (*CP*, 108) |
| XL   Commands to genii | |
| XLI   The world without imagination | Subtitle pt. I, "The Comedian as the Letter C" (*CP*, 27) |

Both the title *Memorias Antiguas* and the formal numbering suggest that Stevens may have had the outline of a single but fairly elaborate poem in mind. But the second, typewritten version of the notebook did not, however, contribute to the organization of a separate poem. Later adaptations were made from both canceled and uncanceled entries. At about the time that Stevens exhausted the sources in *Schemata,* he began the notebook *From Pieces of Paper,* which contains 361 separate entries and which he drew upon for the remainder of his career. And even before *Schemata,* probably before the preparation of the *Harmonium* poems, Stevens wrote out in pencil the following outline, either for a single poem or four separate ones:

I   The Sonnet With The Diamond Ring
II   The Large Blue Sonnet
III   The Sonnet With Two Voices
IV   The Little Old Sonnet Carved In a Bottle

A working list of phrases and ideas in one form or other seems to have been useful to the poet in a minor way throughout his career.

Unlike many entries in *From Pieces of Paper,* the first letters within the entries are not capitalized in *Schemata.* With the later notebook he seems more self-consciously to have had potential titles in mind. Even so, the earlier list also yielded titles and subtitles. Especially in the use of comic titles, where discordant elements produce the unexpected or the absurd, one finds a typical Stevens designation: "Hymn from a water-melon pavilion" (XXI), "Saturday night at the chiropodists" (XXXIII), and "How the constable carried the bed-pot across the public square" (XXXIX). Some entries may have been intended as simple images for later embellishment, such as "Flight of red pigeons" (X) or "Woman with umbrella" (XXXVII). Others he may have considered as potential lines: "This is the emotion of love made visible" (V) or "Is it a goat or a cock you chase now, skeleton death?" (XI). The entry "Holly, kingfisher, grapes and cosmos" (XXIII) implies a still life. "Holly," too, was his daughter's name. Like the references to Mrs. Burfanti (XXX) and Mr. Goldsmith (XXXII), the name may have carried personal associations. Although one expects to find Stevens' typical rhetorical exuberances and surprise metaphorical pairings, there appears nonetheless a different impulse: "The grand simplifications" (VIII), "Cry of the simple man" (XII), "Of the world simple" (XXXVIII), and "The world without imagination" (XLI). Both the creations and decreations of the mind's interplay with the world figure into his notations.

Exactly when the list was collected is impossible to ascertain, but Stevens likely began it while preparing the last *Harmonium* poems. If, for example, "Flight of red pigeons" (X) helped to inspire "Le Monocle de Mon Oncle," *Schemata* may date back to 1918—the poem appeared in *Others* in December of that year. "Peter Parasol," using "Woman with umbrella" (XXXVII), was published in *Poetry* the next year. When the second edition of *Harmonium* appeared in 1931, fourteen new poems were added, and eight entries from *Schemata* contributed to their content in one form or other. Only intermittently did Stevens return to *Schemata* after he resumed writing in about 1933. A poem first published in 1939, "Life on a Battleship," contained "The grand simplifications" (VIII):

> So posed, the captain drafted rules of the world,
> *Regulae mundi,* as apprentice of
> Descartes:
>       First. The grand simplifications reduce
> Themselves to one. (*OP,* 78)

Even later, for "The Lack of Repose," a poem that did not appear until 1943, he made one final adaptation using "A young man fond of his grandmother" (XXVIII). The poem begins with "A young man seated at his table." He reads from a book that distracts him from his identity as "one of the gang, / Andrew Jackson Something." The book becomes a voice from a cloud, transforming the "grandmother" from the entry into the grandfather: "It is the grandfather he liked" (*CP,* 303).

In the context of his later work, *Schemata*'s thirty-fifth item, one of those he marked through, is most significant: "Poetry supreme fiction." It is Stevens' first use of the phrase. The long poem "Notes toward a Supreme Fiction" was not begun until 1942, but the phrase was introduced in the first line of a 1922 poem, "A High-Toned Old Christian Woman": "Poetry is the supreme fiction, madame." Of the three injunctions Stevens later attached to the idea of supreme fiction, "It Must Be Abstract," "It Must Change," and "It Must Give Pleasure," it is only the last that he pleads here. As "supreme fiction," poetry indulges in "fictive things" and challenges the Puritanical "moral law" of the Christian "madame" who distrusts the imagination. In creating the terms of that contest in the poem, Stevens used "Sexual promenades" (XXXVI) and set in motion before the wincing widow just such an extravaganza:

> Allow,
> Therefore, that in the planetary scene
> Your disaffected flagellants, well-stuffed,
> Smacking their muzzy bellies in parade,
> Proud of such novelties of the sublime,
> Such tink and tank and tunk-a-tunk-tunk,
> May, merely may, madame, whip from themselves
> A jovial hullabaloo among the spheres. (*CP,* 59)

If Stevens first intended *Schemata* as the outline of a single poem, that work must have been planned along the lines of "New England Verses." Five entries were worked into that poem. Moreover, the poem's sixteen dialectical couplets, each subtitled, are by design aphoristic and comic and thus conform in tone and attitude to the jottings that served at least in part as their source. John Enck is persuaded that the couplets "ostensibly parody New England primers with their primitive couplets."[2] Two of the notes became subtitles in the poem—"Land of pine and marble" (VI) and "Soupe aux perles" (XVIII)—and "The hairy saints of the north" (XXV) was inserted in part XII. As he did with the other subtitles,

2. John Enck, *Wallace Stevens: Images and Judgments* (Carbondale, 1964), 61.

Stevens found witty rejoinders—"Land of Locust" and "Soupe Sans Perles." There is a possibility that the idea of a poem based upon the rhetorical sparring of outrageously inflated claims and counterclaims may have evolved from *Schemata* itself. In the last two couplets of "New England Verses," for example, Stevens adopted two entries and filled in the context that had originally occurred to him. "The purple dress in autumn" (XV) and "A vivid fruit in vivid atmosphere" (II) had associations with deathlike autumn versus summery nature made into a picture gallery:

XV
*Scène Flétrie*

The purple dress in autumn and the belfry breath
Hinted autumnal farewells of academic death.

XVI
*Scène Fleurie*

A perfect fruit in perfect atmosphere.
Nature as Pinakothek. Whist! Chanticleer. . . .

"New England Verses" is a *tour de force,* and the wit required to sustain it falters; some connotations, instead of balancing incisively, trail off into the private and vague. What should ring as spontaneous is at worst self-consciously labored. Stevens used the technique later and more successfully in "Nudity at the Capital" and "Nudity in the Colonies." But Stevens must have sensed the poem's shortcomings when the *New Republic* rejected it in 1922, one of the few times that happened in his career. He found a place for it shortly afterward in Pitts Sanborn's the *Measure,* along with "How the Constable Carried the Pot Across the Public Square." The title of the latter, from item XXXIX, was later shortened to "The Public Square" when it appeared in the 1931 *Harmonium.* Both poems were withheld from the 1923 *Harmonium,* though they had been completed in time for inclusion; they were added to the second edition.

The fruits of *Schemata* were in part fortuitous. Even canceled items, once reexamined, were found to be serviceable. Although many entries were ill-suited to his original plan, they could still be converted into titles, subtitles, lines, and phrases. Even the designation "supreme fiction" survived its erasure. As we have seen,

"New England Verses," "The Comedian as the Letter C," and "A High-Toned Old Christian Woman" owe more than a casual debt to *Schemata*. Stevens went on to prepare a more formal and detailed notebook, *From Pieces of Paper*. In *Schemata* he seems to have discovered a device that awakened and sustained his powers of invention.

# 7 ✐ *From Pieces of Paper*

This notebook contains 361 entries, all of which are in pencil, on fourteen pages. In the text here, I have numbered entries individually, though Stevens did not do so, and in the order of their appearance in the notebook. Where entries were adopted by Stevens in various texts, I have added the source in the column to the right.

*Page 1*

1. Souvenir of the Heavens & Earth

2. Blessing of Birds

3. Life Without Nature

4. Cold is Our Element      "The Sun This March," l. 9 (*CP*, 134)

5. Carpenter & Fuchsia      "The life and death of this carpenter depend / On a fuchsia in a can"—"An Ordinary Evening in New Haven," pt. XVIII, ll. 10–11 (*CP*, 478)

6. Life Among Drones      "the repeated drone / Of other lives becoming a total drone"— "Americana," ll. 6–7 (*OP*, 94)

7. What They Call Red Cherry Pie      Title of poem first published in *Alcestis* (October, 1934). Reprinted in final form as pt. IV, "Five Grotesque Pieces" (*OP*, 75–76)

8. A Convent In The Woods

9. The Cow In The Clouds

10. Violon d'Ingres

166

11. A Spirit Without A City In A
    City Without A soul

12. A Freshness Of Poetry                    "Polo Ponies Practicing," l. 7 (*OP*,
                                              37)

13. The pine trees shudder in the
    shade

14. The Mind Is A Growth                     "You know that the nucleus of a
                                             time is not / The poet but
                                             the poem, the growth of the
                                             mind / Of the world"—"Reply
                                             to Papini," ll. 7–9 (*CP*, 446)

15. Pierre Laprade

16. To assist them in calamity               "In the little of his voice, or the
                                             like, / Or less, he found a man,
                                             or more, against / Calamity"—
                                             "On an Old Horn," ll. 12–14
                                             (*CP*, 230); "In the sense against
                                             calamity"—"The Auroras of
                                             Autumn," pt. VIII, l. 5 (*CP*,
                                             418)

17. "A world without revolt
    would be one to fly from"

18. la vie ne laisse plus guere de
    place ni à la fantaisie ni aux
    traditions qui lui donnaient
    saveur et couleur

19. Human society as the result of
    human nature

20. Portrait Without Pose

21. All Men In One Man                       "The central man . . . the man of
                                             glass, / Who in a million
                                             diamonds sums us up"—
                                             "Asides on the Oboe," pt. I,
                                             ll. 12–14 (*CP*, 250)

22. The Alp at the end of the
    street

23. The mind is the great poem of            "Man and Bottle," l. 1 (*CP*, 238)
    winter

24. Man & Catsup Bottle

25. Paradise On Paper

26. Health of the Soul

*Page 2*

27. Native speech of the soul

28. The pressure of other people's ideas

29. Invisible men

30. *Sub*-realism

31. Sketches of my solitude

32. Idiom of the hero          Title (*CP*, 200)

33. Music at the world's end

34. Mythological Beast In A Bourgeois Town

35. The Terrible Men

36. Landscape With Boat        Title (*CP*, 241)

37. Contact Now & Later

38. She slung him so bad that he slept in the air. Capt. MacFarland of Christmas Cove — Stevens and his family spent a vacation at Christmas Cove, Maine, in July, 1939.

39. The End Of A Belief — "If ever the search for a tranquil belief should end"—"Like Decorations in a Nigger Cemetery," pt. V, l. 1 (*CP*, 151)

40. Kate The Contrast To Charley

41. Naked And Playing The Harp

42. Mythological Men — "more / Than Tartuffe as myth"—"Paisant Chronicle," ll. 9–10 (*CP*, 335)

43. Et aultres choses solatieuses — "Poetry is a form of melancholia. Or rather, in melancholy, it is one of the '*aultres choses solatieuses*'"—"Adagia" (*OP*, 160)

44. Supersense, exaltation

45. On The Resolving Of Noble
    Enigmas

46. La dées[s]e Imagination, le
    dieu Amour

47. The contemporary romantic is
    a revolutionist

48. This rain was meant to fall in
    Salamanca

49. To feel abnormally

50. Repas de Paysans

51. Dancing

52. The Inadequacy of Landscape      Title rephrased, "On the
                                          Adequacy of Landscape" (*CP*,
                                          243)

53. Une Figure A choix

*Page 3*

54. Lady looking at a vase of      Title rephrased, "Woman Looking
    flowers                                    at a Vase of Flowers" (*CP*, 246)

55. Lady combing her hair      "It must / Be the finding of a
                                          satisfaction, and may / Be of a
                                          man skating, a woman dancing,
                                          a woman / Combing"—"Of
                                          Modern Poetry," ll. 23–26 (*CP*,
                                          240)

56. A quiet normal life      Title (*CP*, 523)
57. The imagination as god      "We say God and the imagination
                                          are one"—"Final Soliloquy of
                                          the Interior Paramour," l. 14
                                          (*CP*, 524); "Proposita: 1. God
                                          and the imagination are one"—
                                          "Adagia" (*OP*, 178).

58. "An Adamant Englishman"

59. The Accordian In the Sun

60. A few modern beads

61. Aphorisms On Society      "While I am uncertain about it,
                                          I think that APHORISMS ON
                                          SOCIETY is a better title than

OWL'S CLOVER. OWL'S CLOVER is a good title, in the sense that, in spite of the owlishness of the poems, there is still enough poetry in them to justify that title. On the other hand, while APHORISMS ON SOCIETY is somewhat pretentious, it brings out for the reader the element that is common to all the poems. After you read the group please let me know which of these titles you prefer" (*L,* 311).

62. Refractions of the world in temperaments

"Now, the poet manifests his personality, first of all, by his choice of subject. Temperament is a more explicit word than personality and would no doubt be the exact word to use, since it emphasizes the manner of thinking and feeling"—"Effects of Analogy" (*NA,* 120).

63. Qualities of a poem
      interesting
      indigenous to a person
      d'un daemon
      felt words
      capable of infuriating
      with
      poetry emotion
      to come from an ever
      free source
      esser
      effortless
      contagious

64. Idyllist & Night Mare

65. Blue In The Tropics

66. gasping magnitude

67. Talcum-powder & Gourd-Vine

68. A child playing with a ball

69. The Admiral Of Their Race      "'The admiral of his race and everyman'"—"A Duck for Dinner," "Owl's Clover," pt. III, l. 4 (*OP*, 62)

70. The Onions of Thirty Years Ago

71. A Grizzly lion

72. Aultres Dieux

73. Bronze Afternoon

*Page 4*

74. Solar Repertoire

75. Public Ferns      "Examination of the Hero in a Time of War," pt. VII, l. 12 (*CP*, 276)

76. La Douceur d'une [*sic*] Café

77. Poor Men's Poems

78. Sur Le Motif

79. The Halo That Would Not Light

80. Shrinking From Sweden      "Now, I have not the slightest desire to sing Swedish songs correctly or incorrectly and at the moment a Swedish anthology is the last thing in the world that I should ever look at" (*L*, 712).

81. Loud Night

82. An American Monster

83. A truce to tragedy

84. More than any scene of the guillotine, any glamorous hanging      "It is more than any scene: / Of the guillotine or of any glamorous hanging"— "Parochial Theme," ll. 26–27 (*CP*, 192)

85. An Idea Without A Form

| | |
|---|---|
| 86. loud-tooting spring | |
| 87. The mind in its cloister | "The self is a cloister full of remembered sounds"—"The Woman That Had More Babies Than That," pt. II, l. 8 (*OP*, 82) |
| 88. As a prairie | |
| 89. Le Poète Soleil | "Master Soleil"—"Of Hartford in a Purple Light," l. 2 (*CP*, 226) |
| 90. Chasseurs d'Image | |
| 91. The True Temper | |
| 92. Bobbins Spinning In A Mill | |
| 93. Revolution Against The Rose | |
| 94. anatomy of form | |
| 95. All the vices of a chambermaid | |
| 96. modesty before the saints | |
| 97. to make memorable the life we actually live | |
| 98. the poem of the ignorant man | The image of "the ignorant man" is incorporated into "The Sense of the Sleight-of-hand Man," l. 16 (*CP*, 222); "Crude Foyer," l. 18 (*CP*, 305); and "Notes toward a Supreme Fiction," "It Must Be Abstract," pt. I, l. 4 (*CP*, 380) and "It Must Change," pt. VII, l. 17 (*CP*, 395). |
| 99. not ideas about the thing but the thing itself | Title (*CP*, 534) |
| 100. vegetation for a public garden | "The idea of things for public gardens"—"Examination of the Hero in a Time of War," pt. VII, l. 11 (*CP*, 276) |
| 101. Theme Without Variations | "How close / To the unstated theme each variation comes"— "Thinking of a Relation |

between the Images of
Metaphors," ll. 10–11 (*CP*,
356–57)

*Page 5*

102. beautiful as a cemetery

103. Prayers without a book

104. Arrival At The Waldorf      Title (*CP*, 240)

105. The sun is cheap in Italy

106. sitting in a pine-wood

107. Morgue near Heaven

108. no time for the solemn

109. to feel the world not merely
to see it

    "So to feel / Those feelings that
the body balks, / The feelings
of the natures round us here"—
"Variations on a Summer Day,"
pt. X, ll. 2–4 (*CP*, 234)

110. Poetry American Type

111. Mountain Disappearing In
Twilight

112. Honest, well-meaning,
inferior people

113. How A Church Bell Should
Sound

114. He's fought his duels

115. We are all Indians

116. Cats & Marigolds

117. Conversation On A Hillside

118. to redeem myself from this
world

119. The Death of A Class

120. A Jackass In His Own
Clothes

121. Embellishments &
Emoluments

122.  the continuous definition of poetry

123.  A poem like a season of the mind

124.  Remonstrances with the People
1. de demeurer en la foy de leur[s] Ancestres

125.  Women & Silence

126.  Organa

127.  Deep Sky

128.  Works & Feasts

*Page 6*

129.  Ah, yes! Desire . .                    "Ah! Yes, desire. . . ."—"The Men That Are Falling," l. 7 (*CP*, 187)

130.  A Poet Without Peculiarity      Title rephrased, "World without Peculiarity" (*CP*, 453)

131.  God and all angels sing the world to sleep      "The Men That Are Falling," l. 1 (*CP*, 187)

132.  Brahms Roundé[?]

133.  A new manner is equal to a new word      "A new meaning is the equivalent of a new word"—"Adagia" (*OP*, 159).

134.  Black Gloves for the Bishop

135.  Brochure On Eden

136.  the cadets of cigarette Road

137.  And where ye spend much, though ye spent but lickell,
Yet little by little the cat eateth the flickell

138.  In the mud                          "The Man with the Blue Guitar," pt. XXIV, l. 2, and pt. XXXIII, l. 2 (*CP*, 177, 183)

139.  The last of the rich men

140. Peacock covered with fleas
141. sensual realism
142. Dogwool [*sic*] & Oakum
143. Fame & Fright
144. Woman surrounded by her children under a parasol
145. Loggia au bord de la Mer
146. Period spirit
147. gaudium scribendi
148. Possum & Sop & Taters

Title rephrased, "No Possum, No Sop, No Taters" (*CP*, 293). "How happy you all seem to be down there [Jacksonville, Florida]; how you go on living in a land of milk and honey, or, to be more exact, possum, sop and taters" (Stevens to Philip S. May, January 31, 1940, quoted in Brazeau, *Parts of a World,* 109).

149. The Skeleton & The Joyful Voice
150. Two Prides
151. As one of the Characters
152. The Pleasure of Being
153. Rocks, Roses

"He would compose / The scene in his gray-rose with violet rocks"—"From the Packet of Anacharsis," ll. 7–8 (*CP*, 366)

*Page* 7
154. Already The Judas Tree
155. Dont You Love Yams?
156. One of Those Hibiscuses of Damozels

Subtitle pt. I, "Five Grotesque Pieces" (*OP*, 74)

157. Really A Nun
158. An American Gorge

159. Bush Arbor Meeting

160. Chips & Whetstones

161. A Pre-Proustian Past

162. Sparkling Harness of Rich Horses

163. Sketch Of A River

164. For An Old Man Facing Death

165. Figure of A Woman Reading a Letter, Newspaper, Book etc.

166. A Favorite With Cats

167. Rocking Chair Reef

168. Aspects—Sum Total         "or else / An object the sum of its complications, seen / And unseen"—"Someone Puts a Pineapple Together," pt. III, ll. 33–35 (*NA*, 87)

169. Living In Books and Living in Paintings

170. A Great Big Handsome Cow-Boy

171. Winter's Dirt         "And dirt. The wind blew in the empty place. / The winter wind blew in an empty place"— "Extracts from Addresses to the Academy of Fine Ideas," pt. IV, ll. 8–9 (*CP*, 255)

172. Reflections Of Words On Other Words

173. Asides On The Oboe         Title (*CP*, 250)

174. Address To A Town

175. La Mère Qui Tousse

176. A Little Boy With Wax In His Ear

177. And Brussells [*sic*] Sprouts And A Raspberry Tart

178. Words About Death

179. Pretty Hot Weather For Dead Horses

180. A Lake With A Fence Around It

181. Cemetery Language

*Page 8*

182. Parade of Poets

183. Preparing A Child To Eat Eclairs

184. The Artificial Man Coming Into Contact With Reality

"an artificial man / At a distance"—"The Creations of Sound," ll. 12–13 (*CP*, 311)

185. Alcohol & Alms

186. Women & Nationalism

187. L'Humain Depourvu

188. The Negation Of The Artist

189. I Was Born In Europe

190. Reine Cimetière

191. Pax, Ajax & The Crocuses

192. Seelensfriede [*sic*] durch Dichtung

"This memorandum makes it look as if I were trying to bring about a *seelensfriede durch dichtung*" (*L*, 377). "Adagia I" ("Particles of Order: The Unpublished Adagia," ed. A. Walton Litz, in Doggett and Buttel (eds.), *Wallace Stevens*, 72).

193. Sure[?] foreword

194. Life Without Any Dream

195. It's going to be pretty around here

196. Precis Of A Fiction Quasi Divine

197. Some Figures Of The Future

198. The bees get all the new ones, the flies get all the old ones.

199. Last Illumination

200. Swiss Widow

201. Sketches of A Man Walking Round A Lake — "Perhaps / The truth depends on a walk around a lake"—"Notes toward a Supreme Fiction," "It Must Be Abstract," pt. VII, ll. 2–3 (*CP*, 386)

202. Poesie Abrutie — Title (*CP*, 302)

203. The Doves Come Home

204. Emotion Complicated By The Viola

205. Paradise, Paris & Home

206. Chant of Mere Being — Title rephrased, "Of Mere Being" (*OP*, 117)

207. A Centre For Poetry

208. Idols

209. To Seize The Actual

*Page 9*

210. Death's Orator

211. Goldstein In Heaven

212. The Little Animal That's All One Knows — "The Man, That's All One Knows," was considered as the title for the volume that eventually became *Parts of a World*.

213. The Need For Ideas

214. The Last Private Opinion

215. Monsieur Diabète

216. Man Carrying A Thing — Title rephrased, "Man Carrying Thing" (*CP*, 350)

217. God exists by grace of
     Racine.

218. Dew–Masters

219. The great wars between
     civilizations in place of the wars
     of civilizations against savages.

220. Egotism & Beverages

221. La Pensée à L'Après-Midi

222. The Souvenirs of Older Men

223. The Pure good of theory        Title (*CP*, 329)

224. On Melody In Poetry

225. Underglazia

226. Ingenious machine

227. Sketches of the Ultimate        Title rephrased, "Sketch of the
     Politician                      Ultimate Politician" (*CP*, 335)

228. The poet who lived with his
     words

229. For people who enjoy clouds

230. Description of a cartwheel      "The broken cartwheel on the
                                     hill"—"Continual Conversation
                                     with a Silent Man," l. 3 (*CP*,
                                     359)

231. Man's Place In Music           "Notes toward a Supreme Fic-
                                     tion," "It Must Be Abstract,"
                                     pt. II, l. 11 (*CP*, 382)

232. Ennui des Arts

233. On dit Vladimir

234. Defense de la vie même

235. A Foreign Mind

236. Why Flies Dont Fight

*Page 10*

237. Dynamics of Ideas

238. Effect of Metaphor
     (Exhilarating)

239. A Poem For Liadoff                 "Chocorua to Its Neighbor," pt.
                                        IV, l. 4 (*CP*, 297). See also "Two
                                        Tales of Liadoff" (*CP*, 346)

240. Men Made Out of Words              Title (*CP*, 355)

241. Why The Past Doesn't Smile

242. The Storm of Morning

243. Bad Money At The Six
     O'Clock Mass

244. Motive for Metaphor                Title rephrased, "The Motive for
                                        Metaphor" (*CP*, 288)

245. So-And-So Reclining On             Title (*CP*, 295)
     Her Couch

246. Poem Of Distance And               Title may have been rephrased,
     Flight                             "Wild Ducks, People and
                                        Distances" (*CP*, 328)

247. Poems For Meditation

248. The Houses Show The
     Experience Of Night

249. —della sua virtu

250. Two Women & Their
     Children

251. A Basic Poem In A Basic
     Tongue

252. Poems Of Observation

253. Personal Rapport

254. Private Creatures & Public
     Creatures

255. Catalogue Of Past Mind

256. Museo Olympica (botched           "*Museo Olimpico*"—"Description
     words)                            without Place," pt. III, l. 29
                                       (*CP*, 342)

257. How soon the priest of            "The priest of nothingness who
     nothingness intones               intones"—"This as Including
                                       That," l. 4 (*OP*, 88)

258. Dry birds are fluttering in        Subtitle pt. IV, "The Pure Good of
     blue leaves                        Theory" (*CP*, 332)

259.  Provincial Elegance &
Metropolitan Elegance

260.  The Difficulty of Fixing on a
Final Color (a single color:
blue) for Daylight

261.  Non-Human Days

262.  The Poet's Sense of His own
Merit

263.  Men As Animals

"The bird kept saying that birds
had once been men, / Or were
to be, animals with men's
eyes"—"On an Old Horn," ll.
1–2 (*CP*, 230)

*Page 11*

264.  Mittelmässigkeit

265.  A Peculiar Duck

266.  The President Of The Union

"The President ordains the bee to
be / Immortal"—"Notes
toward a Supreme Fiction," "It
Must Change," pt. II, ll. 1–2
(*CP*, 390)

267.  the quality of the *irreductible*
in reality

268.  Realité Fatale

269.  American Poverty

270.  Debris of N's[?] Life & Mind

Title rephrased, "Debris of Life
and Mind" (*CP*, 338)

271.  A Kind of Surradio

272.  The Prejudice Against The
Past

Title (*CP*, 368)

273.  Holiday In Reality

Title (*CP*, 312)

274.  Springs Infuriation

"And spring's infuriations over"—
"Credences of Summer," pt. I,
l. 2 (*CP*, 372)

275.  Dessins d'un (Embryo) pour
un beau monde à venir

276. This Structure of Ideas, These Ghostly Sequences of the Mind — "The Bed of Old John Zeller," ll. 1–2 (*CP*, 326)

277. Little White Houses Like Wash out[?] On A Line

278. Considerations Of The Ego

279. Familiar Sophomore — "Man is an eternal sophomore"— "Adagia" (*OP*, 169)

280. The Passing Of The Tiger

281. Plato's Ghost & Aristotle's Skeleton — "Let him move as the sunlight moves on the floor, / Or moonlight, silently, as Plato's ghost / Or Aristotle's skeleton"—"Less and Less Human, O Savage Spirit," ll. 3–5 (*CP*, 327); "Aristotle is a skeleton"—"Adagia" (*OP*, 168)

282. The Fault In Our Too Human God — "The fault lies with an overhuman god"—"Esthétique du Mal," pt. III, l. 4 (*CP*, 315)

283. Nights Among Beetles b-bats

284. Communism As Spite

285. Explanation. Consolation.

286. Discharge of the Past

287. Psychologia Poetica (doctrine of poetic power as a phase of abnormal psychology.) — Stevens treats this issue in "Imagination as Value" (*NA*, 153–56).

288. The Relation Between the Images of Metaphors — Title rephrased, "Thinking of a Relation between the Images of Metaphors" (*CP*, 356)

289. Concerning Humanity As A Single Thing (Machine)

290. Continual Conversation With A Silent Man — Title (*CP*, 359)

*Page 12*

291. Scrutiny Of The Hour of Twelve[?]

292. The Concept Of The
    Arrière-Penseur
293. A People Without A Capital
294. Water in Autumn Sunlight
    (Silence)
295. Ivory Tower of Nature

"One of these days I should like to do something for the Ivory Tower. There are a lot of exceedingly stupid people saying things about the Ivory Tower who ought to be made to regret it" (*L*, 403). Stevens discusses the poet's "ivory tower" in "Effects of Analogy" (*NA*, 121–23).

296. The Wagon of Heaven
297. How Now, O,
    Brightener . . .

Title (*OP*, 97)

298. Transport To Summer

Title of volume (1947)

299. The Contemplative
    Playground
300. Reason's Constant Ruin

"Two Versions of the Same Poem," pt. I, l. 19 (*CP*, 354)

301. Verklärung durch Erklärung
302. Packet of Anacharsis

Title rephrased, "From the Packet of Anacharsis" (*CP*, 365)

303. One More[?] Vladimir
304. The Good Man Has No
    Shape

Title (*CP*, 364)

305. A Few Pages in C Major

"You might like to know of a remark that Gounod made concerning Charpentier. He said . . . 'At last, a true musician! He composes in C-natural and no one else but the Almighty could do that'" (*L*, 393).

306. The Master Of The Mind

"Mud Master," l. 18 (*CP*, 148)

307. The Arches Of The
    Afternoons (Arles)

308. Poetry As The Switzerland          "I assume that you will see
    Of The Mind                         something of Switzerland,
                                        which has been everywhere in
                                        my mind recently" (*L*, 665).

309. Souvenirs Of A Man I Never
    Knew

310. There's Nothing Like A
    View

311. Three Legged Men & Five
    Armed Women

312. The Large Populations of the
    Horizons

313. Lack of Choice

314. Resemblance As The Source          "It is not too extravagant to think
    Of The Ideal                        of resemblances and of the
                                        repetitions of resemblances as a
                                        source of the ideal"—"Three
                                        Academic Pieces" (*NA*, 81).

315. The First Days After A
    Death

316. All About the Bride's
    Grandparents

317. Snow Under The North

318. An Object of the Mind

*Page 13*

319. On The Validity of Analogy

320. Without Any Of The
    Categories of Reality

321. The Interest Of People
    In
    Each Other
    The Wild Fury Of
    Other Men

322. The Obligation To Be
    Dismal

323. The Auroras of Autumn    Title of volume (1950) and of poem (*CP*, 411)

324. The Guide Through Poetic Dogma

325. (The) Degrees Of Abstraction

326. The Accretion Of Lives In A University    "To me, the accumulation of lives at a university has seemed to be a subject that might disclose something extraordinary"— "Imagination as Value" (*NA*, 146).

327. Of Meta-men and Para-things    "The Bouquet," pt. II, l. 3 (*CP*, 448)

328. A World Without Glory

329. Space In Poverty    "that life / Itself is like a poverty in the space of life"— "Chocorua to Its Neighbor," pt. XII, ll. 2–3 (*CP*, 298–99)

330. Autour de la Misère
    1. Boy With Pin-Wheel In His Hat
    2. Pursuit of Pleasure In Canoes
    3. Child Surrounded By Pigeons
    4. The Aimless Reportage & Three Successive [indecipherable word]

331. Metaphor As Degeneration    Title (*CP*, 444)

332. Among The Pheasants    "A poem is a pheasant"; "Poetry is a pheasant disappearing in the brush"—"Adagia" (*OP*, 168, 173).

333. A Sudden Importance of Switzerland    "But, suddenly, I began to think about Switzerland. There is a great deal coming from Switzerland. Then, too, Switzerland is something that

one ought to think about in the summertime" (L, 594).

334. Ideas On Emerging From Miscellany

335. The Reportage of Tragedy

336. The One Theme Of Which Everything Else Is A Variation

"How close / To the unstated theme each variation comes"— "Thinking of a Relation between the Images of Metaphors," ll. 10–11 (CP, 356–57)

337. Winter Women

338. Enlargements

339. An Ordinary Evening In New Haven

Title (CP, 465)

340. The Art Of Metaphor

341. Imagination & The Sun

*Page 14*

342. On The Resemblances Between Sight & Thought

"The eye does not beget in resemblance. It sees. But the mind begets in resemblance as the painter begets in representation; that is to say, as the painter makes his world within a world"—"Three Academic Pieces" (NA, 76).

343. Serenades Even Now

344. Angel Surrounded by Peasants

Title rephrased, "Angel Surrounded by Paysans" (CP, 496). "Tal Coat is supposed to be a man of violence but one soon becomes accustomed to the present picture. I have even given it a title of my own: *Angel Surrounded By Peasants*" (L, 649–50).

345. Lunch Without A Fork

346. The Role Of the Idea In Poetry | Title (*OP*, 93)

347. The Identity of The Bridegroom

348. On The Presence of Italians In Parks | The association was an old one for Stevens, as this 1906 journal entry indicates: "Parks (excepting the drives in them) are, generally, filled with the lower classes. Our park here, today, was thick with Italians and negroes" (SP, 166).

349. Ecstatic Perçu

350. The World Made Artifice | "I tried to pretend that everything in nature is artificial and that everything artificial is natural, as, for example, that the roses in Elizabeth Park are placed there daily by some lover of mankind and that Paris is an eruption of nature" (*L,* 684).

351. The young Perch

352. The Month Of Mid Winter (Exploration of Aesthetics)

353. The All-Together Of All Conversations

354. The Identity of Poetry and Style | "My first proposition is that the style of a poem and the poem itself are one"—"Two or Three Ideas" (*OP*, 202).

355. Poetry As Myth

356. The Potentialities Of Poetry

357. The Nature of The Abstract

358. Exact Speech

359. Still Life With Aspirin

360. The Absence[?] of Mythology

361.  One Must Sit Still To
      Discover The World

*From Pieces of Paper* discloses a unique view of one device adopted
by the poet in plotting his poems. The notebook also underscores
certain habits of Stevens' mind: its playfulness, its penchant for the
aphoristic, its experimentation, its fondness for other languages
(especially French), its alliance with metaphor both in theory and
in practice. Stevens' fondness for music and painting is manifest.
The notations vary in tone from the formal and decorous to the
idiomatic.

Stevens was a collector of random notes throughout his life. He
described for Elsie the result of his reading at the Astor Library in
1909: "Scraps of paper covered with scribbling—Chinese antiq-
uities, names of colors, in lists like rainbows, jottings of things to
think about, like the difference, for example, between the *expression* on men's faces and on women's, extracts, like this glorious one
from Shakespeare: 'What a piece of work is man! how noble in reason! how infinite in faculty!' and so on" (*L,* 143). Carl Van Vechten
recalls that as early as 1914 and 1915, Stevens composed "his tiny
verses on tiny bits of paper cunningly disposed in big books which
he held against the curious inspection of the eyes of his associates
and underlings."[1] The title of the notebook may be a literal description of how it came to be.

The notebook item that found its way into print first was "Cold is
Our Element" (4). It was incorporated into "The Sun This March,"
which was published in the *New Republic* on April 16, 1930. The
date parallels Stevens' renewed interest in poetry—for several years
after *Harmonium* he published almost nothing—and suggests that
the notebook itself may have hastened his return to writing. If
Samuel French Morse is correct that "Of Mere Being" was written
in 1955 (*OP,* 300), "Chant of Mere Being" (206) was modified into
the title of one of Stevens' last poems. The poem on the last page
of *The Collected Poems of Wallace Stevens,* "Not Ideas about the
Thing But the Thing Itself," was first published in 1954; the title is
present here as 99.

The evidence suggests that the items may have been entered ran-

---

1. Carl Van Vechten, "Rogue Elephant in Porcelain," *Yale University Library Gazette,*
XXXVIII (October, 1963), 45.

domly from papers collected for a number of years. This would account for the fact that the order of presentation does not always correspond to the order of appropriation. A fairly late entry, for example, "The Master Of The Mind" (306), became the last line of "Mud Master," which was published in *Ideas of Order* in 1935. Either directly or from memory, Stevens turned to *From Pieces of Paper* for the last twenty-five years of his career as a poet. According to dates of first publication, the poems of the mid-1940s derive most frequently from the notebook, but every volume except *Harmonium* contains adaptations from the entries.

It seems most likely that Stevens began the notations as a gathering of potential titles for poems. Most of them, for example, were recorded with the beginning of each word capitalized. He told Ronald Lane Latimer in 1935: "Titles with me are, of course, of the highest importance. Some years ago a student of Wesleyan came up to the office. Apparently he had been given the job of writing a paper on HARMONIUM. He was under the impression that there was no relation whatever between the titles and the poems. Possibly the relation is not as direct and as literal as it ought to be. Very often the title occurs to me before anything else occurs to me" (*L,* 297). For "To the One of Fictive Music," one of the few poems that survives in manuscript, Stevens considered the following titles: "To the Fictive Virgin," "Souvenir de la Muse De la Belle Terre," "De la Terre Belle et Simple," "Souvenir of the Muse of Archaic Earth," "Souvenir of the Archaic Muse," "Souvenir of a Muse," "Of Fictive Music," "To the ["Fictive" crossed out] One of Fictive Music."[2] Although many of the entries in *From Pieces of Paper* were adapted to other uses and most were never used at all, approximately one-tenth became titles, some directly (twenty entries) and some by slight modification (twelve items). Two eventually became volume titles—"Transport To Summer" (298) and "The Auroras Of Autumn" (323).

The modification of titles between notebook and poem is itself a subject that invites conjecture. When Paule Vidal, his Paris art agent, sent Stevens a new still life by Tal Coat in the autumn of 1949, for example, the poet named it "Angel Surrounded by Peasants"—directly from the notebook (344). Within days, however,

2. Louis L. Martz, "Manuscripts of Wallace Stevens," *Yale University Library Gazette,* LIV (October, 1979), 52.

he finished a short poem for Nicholas Moore of *Poetry London,* one no doubt inspired by the same painting, and in the title he substituted "Paysans" for "Peasants." In other cases, the notebook may have provided a poem's *donnée,* but when Stevens actually began to write, the work took on a life beyond the limits of the proposed title. The change from "The Inadequacy of Landscape" (52) to "On the Adequacy of Landscape" was dictated by the poem's unfolding statement, in which the landscape of day, bird, and sun is preferable to the people in the first stanzas who shrink from the "blood–red redness of the sun" (*CP,* 243). What began as inadequacy emerged as sufficiency, and even triumph, by the end of the poem. Similarly, in a much later poem, the modification of "A Poet Without Peculiarity" (130) to "World without Peculiarity" accents the poem's shift from a human figure alone ("he") to the earth and day ("world") personified as a human: "It is the earth itself that is humanity." Without peculiarity, self and world are finally one, "a single being, sure and true" (*CP,* 454). The alteration of "Possum & Sop & Taters" (148) to "No Possum, No Sop, No Taters" retains its antipoetic humor but reinforces the series of reductions and cancellations imposed by the stark winter scene described in the poem. "Of Mere Being" was an abbreviation of "Chant of Mere Being" (206), perhaps because the poem itself emphasizes the visual ("The bird's fire-fangled feathers") over the audible (*OP,* 188).

Another tenth of the entries in *From Pieces of Paper* were reproduced in the poems. "Man and Bottle," "The Men That Are Falling," and "The Bed of Old John Zeller" are launched from jottings in the notebook. In the case of "The Men That Are Falling," he informed Bernard Heringman in 1953 that he had the Republicans of the Spanish civil war in mind when he completed it in 1936. But he must have turned to his notebook to find a beginning:

> God and all angels sing the world to sleep,
> Now that the moon is rising in the heat
>
> And crickets are loud again in the grass. The moon
> Burns in the mind on lost remembrances.
>
> He lies down and the night wind blows upon him here.
> The bells grow longer. This is not sleep. This is desire.
>
> Ah! Yes, desire. . . . (*CP,* 187)

Line 1 is a direct transcription of entry 131, and the last line here appears as item 129. The tension between passive sleep and active desire may well have stimulated the other associations that issue in the poem. The unnamed man is the dying poet-soldier, the speaker of the "immaculate syllables" in the "catastrophic room" of war. In the poem's conclusion, Stevens brings together the two entries, sleep of death and the desire for life, in order to impugn the celestial and to establish the terrestrial as the valid object of desire in the face of death: "This man loved earth, not heaven, enough to die."

Almost all of Stevens' contributions to magazines after 1930 were occasioned by editors' soliciting his work. As a result, it was his practice to compose poems, both in length and in number, according to the particular request. For example, Stevens sent "Man and Bottle" and "Of Modern Poetry" to the editor of *Hika* in 1940, and he had apparently consulted *From Pieces of Paper* (23 and 55) in preparing both poems. A few years later, Oscar Williams requested some poems for an anthology to be published in 1943. Stevens gathered four previously unpublished poems, and here again he used the notebook. Two titles, "No Possum, No Sop, No Taters" and "So-And-So Reclining on Her Couch," were adopted from entries 148 and 245. The third poem, "Return," seems independent of the notebook, but perhaps not. When it was assigned a new title for *Transport to Summer* four years later, Stevens discovered in the notebook its permanent title, "Poesie Abrutie" (202). The fourth poem, "Chocorua to Its Neighbor," evidences Stevens' using his collection only for certain phrases. The abstract "Space In Poverty" (329) was shaped into the speech of the mountain Chocorua, who in his largeness is one with the misery of war and death:

> "There lies the misery, the coldest coil
> That grips the centre, the actual bite, that life
> Itself is like a poverty in the space of life,
> So that the flapping of wind around me here
> Is something in tatters that I cannot hold." (*CP*, 298–99)

Chocorua, however, possesses the "central mind"; he is another of Stevens' hero-figures whom the poet set out to define in poem after poem in the 1940s. Chocorua's strength and bulk are given many configurations, one of which is rather curious: "He was the figure in / A poem for Liadoff, the self of selves" (*CP*, 297). Whatever the poet's fondness for the music of Anatol Liadoff, the Russian composer who died in 1914, Stevens did not forget to write "A Poem For Liadoff" (239).[3] "Two Tales of Liadoff" was completed two years later, and in 1946 he gathered twelve poems for the *Quarterly Review of Literature* under the title "More Poems for Liadoff."

Stevens' interest in the figure of the hero, the giant, the major man, the central man, the man of glass, is representative of his search for the fully human but ideal poet who could assuage those whose faith in the traditional gods had collapsed. Being fully human, the hero could not, however, be reduced to a single individual. He was to be an object of faith abstracted and proposed, but not yet realized, "The impossible possible philosophers' man" (*CP*, 250). During World War II, the hero frequently appeared in Stevens' poems as a soldier, and "Examination of the Hero in a Time of War" is typical of Stevens' portraying the abstraction. In stanza VII, for example, two unlikely entries from the notebook, "vegetation for a public garden" (100) and "Public Ferns" (75), converge:

> There are more heroes than marbles of them.
> The marbles are pinchings of an idea,
> Yet there is that idea behind the marbles,
> The idea of things for public gardens,
> Of men suited to public ferns . . . The hero
> Glides to his meeting like a lover
> Mumbling a secret, passionate message. (*CP*, 276)

The notebook here provides little more than a setting for the potential effigies of the hero. One wonders whether the stanza itself, if not the entire poem, might not have sprung from the images of public gardens and public ferns already associated in the poet's mind with "that idea behind the marbles."

Like Chocorua and the soldier-hero, other representations of the major man are hinted at in *From Pieces of Paper,* though they

---

3. Stevens' personal library of records included at least two works by Liadoff: "(The) Enchanted Lake, Op. 62, Boston Symphony—Koussevitsky, (Vic. 14078)" and "(8) Russian Folk Songs, Op. 58, L.S.O.—Coates (Vic. 9797/8)." Michael O. Stegman, "Wallace Stevens and Music: A Discography of Stevens' Phonograph Record Collection," *Wallace Stevens Journal,* III (Fall, 1979), 89.

were not always directly incorporated into poems. "All Men In One Man" (21) points to "the man of glass" in "Asides on the Oboe," "Who in a million diamonds sums us up" (*CP*, 250). "Mythological Men" (42) is like "Tartuffe as myth" in "Paisant Chronicle" (*CP*, 335), wherein Stevens set out to define major man. Another exalted figure, "The Admiral Of Their Race" (69), becomes the definition of the evolving common man as seen by the Bulgar in "A Duck for Dinner":

> "This man
> Is all the birds he ever heard and that,
> The admiral of his race and everyman,
> Infected by unreality, rapt round
> By dense unreason, irreproachable force,
> Is cast in pandemonium, flittered, howled
> By harmonies beyond known harmony." (*OP*, 62)

The central images of part II of "The Bouquet" also derive from the notebook—"Of Meta-men and Para-things" (327). The meta-men, superior beholders, view the world of the duck, the table-cloth, and the bouquet itself as "transfixed, transpierced and well / Perceived" (*CP*, 449). Finally, "Idiom of the hero" (32) reappears as the title of a 1938 poem.

Like "The Men That Are Falling," "Chocorua to Its Neighbor," and "Examination of the Hero in a Time of War," other poems testify to Stevens' use of the notebook. In longer works, the poet needed to sustain a flow of images and metaphors. "Notes toward a Supreme Fiction" is a good example. "The poem of the ignorant man" (98) provides the central theme for the first canto, though this entry had been used in earlier poems. Further, "Man's Plan In Music" (231) is transcribed directly into the second canto: "The philosopher / Appoints man's place in music, say, today. / But the priest desires. The philosopher desires" (*CP*, 382). "Sketches of A Man Walking Round A Lake" (201), though perhaps conceived originally as a future title, was recast as a declaration in canto VII: "Perhaps / The truth depends on a walk around a lake" (*CP*, 386). And "The President Of The Union" (266) may have given rise to "The President ordains the bee to be / Immortal" in the second canto of "It Must Change" (*CP*, 390).

The title "Thinking of a Relation between the Images of Metaphors" derives from a notebook entry (288) as do certain images in the sixteen-line poem. In the metaphorical identities among doves, fish, and fisherman, each is keenly attuned to the other: "How close / To the unstated theme each variation comes" (*CP,* 356–57), the poem summarizes. The lines reflect two entries—"Theme Without Variations" (101) and "The One Theme Of Which Everything Else Is A Variation" (336)—and the first is invalidated while the second is ratified. "Continual Conversation with a Silent Man" is a title that is traceable to the notebook (290), and the poem assimilates an image Stevens had jotted down (230) as one to be recalled for later use:

> The old brown hen and the old blue sky,
> Between the two we live and die—
> The broken cartwheel on the hill. (*CP,* 359)

Taking both its title and an image from the notebook, "From the Packet of Anacharsis" adapts "Rocks, Roses" (153) to the visual tonalities of the nineteenth-century French painter Puvis de Chavannes: "He would compose / The scene in his gray-rose with violet rocks" (*CP,* 366). The entry itself may be a shorthand description of a painting Stevens had seen in a New York museum.

The notebook assisted Stevens in his writing essays throughout the 1940s. Many of these were prepared initially as lectures he was invited to give at various universities, and they were later collected in *The Necessary Angel: Essays on Reality and the Imagination* (1951). "The pressure of other people's ideas" (28), for example, recalls the various pressures of reality outlined in the first of these essays, "The Noble Rider and the Sound of Words." Only the imagination, "pressing back against the pressure of reality" (*NA,* 36) as a "violence from within," could successfully combat that modern force.

"Three Academic Pieces," read by Stevens at Harvard in 1947, treats the role of resemblances in human perception. Although the subject was a familiar one, his reading of Charles Mauron's *Aesthetics and Psychology* (1935), a book he both owned and marked, offered further corroboration. Stevens drew a line in the margin, for example, beside this passage: "If I wished to give this discussion all the philosophic breadth of which it is capable, I should point out that the search for resemblances is an essential characteristic of the human mind." A page later he underlined: "In active life the intellect looks for resemblances because it wishes to foresee efficiently: in art this aim disappears, but the intellect still looks for analogies—that is its function—and now, it seems, for the pure pleasure of discovering them." "On The Resemblances Between Sight & Thought" (342) provided the nucleus for a distinction he drew in his own essay. The eye begets directly, independent of resemblances; the mind, however, is freer: "But the mind begets in resemblance as the painter begets in representation; that is to say, as the painter makes his world within a world; or as the musician begets in music" (*NA*, 76). The resemblances the mind begets take the perceiver closer to the ideal, a point with which the essay concludes. Resemblances make the ideal possible and accessible: "Since . . . it is easy for perfectionism of a sort to evolve, it is not too extravagant to think of resemblances and of the repetitions of resemblances as a source of the ideal" (*NA*, 81), a notion incorporated from entry 314, "Resemblance As The Source Of The Ideal."

"Imagination as Value" was delivered in 1948 at Columbia. Here the notebook phrase "The Accretion Of Lives In A University" (326) took on an illustrative function. For Stevens, it demonstrated one of the social consequences of the imagination: "To me, the accumulation of lives at a university has seemed to be a subject that might disclose something extraordinary. What is the residual effect of the years we spend at a university, the years of imaginative life?" (*NA*, 146). Stevens cites Rimbaud's poetry and Kafka's fiction as imaginative, but also "exploits of the abnormal." He adds, "Ordinarily we regard the imagination as abnormal per se," an issue also raised in the notebook—"Psychologia Poetica (doctrine of poetic power as a phase of abnormal psychology)" (287). The essay, however, concludes that even though we live in images of the imagination before the reason has ratified them, it is equally true that "the imagination is the power that enables us to perceive the normal in the abnormal, the opposite of chaos in chaos" (*NA*, 153).

The discourse that appears most indebted to *From Pieces of Paper* is "Effects of Analogy," a 1948 Yale lecture. Never remote from Stevens' interest, the general topic had been introduced in his notes as "On The Validity of Analogy" (319), and as he organized his subject he likely referred to other entries as well. Like "resemblances" in "Three Academic Pieces," analogy making is defined as a function of the imagination, originating in emotions and organized in images. Stevens proceeds to demonstrate that "another mode of analogy is to be found in the personality of the poet," his unique "sense of the world" (*NA,* 118). As if contesting Eliot's denigration of the role of individual personality in poetry, Stevens defends it in terms of the poet's temperament (p. 120), his ivory tower as his immediate and legitimate world (p. 121), and his style (p. 123). All three categories are in the notebook: "Refractions of the world in temperaments" (62), "Ivory Tower of Nature" (295), and "The Identity of Poetry and Style" (354). The last proposition was revived three years later in the first sentence of "Two or Three Ideas": "My first proposition is that the style of a poem and the poem itself are one" (*OP,* 202).

Fully three-quarters of the notations in *From Pieces of Paper* were never discernibly worked into Stevens' poetry and prose. It is possible and even likely, given the number of items and the frequency with which he consulted the notebook, that some entries set off associations in the poet's mind that stimulated his writing. For this, of course, there can be no verification and hardly even speculation. Even though Stevens ultimately elected to leave untouched most of his "pieces of paper," an examination of many of them reveals predilections and habits of mind typical of the poet and his work.

Any reader of Stevens notes with pleasure the jauntiness of his titles, and, as we have seen, he compiled *From Pieces of Paper* to have a store of them for later use. He was fond of joining two unlikely elements in creating titles. Among the published poems, for example, one thinks of "Hymn from a Watermelon Pavilion," "Saint John and the Back-Ache," and "Lytton Strachey, Also, Enters into Heaven." Many entries in the notebook attest to the same pattern of sportive juxtapositions: "Naked And Playing The Harp" (41), "Talcum-powder & Gourd-Vine" (67), "Morgue near Heaven" (107), and "Bad Money At The Six O'Clock Mass" (243), along with many others.

Sometimes Stevens enjoys inserting deliberately antipoetic or commonplace objects into the decorous frame of a title, and the effect is one of comic surprise. "A Rabbit as King of the Ghosts," "The Man on the Dump," and "Mountains Covered with Cats" are illustrations. Similar instances from the notebook include:

"The Onions of Thirty Years Ago" (70), "A Jackass In His Own Clothes" (120), "Dont You Love Yams?" (155), "A Little Boy With Wax In His Ear" (176), "And Brussells Sprouts And A Raspberry Tart" (177), and "Pretty Hot Weather For Dead Horses" (179).

The reader of *From Pieces of Paper* inevitably notes the shifts in tone from one formulation to the next. The variations range from the formal, such as "This Structure of Ideas, These Ghostly Sequences of the Mind" (276), to the bathetic "Possum & Sop & Taters" (148); and such dramatic installments as "More than any scene of the guillotine, any glamorous hanging" (84) or "Plato's Ghost & Aristotle's Skeleton" (281) are countered by the breeziness of "Arrival At the Waldorf" (104) or "So-And-So Reclining On Her Couch" (245). A few suggest colloquialisms of actual speech. Captain MacFarland of Christmas Cove, Maine, is even cited as the source for entry 38, "She slung him so bad that he slept in the air." Other items seem to be conversational novelties overheard in passing—"Pretty Hot Weather For Dead Horses" (179), "It's going to be pretty around here" (195), and "The bees get all the new ones, the flies get all the old ones" (198). Although it is not everywhere typical of his work, Stevens occasionally interjects into his poetry idiomatic and aphoristic expressions. In "Nudity at the Capital," for example (a companion to "Nudity in the Colonies"), he tosses off a couplet: "But nakedness, woolen massa, concerns an innermost atom. / If that remains concealed, what does the bottom matter?" (*CP,* 145). The epigrammatic wit of entry 137 is similar: "And where ye spend much, though ye spent but lickell, / Yet little by little the cat eateth the flickell." "Dancing" (51), "As a prairie" (88), "Idols" (208), and "Exact Speech" (358) are among the entries that seem to be private memoranda.

Stevens' frequent use of images related to the fine arts, and especially music and painting, is well known. "The Man with the Blue Guitar" associates the activity of the imagination with Picasso's musician. In the notebook we find "Violon d'Ingres" (10), though it also idiomatically denotes an amateurish hobby. The theory and rhythm of music are integral to "Peter Quince at the Clavier" and "Mozart 1935." In various entries in *From Pieces of Paper,* Stevens shows the appeal of this resource: "Music at the world's end" (33), "Brahms Roundé" (132), "Asides On The Oboe" (173), "Emotion

Complicated By The Viola" (204), "On Melody In Poetry" (224), "Man's Place In Music" (231), "A Few Pages in C Major" (305), and "Serenades Even Now" (343). Techniques of modern painting are explored in "Study of Two Pears" and "So-And-So Reclining on Her Couch." "The Relations between Poetry and Painting," a lecture he delivered at the Museum of Modern Art in 1951, best summarized his views on the subject. And the notebook reflects this lifelong interest: "Portrait Without Pose" (20), "Lady looking at a vase of flowers" (54), "Sketch Of A River" (163), "Sketches of A Man Walking Round A Lake" (201), "Sketches of the Ultimate Politician" (227), "The Difficulty of Fixing on a Final Color (a single color: blue) for Daylight" (260), and "Still Life With Aspirin" (359).

In *Souvenirs and Prophecies: The Young Wallace Stevens*, Holly Stevens speculates that her father may have begun studying French when he was in kindergarten. We know that he enrolled in French courses at Harvard, and years later in his "Adagia," Stevens concludes that "French and English constitute a single language" (*OP*, 178). Although "Poesie Abrutie" is the only French entry in the notebook that actually became a title, the other twenty-eight notations in that language attest to Stevens' feeling about it: "What a great many people fail to see is that one uses French for the pleasure that it gives" (*L*, 792). His delight in the sounds and idioms of the language is evidenced in some otherwise casual phrases— "Repas de Paysans" (50), "Une Figure A choix" (53), and "La Douceur d'une Café" (76). Other phrases, however, reflect the poet's interest in the French arts. The early entry "Pierre Laprade" (15) is the name of the early-twentieth-century painter. "Le Poète Soleil" (89) plays upon the designation of Louis XIV as the Sun King; it also recalls Baudelaire's "Le Soleil," in which the sun, "ainsi qu'un poète," descends upon the city and "s'introduit en roi." More general observations indicate Stevens' interest in French painting and poetry—"Chasseurs d'Image" (90), "Ennui des Arts" (232), and "Dessins d'un (Embryo) pour un beau monde à venir" (275).

Entry 18, especially congenial to the Stevens temperament, may actually be a quotation: "la vie ne laisse plus guere de place ni à la fantaisie ni aux traditions qui lui donnaient saveur et couleur" (there is no more room in life either for fantasy or for traditions that used to give life its savor and its color). It was recopied in *Sur*

*Plusieurs Beaux Sujects* [*sic*], II, a commonplace book. His venerating the human imagination in divine terms is hinted at with "Aultres Dieux" (72) and is made specific in "La dées[s]e Imagination, le dieu Amour" (46). "Et aultres choses solatieuses" (43) became one of the "Adagia": "Poetry is a form of melancholia. Or rather, in melancholy, it is one of the '*aultres choses solatieuses*'" (*OP,* 160).

Other entries in *From Pieces of Paper* reflect Stevens' penchant for capturing a language's unique eloquence in subjects consistent with his poetic composition, real or potential: "gaudium scribendi" (147); "Seelensfriede durch Dichtung" (192) and "Verklärung durch Erklärung" (301); and "della sua virtu" (249). Stevens' mind habitually roamed in the larger world. In his native tongue, there are additional references to Europe (189), the tropics (65), England (58), Spain (48), Italy (105), Sweden (80), and Switzerland (22, 200, 308, 333).

One other category emerges from the entries not incorporated into poems. These are expressions that seem so typical of Stevens that in a sense they belong to poems ranging from *Harmonium* to *Opus Posthumous*. As topics, they are endemic and can hardly be attributed to another poet: "the continuous definition of poetry" (122), "A poem like a season of the mind" (123), "The Pleasure of Being" (152), "To Seize The Actual" (209), "The poet who lived with his words" (228), "Poems Of Observation" (252), "the quality of the *irreductible* in reality" (267), "An Object of the Mind" (318), "The World Made Artifice" (350), and "The Nature of The Abstract" (357).

In the context of Stevens' complete work, *From Pieces of Paper* plays a relatively minor role. In fact, what often stands out is the casual, even whimsical, way in which an isolated item falls into a poem. But the poet valued the notebook as a gathering of potential titles, as a source of ideas and topics, and as a catalog of apothegms for poems and essays. It may have been especially useful when the imagination's store was exhausted and a poem was due. Many of the entries clearly had connotations and associations for Stevens that the notebook itself cannot disclose. *From Pieces of Paper* is a valuable instrument from the poet's laboratory. It affords a unique chance to imagine, if not to see directly, the poet at work. For Stevens, who apparently did little by way of outlines or rough

drafts and almost no revising after publication, such insights are
uncommon. In a different way, the notebook also verifies the larger
range of Stevens' poetic temperament, his play of mind, his delight
in unexpected metaphors, the intimate bond he established between poetry and music and painting, his cosmopolitanism, both
in language and allusion, and, everywhere manifest, his pleasure in
the "gaiety of language."

# 8 ✐ Epigraphs

Stevens was sparing in his use of epigraphs. More often than not, his poems seem born of impressions and sensations rather than fragments of erudition. The epigraphs derive from his wide and somewhat unsystematic reading, especially in French. With two exceptions (Pascal and Anacreon), the sources are not classical texts, like those of Eliot, but popular essays or journalistic articles. The epigraph typically provided Stevens with a conceptual frame that the poem itself proceeds to ratify, qualify, or dispute. "Nuances of a Theme by Williams" and "Colloquy with a Polish Aunt" are indeed nuances and colloquy in response to their respective epigraphs. "Reply to Papini," on the other hand, debates the poem's introductory words. From the letters of Eugène Lemercier in "Lettres d'un Soldat" or the statements of Mario Rossi in "Evening without Angels" and Georges Enesco in "The World as Meditation," Stevens culls major images for the respective poems—even a pattern of poetic organization. In short, we can observe the ties between private reading and subsequent poems and recognize the poems themselves as creative responses to their epigraphic foci.

As the gateway to a poem, the epigraph possesses a strategic importance. It is, in effect, the poet's way of saying to his reader, This is the lens through which I wish you to view the poem. Enlarging upon its compressed introduction, the poem takes its temper and tack from the epigraph. Although there are virtually no comments in Stevens' letters and essays on the device, its use covers the whole of his career, from his first offerings to *Poetry* in 1914 ("Phases") to "The World as Meditation" three years before his death. Moreover, Stevens' fondness for "adagia" and his notebook collections suggest that he might have employed epigraphs more liberally. *Sur Plusieurs Beaux Sujects,* I and II, are commonplace books in which he recorded excerpts from his reading, and, indeed, the epigraphs by Jules Renard (for "United Dames of America") and Mario Rossi (for "Evening without Angels") are preserved there. Yet Stevens' use of the epigraph, while revealing, remained intermittent.

With the submission of eleven war poems to *Poetry* in 1914, the thirty-five-year-old poet signaled both his recovered interest in writing poetry and his desire to address the international topic of the hour. To bring together his uneven collection, he assigned the poems the general title "Phases" and selected his first epigraph from Pascal's *Pensées,* No. 416: "La justice sans force est contredite, parce qu'il y a toujours des méchants; la force sans la justice est accusée" (Justice without force is a contradiction because there will always be the unjust; force without justice is condemned).[1] One is struck at once by the disparity between the implied evanescence in the title and the emphatic finality of "la justice" and "la force" in the epigraph. The oracular pronouncement of the epigraph is further modulated by the impressionistic lyricism of several of the poems:

> Peace means long, delicious valleys,
> In the mode of Claude Lorraine;
> Rivers of jade,
> In serpentines,
> About the heavy grain.

It is possible that Stevens saw a consistency between the general notion of "phases" and "pensées." But the actual poems nowhere address the issue of the mutual dependence of justice and force, except for the obvious implication that war is the force that Hopkins and fallen Winkle and the other combatants deploy in their struggle. The closest Stevens comes to defining the epigraph occurs in one of the weakest poems (the eighth):

> Shall we, then, say to the lovers of freedom
> That force, and not freedom, must always prevail?
> Say that the fighter is master of men.
>
> Or shall we say to the lovers of freedom
> That freedom will conquer and always prevail?
> Say that the fighter is master of men.

1. The "Phases" poems and "Lettres d'un Soldat" poems are reproduced in A. Walton Litz, *Introspective Voyager: The Poetic Development of Wallace Stevens* (New York, 1972), 305–15.

As if to mock his own gravity, Stevens originally added the name "Peter Parasol" to the end of the series. Not yet having mastered the devices of irony, he could belittle the poem's artificiality and overstatement only by the weak gesture of attaching the signature of a bodiless dandy. Stevens' first epigraph is a literary mannerism, not unlike most of the poems in the sequence. Harriet Monroe can hardly be censured for omitting it when she published four of the poems. This epigraph is the most formally literary that Stevens selected, and, never reprinting the poem in his various collections, he must have recognized that manipulating Pascal's words, imposing their authority and conviction upon the work, was not successful.

Four years after "Phases," Stevens published a sequence of war poems in *Poetry* under the title "Lettres d'un Soldat." His manuscript may have consisted of as many as seventeen poems, each containing an epigraph from Eugène Lemercier's *Lettres d'un Soldat.* Like Wilfred Owen, the French soldier had corresponded faithfully with his mother, recording his impressions of war amid the certainty of doom. He lost his life on the front in 1915. Although Stevens and Monroe eventually selected only nine of the poems for *Poetry,* the total number of borrowings from Lemercier represents Stevens' most extensive use of the epigraph. The quoted lines have, moreover, a direct congruence with the poems flowing out of them. And in the letters of the sensitive young soldier-painter, Stevens found a moral posture toward the reality of war that he was to develop and refine in later poems, including those of the 1940s: resignation to battle and death, not in pursuit of glory, but as natural fulfillment of a sensuously rich earthly existence. André Chevrillon, in his preface, offered Stevens the general epigraph to the sequence: "Combattre avec ses frères, à sa place, à son rang, avec des yeux dessillés, sans espoir de gloire et de profit, et simplement parce que telle est la loi, voilà le commandement que donne le dieu au guerrier Arjuna, quand celui-ci doute s'il doit se détourner de l'absolu pour le cauchemar humain de la bataille. . . . Simplement, au'Arjuna bande son arc avec les autres Kshettryas!" (To fight with his brothers, at his own place, in his own rank, with open eyes, without hope of glory or of gain, and simply because such is the law: this is the commandment of the god to the warrior Arjuna, who had doubted whether he were right in turning from the abso-

lute to take part in the human nightmare of war. . . . Plainly it is
for Arjuna to bend his bow among the other Kshettryas!). The
command to Arjuna, taken from the Bhagavad Gita, would provide Eliot an allusion in "The Dry Salvages" in 1941; for Stevens in
1918, it introduces the life and fate of a twenty-eight-year-old soldier who sought the compensation of beauty amid the havoc of
war. "I have amassed a stock of beauty sufficient to furnish my
whole life," Lemercier wrote from the front.[2] Stevens also found in
the soldier's stubborn idealism and religious faith a field for ironic
reversals.

Stevens acknowledged to Monroe in submitting the poems that
they were based on Lemercier's letters (*L,* 202), and he enclosed a
copy for her convenience. In the passages he selected, he found
an attitude and frame for his lyrics. The epigraph of the fifth
poem, for example, describes the forest animals as "une estampe
japonaise" (a Japanese picture) and the mice "avec l'interieur de
leurs oreilles rose comme un coquillage" (with the inside of their
ears as pink as a shell; Lemercier, p. 38). Stevens here discovered a
pictorial delicacy and freshness that he was copying from Japanese
prints:

> Here I keep thinking of the Primitives—
> The sensitive and conscientious schemes
> Of mountain pallors ebbing into air;
>
> And I remember sharp Japonica—
> The driving rain, the willows in the rain,
> The birds that wait out rain in willow leaves.
>
> Although life seems a goblin mummery,
> These images return and are increased,
> As for a child in an oblivion:
>
> Even by mice—these scamper and are still;
> They cock small ears, more glistening and pale
> Than fragile volutes in a rose sea-shell.

Glen MacLeod has demonstrated that the poems occasionally draw
from letters in addition to the one indicated in the epigraph. He

2. Eugène Lemercier, *A Soldier of France to His Mother: Letters from the Trenches on the
Western Front,* trans. Theodore Stanton (Chicago, 1917), 18. This translation, though not
always accurate or idiomatic, is the one Stevens recommended to Harriet Monroe. Subsequent references to this book will occur in parentheses.

suggests that the sequence is, in fact, "a poetic summary of the entire book."[3] Here, for example, the memory of the Primitives and the subtitle of the poem, "Comme Dieu Dispense de Graces," come directly from a letter written three days before the one in which the mice were described: "We remarked hills, covered with trees, which presented charming contours. It all made me think of the primitives and their landscapes so full of feeling and so conscientious. What fastidious majesty, whose grandeur seizes you at the first glance and whose details make a profound impression on you. You perceive, dear Mother, how God dispenses graces which are far above the reach of the miseries of the hour" (Lemercier, p. 34).

The third poem in the sequence shows a different use of the epigraph—one of ironic retort. The majesty of Lemercier's exclamation, "Ce qu'il faut, c'est reconnaître l'amour et la beauté triomphant de toute violence" (What you must accustom yourself to is to recognize love and beauty triumphant over every kind of violence; p. 25), struck Stevens as false. In jagged and clipped lines, he presents "a crowd / Of blind men tapping their way" through the streets of a city. The speaker, however, has little patience with "these crickets":

> Permit me, gentlemen,
> I have killed the mayor,
> And am escaping from you.
> Get out of the way!
> (*The blind men strike him down with their sticks.*)

Lemercier's "beauté triomphant" has been reduced in the poem to a sniggering *grotesquerie triomphant*.

Four of the poems from "Lettres d'un Soldat" were published without their original epigraphs in the second edition of *Harmonium*—"The Surprises of the Superhuman," "Lunar Paraphrase," "Negation," and "The Death of a Soldier." The three couplets of "The Surprises of the Superhuman" are minor except as an anticipation of some of the later hero-poems. Lemercier's "surprise" is based on a contrast: "J'ai la ferme espérance, mais surtout j'ai confiance en la justice éternelle, quelque surprise qu'elle cause à l'humaine idée que nous en avons" (I have a firm hope and a real confi-

---

3. Glen MacLeod, *Wallace Stevens and Company: The "Harmonium" Years, 1913–1923* (Ann Arbor, 1983), 55.

dence in eternal justice, whatever may be the surprise that this eternal justice sometimes causes in us because of our preconceived human idea of what it should be; pp. 68–69). The young soldier's confidence sprang from his religious faith; he had expressed a similar statement to his mother one month earlier: "The duty lies in accepting whatever comes and having, at the same time, perfect confidence in eternal justice" (p. 30). Stevens toys, somewhat coyly, with the notion that the centralized leadership of a "superhuman" figure holds out more promise for society than the justice of chambermaids. The recommendation of the "Übermenschlichkeit" over the "palais de justice" is indeed a surprise in the context of the war. Is it so startling that Stevens expected his reader to take the proposal as sarcastic and absurd? Or is he challenging, in the words of the epigraph, our "preconceived human idea" of justice by earnestly proposing the remedy of the German superman? The confusion was reduced in part when the poem was published without the epigraph—thus removing it from the context of the war—in the 1931 edition of *Harmonium*. As a result, the poem's praise of Nietzschean "Übermenschlichkeit" is inevitably read as an early and unironic anticipation of his hero-figure, often described in the poems of the 1940s as a soldier.

"Lunar Paraphrase," the poem Monroe eliminated from the series in 1918, is also a variation on Lemercier: "Telle fut la beauté d'hier. Te parlerai-je des soirées précédentes, alors que sur la route, la lune me dessinait la broderie des arbres, le pathétique des calvaires, l'attendrissement de ces maisons que l'on sait des ruines, mais que la nuit fait surgir comme une évocation de la paix" (Such were some of the beauties of yesterday. What can I tell thee of the preceding evenings when the moon reflected on the roads the embroidery made by the bare branches of the trees, the pathetic outlines of the calvaries, and the shadows of houses which we know to be only heaps of ruins but which the obscurity of the night presents as if peace had built them up again; p. 72). The moon embroidering the outline of trees, the pathetic calvaries, and the houses all reappear in the poem:

> The moon is the mother of pathos and pity.
>
> When, at the wearier end of November,
> Her old light moves along the branches,
> Feebly, slowly, depending upon them;

When the body of Jesus hangs in a pallor,
Humanly near, and the figure of Mary,
Touched on by hoar-frost, shrinks in a shelter
Made by the leaves, that have rotted and fallen;
When over the houses, a golden illusion
Brings back an earlier season of quiet
And quieting dreams in the sleepers in darkness—

The moon is the mother of pathos and pity.

Lemercier's letter, dated the morning of November 29, sets the poem "at the wearier end of November." The soldier's "pathetic outlines of the calvaries" are apparently outdoor shrines he encountered along the roadside during his company's maneuvers; he had mentioned similar "calvaries" in letters of November 15 and 23. Stevens' image is more explicit: "the body of Jesus hangs in a pallor, / Humanly near." The setting for Mary's presence appears to have been taken from another letter written eleven days earlier: "When we awoke this morning, we found the ground covered with a hoar frost, a whiteness spread alike over hill and forest. . . . I spent most of the night in a warmed shelter" (p. 54). "Lunar Paraphrase" concludes with the "golden illusion" that restores "an earlier season of quiet / And quieting dreams." In a previous letter, Lemercier had spoken of "the contrast between the consequences of these military activities and the peace accustomed to reign in this spot" (p. 70).

Stevens' poem is a mood piece, a succession of images and emotions aroused by various passages in the young Frenchman's correspondence. In the context of the letters, the "pathos and pity" are inspired by the doom of war. Without the epigraph (supplied only by Litz as the source "Stevens must have had in mind")[4] and the other recognized references to Lemercier's letters, the "pathos and pity" center on the figures of Jesus near death and Mary "Touched on by hoar-frost"—both stripped of divine associations, hovering "Humanly near" in anguish.

The impertinence of "Negation" ("Hi! The creator too is blind . . .") is Stevens' irreverent answer to Lemercier's testimony on behalf of "une justice impersonelle" and a "destinée utile et harmonieuse." He devises a personal creator manqué who, like

4. Litz, *Introspective Voyager*, 316.

Lemercier's impersonal abstraction, struggles toward "his harmonious whole," rejecting "Horrors and falsities and wrongs." But his "meticulous potter's thumb" is not really meticulous at all, for he is "blind," an "Incapable master," and "Too vague idealist." Like "The Surprises of the Superhuman," the poem dispenses irony and adds blasphemy to correct Lemercier's lofty edicts. The soldier's plea for "faith" finds only negation in Stevens' poem.

"The Death of a Soldier" does not mock its epigraph, however, but finds in it the congenial serenity between "La mort du soldat" and "choses naturelles." This summarizes a lesson Lemercier had learned almost three months earlier: "During a recent march, the courage that is in me was greatly strengthened by a grand lesson taught me by a fine tree. Ah! dear Mother, the whole of us may disappear and yet nature will go right on just the same and be as splendid as ever; and the gift of herself which now and then she makes me for an instant suffices to justify my whole existence. That tree was like a soldier!" (p. 87). The poem restates the lesson:

> Life contracts and death is expected,
> As in a season of autumn.
> The soldier falls.
>
> He does not become a three-days personage,
> Imposing his separation,
> Calling for pomp.
>
> Death is absolute and without memorial,
> As in a season of autumn,
> When the wind stops,
>
> When the wind stops and, over the heavens,
> The clouds go, nevertheless,
> In their direction. (*CP*, 97)

Of the four poems Stevens rescued from "Lettres d'un Soldat," this uniquely maintains its identity as a war poem. In what was to be his favorite stanzaic form, the tercet, he modulates a rhythmic deceleration accompanying the ever-shortening lines. The poem's treatment of death delicately plays off the processes of retardation ("contracts," "falls," "stops," "stops") and of continuity ("As in a season of autumn," "As in a season of autumn," "The clouds go, nevertheless, / In their direction"). Like "Negation," the poem ex-

pels the divine, but now reverentially instead of comically. There is
only a faint hint of irony in the word "heavens" in the final tercet.

Stevens must have found Lemercier's piety to be near his own
predilection. The soldier had written in November of a visit to a
Catholic church, but he was not "led there by any sentimental feelings or desire for outside comfort. My conception of divine harmony doesn't need to be bolstered up by any formalism or popular
symbolism" (pp. 64–65). His religion was a private one wherein
he consigned his fate to God's plan. Two weeks later he contrasted
his own understanding of religion with the more commonly held
notion, and his terms recall Stevens' resolution in 1902. Lemercier
wrote:

> You know what I call religion. It is that which links man with all his
> conceptions of the universal and the eternal—those two forms of God.
> Religion, in the ordinary sense of the word, is only the link which
> unites certain moral and disciplinary formulas which are associated
> with an admirably poetic figuration, that is, the external form and
> shape which are given to the vigorous philosophy of the Bible and
> Christianity. But don't let us wound anybody's feelings while we hold to
> our own beliefs, for when carefully examined, these religious formulas,
> however foreign they may be to my own intellectual assumptions, seem
> to me praiseworthy and deserving of our sympathy for what they con-
> tain of aspirations toward beauty and esthetic form. (p. 79)

"The Death of a Soldier" is the preeminent poem of "Lettres
d'un Soldat." It anticipates, for example, part VII of "Esthétique
du Mal":

> How red the rose that is the soldier's wound,
> The wounds of many soldiers, the wounds of all
> The soldiers that have fallen, red in blood,
> The soldier of time grown deathless in great size. (*CP*, 318–19)

The poignancy of life's cessation, and it hardly need be the context
of war, is something deeper than stoic pathos. Death is no mother
here, as in "Sunday Morning," but life stops as "the wind stops"
and life resumes as "The clouds go." Not a begetter, death neither
denies nor detracts. Lemercier's sentence encapsulates the poem:
"La mort du soldat est près des choses naturelles."

With the poems of "Lettres d'un Soldat," Stevens showed not

only his poetic advance over "Phases" but also a more organic utilization of the epigraph. The excerpts from Lemercier could serve for lyrical increment and for ironic countermand. So successful had the epigraph been in launching and forming the poems that when he chose to publish them later as independent poems, he could simply cancel the epigraphs.

When he reproduced in italics the four lines of William Carlos Williams' "El Hombre" at the beginning of "Nuances of a Theme by Williams," Stevens was modifying the epigraphic form. The effect is the direct interaction of two complete statements.

> *It's a strange courage*
> *you give me, ancient star:*
>
> *Shine alone in the sunrise*
> *toward which you lend no part!*

I

Shine alone, shine nakedly, shine like bronze,
that reflects neither my face nor any inner part
of my being, shine like fire, that mirrors nothing.

II

Lend no part to any humanity that suffuses
you in its own light.
Be not chimera of morning,
Half-man, half-star.
Be not an intelligence,
Like a widow's bird
Or an old horse. (*CP*, 18)

The poem as a literary dialogue is rare in Stevens' verse, though he was to take phrases and lines from Yeats's "The Lake Isle of Innisfree" and weave them into "Page from a Tale" many years later. Williams was a personal friend, however, when Stevens published the poem in 1918, and Stevens was later to write: "What Williams gives, on the whole, is not sentiment but the reaction from sentiment, or, rather, a little sentiment, very little, together with acute reaction" (*OP*, 255).

In "El Hombre," Williams does concede his "very little sentiment" in the form of the "strange courage" the beholder derives from the single star. But he reacts against the sentiment—the star's separateness from the sunrise allows no bonding between them. In what Stevens calls Williams' "anti-poetic" fashion, "El Hombre" rebuffs the more conventional romantic union as expressed in Keats's "Bright Star" or Stevens' own undergraduate sonnet, "There shines the morning star!" In the lines after Williams', Stevens presents his own "nuances." Joseph Riddel accurately concludes that Stevens' poem is "at once more objective than Williams' and more intensely concerned with the separation between self and thing." [5] Not even Williams' "strange courage" derived from the star will appease Stevens, who instructs, "Lend no part to any humanity." The starlight should reflect neither "my face" nor "any inner part / of my being." But the nuances do not end there. In the last three lines, the introduction of the widow with her bird as an illustration of the *absence* of human intelligence is mildly ironic, even though as a widow she also represents another kind of severance. "Widow's bird" itself implies a unity between human and nonhuman life rather than a cleavage. The differences between Williams and Stevens in the poem are hardly extreme. Stevens appears to outdistance Williams at his own game, until the irony of the "widow's bird" faintly hedges his claim.

The epigraph for "Colloquy with a Polish Aunt" comes from an unlikely source. Shortly after the death of Teodor de Wyzewa in 1917, Stevens came across an essay on his life by René Doumic in the *Revue des Deux Mondes.* Wyzewa, a Pole, settled in Paris in 1889 and began a career as a journalist and music critic; he is remembered principally for his two-volume biography of Mozart. Stevens was attracted, first, by Wyzewa's French translation of Jacobus de Voragine's *Golden Legend,* the work that Stevens described to Harriet Monroe as "the best known book of the Middle Ages" (*L,* 216). Stevens noted, second, that the man who would later translate the lives of the saints had been under the strong influence of his Aunt Vincentine, who knew, as the epigraph has it, "toutes les légendes du Paradis et tous les contes de la Pologne." The connection between the aunt's "légendes" and Voragine's account is not made in the essay itself, though it is in the poem. The essay describes the old woman: "Savait-elle lire? Mais elle savait toutes les légendes du Paradis et tous les contes de la Pologne. Et elle en inventait d'autres,

---

5. Joseph N. Riddel, *The Clairvoyant Eye: The Poetry and Poetics of Wallace Stevens* (Baton Rouge, 1965), 281.

toute sorte d'autres, qu'elle croyait seulement raconter, ayant en elle ce don de création qu'on prête à l'imagination populaire" (Did she know how to read? But she knew all the legends of paradise and all the tales of Poland. And she invented others, all sorts of them, which she believed she was only repeating, having in her this gift of creation that one attributes to the popular imagination). Stevens' inevitable sympathies were touched by Wyzewa's personal recollection of Aunt Vincentine, together with the Pole's defense of the imagination:

> Ce sont eux, ces contes de mon enfance, qui m'ont enseigné à admettre toujours la possibilité des choses impossibles, à me défier de toute pré-tendue science imposant des limites arbitraires aux faits, sous prétexte de "lois," et à tenir pour étrangement incomplète et indigente la réalité de nos sensations présentes en regard de celle de nos libres rêves. Aussi bien ma préférence invincible de la póesie à la prose, cette préférence qui, malgré toutes mes misères et toutes mes fautes, m'a cependant permis de goûter à la vie un plaisir merveilleux, suffirait, à elle seule, pour me faire apparaître les récits de ma tante comme ma grande source d'éducation intellectuelle et morale.
>
> (It was these, these stories of my youth, that taught me always to admit the possibility of impossible things, to beware of all scientific conten-tions imposing arbitrary limits upon facts under the pretext of "laws," and to hold as strangely incomplete and impoverished the reality of our present sensations in comparison with the reality of our free dreams. Moreover, my invincible preference for poetry over prose— this preference that, in spite of all my miseries and all my faults, none-theless has permitted me to taste in life a marvelous pleasure—was suf-ficient in itself to make these accounts by my aunt appear to be the great source of my intellectual and moral education.)[6]

In "Colloquy with a Polish Aunt," Aunt Vincentine and Wyzewa are identified only as SHE and HE. But it is the aunt, in her role as "ma grande source d'éducation intellectuelle et morale," who jus-tifies the imagination:

SHE

How is it that my saints from Voragine,
In their embroidered slippers, touch your spleen?

6. René Doumic, "Teodor de Wyzewa," *Revue des Deux Mondes,* September 15, 1917, p. 344 (my translation).

> HE
> Old pantaloons, duenna of the spring!
> SHE
> Imagination is the will of things. . . .
> Thus, on the basis of the common drudge,
> You dream of women, swathed in indigo,
> Holding their books toward the nearer stars,
> To read, in secret, burning secrecies. . . . (*CP,* 84)

That Wyzewa's "spleen" was "touched by my saints" is clear from the prose description of the aunt. Her instruction in the superiority of "nos libres rêves" to "toute prétendue science" is echoed in the poem by her interpreting his dream of women in slippers and indigo. Wyzewa's translation of Voragine evolved from the aunt's accounts of the saints' lives, but her "légendes" and his translation yield in the poem to other books, which the women of his dream grasp in order to "read, in secret, burning secrecies." Stevens, however, does not uphold the sanctity of Voragine's canon or of Wyzewa's sainted aunt—"Teodor . . . a écrit la vie de l'humble créature, à la manière d'une vie de sainte" (Teodore . . . wrote the life of the humble creature in the mode of a saint's life).[7] Stevens emphasizes, rather, the seductiveness of saints beautified instead of beatified. The virginal saint made over into the voluptuary by the beholder was a motif Stevens had already cultivated with Susanna in "Peter Quince at the Clavier" and with Saint Ursula in "Cy Est Pourtraicte, Madame Ste Ursule, et Les Unze Mille Vierges." "The Apostrophe to Vincentine," first published late in 1918, may have also been suggested by the aunt's name. "Heavenly Vincentine" is another of Stevens' sensual female apparitions: "I figured you as nude between / Monotonous earth and dark blue sky" (*CP,* 52).

When Stevens submitted "Colloquy with a Polish Aunt" to *Poetry* in 1919, another poem, "Aux Taureaux Dieu cornes donne," was part of the "Pecksniffiana" collection. He later sent Monroe "The Weeping Burgher" to replace the latter poem, but she published it anyway under the title "Peter Parasol," the name he had used at the end of the "Phases" poems. Stevens had feared that the poem would "go off on its substance and not on its style" (*L,* 214). The new title relegated the previous one to an epigraph of sorts:

7. *Ibid.*

"Aux taureaux Dieu cornes donne / Et sabots durs aux chevaux" (To bulls God gives horns / And hard hooves to horses).

The whole of the poem is indebted directly to the source of the epigraph, one of the Greek songs of Anacreon, who was born around 500 B.C. Stevens owned a copy of Richard Aldington's translation, *Greek Songs in the Manner of Anacreon*. The small collection was published in the same year as Stevens' poem, and Stevens actually inscribed the French lines above Aldington's translation (now at the University of Massachusetts). Anacreon's poem, "Women's Gift," is translated as a prose poem:

> Nature gave horns to the bull and hoofs to horses, fleetness to hares and a wide mouth of teeth to the lion, swimming to fish, flight to birds, and wisdom to men, but to women nothing.
>
> Nothing? Beauty is a gift beyond all shields and swords and she who is beautiful conquers steel and fire.[8]

Although the horns of the bull and the hooves of horses come directly from Anacreon through Aldington to what is apparently Stevens' own French translation, Stevens made other modifications. Hares, lion, fish, and birds are recast as elephant and tigers. Stevens' poem concludes:

> Ah, good God! That all beasts should have
> The tusks of the elephant,
> Or be beautiful
> As large ferocious tigers are.
>
> It is not so with women.
> I wish they were all fair
> And walked in fine clothes,
> With parasols, in the afternoon air. (*OP*, 20)

Although Anacreon contradicts his notion that nature gave to women "nothing" by going on to exalt their beauty as "beyond all shields / and swords," Stevens ironically agrees that nature has given them nothing. He only wishes them in fine clothes and with parasols.

The poem is little more than a playful exercise directed toward

---

8. *Greek Songs in the Manner of Anacreon*, trans. Richard Aldington (London, 1919), 17. I am indebted to Milton Bates's *Wallace Stevens: A Mythology of Self* (Berkeley, 1985), 101–102, for leading me to this source.

its unidentified source. Stevens rightly recognized its slightness and did not reprint the poem. He told Herbert Weinstock at Knopf in 1953 that he had "discarded" it and was unable to recall it (*L,* 794).

Stevens' best-known epigraph introduces one of his major poems, "Evening without Angels." Ascribed to Mario Rossi, the lines are recognizably Stevensian: "the great interests of man: air and light, the joy of having a body, the voluptuousness of looking." Six years after its publication, Hi Simons wondered about the origin of Rossi's words. Stevens was not certain: "I enclose a letter from Elizabeth Yeats, sending me a photograph of Rossi together with a letter from Rossi himself. . . . I don't remember where I picked up the quotation; as you will see from his letter, Rossi is a bit uncertain. It does not seem to come from his book on Swift, which I looked through last night; it may come from LIFE AND LETTERS, as he says; on the other hand, it was my impression that it came from something in the LONDON MERCURY" (*L,* 347). Rossi, in fact, was right. The words had come not from his book *Swift or the Egotist* but from an earlier essay on the eighteenth-century satirist in *Life and Letters.* Rossi, a teacher at the University of Bologna and translator of Bishop Berkeley, deplores in his essay Swift's inability to escape the "wretched sorrows" and "spiteful pleasures" that had nurtured his art: "So he passed through life—a blind arrow that ever missed the target. Stretched out taut in what related to the petty interests of the hour, he relinquished for all eternity the great interests of man: air and light, the joy of having a body, the voluptuousness of looking."[9]

In the process of writing the poem, Stevens found himself sufficiently absorbed by the lines to locate Rossi's address through Elizabeth Yeats, sister of William Butler Yeats and editor of the Cuala Press, and to write requesting an elaboration. His commonplace book, *Sur Plusieurs Beaux Sujects,* I, contains a record of his and Rossi's impressions touching on "the great interests of man":

> Miss Yeats, who published one of Dr. Rossi's works, gave me his address. He wrote to me in April, 1934, from Reggio Emilia.
> "I don't think indeed man has only such interests. I meant to say that amongst human interests, the simple pleasures of life—living pure, as

---

9. M. Manlio Rossi, "Essay on the Character of Swift," trans. J. M. Hone, *Life and Letters,* VIII (September, 1932), 356.

it were, have a paramount importance . . . The glory and glamour of the world is enough in itself to make man happy with his destiny . . But this implies . . that reality is further on . . Yes, a Pagan if you like. But dont forget . . there was the imperscrutable Ananke. Call it destiny, call it God, call it predestination—it comes all alike. It gives a sense to the marvelous spectacle of the world."

Imperscrutable is Dr. Rossi's magnificent word and Ananke is necessity or fate personified: the saeva Necessitas of Horace Odes Book I No. 35, to Fortune: "Inexorable necessity always marches before thee, holding in her brazen hand huge spikes and wedges . ." etc.

Ex Divina Pulchritudine esse omnium Derivatur, and, above all, poetry. And in reflecting on this think of it in connection with the association of poetry and pleasure and, also, in connection with "instinct du bonheur." If happiness is in our selves, divine pulchritude is in our selves and poetry is a revelation or a contact.[10]

Stevens would return to Rossi's "imperscrutable Ananke" in "Like Decorations in a Nigger Cemetery" and in "The Greenest Continent" in "Owl's Clover." To establish divine pulchritude in our selves and to elaborate on the gifts withheld from Swift, he wrote "Evening without Angels."

From the epigraph, Stevens took air and light and organized the poem around them:

> Air is air.
> Its vacancy glitters round us everywhere.
> Its sounds are not angelic syllables
> But our unfashioned spirits realized
> More sharply in more furious selves.

> And light
> That fosters seraphim and is to them
> Coiffeur of haloes, fecund jeweller—
> Was the sun concoct for angels or for men?

The "voluptuousness of looking" is the enjoyment of air and light, but, as the poem makes clear, the pleasures of visibility are also within: "Light, too, encrusts us making visible / The motions of the mind." Thus, the joy of having a body is one with the satisfactions of thought. The images of light in the poem are subtly reshaped in the movement from morning to evening. In the first

---

10. *Sur Plusieurs Beaux Sujets*, I, 7–9 (Both volumes in Huntington Library).

part, "We are men of sun / And men of day." The sun of the "immensely flashing East" replaces the angels' "Coiffeur of haloes, fecund jeweller." The sun then yields in the final lines to darkness. The "voluptuousness of looking" is tempered by the now austere gaze at the single rounded light:

> Bare night is best. Bare earth is best. Bare, bare,
> Except for our own houses, huddled low
> Beneath the arches and their spangled air,
> Beneath the rhapsodies of fire and fire,
> Where the voice that is in us makes a true response,
> Where the voice that is great within us rises up,
> As we stand gazing at the rounded moon. (*CP*, 136–38)

What had been a casual aside by Rossi captured for Stevens life's extraordinary endowments—air, light, sensation, vision within and without, *l'instinct du bonheur*.

"United Dames of America," first published in the New York *Times* in 1937, has been largely ignored by Stevens' readers. Typical of the poems of the late 1930s and early 1940s, it is an exercise on the idea of the hero, and, in this case, his relation to the masses, the united dames of America. Stevens' hero-poems tend to be among his most daring conceptually and his most damning aesthetically, and for reasons that are not hard to fathom. The hero represents the indulgence of the imagination to the detriment of the real, a wish indulged, even as an article of faith, but not realized. Major man, as Stevens later called him, remained theoretically, and thus poetically, an abstraction, even though Stevens wanted desperately to believe in his palpable presence. He turned not to the politician, but rather to the poet as the truest figuration of a major man. Here, the lines that serve as the epigraph to "United Dames of America" are especially pertinent: "Je tâche, en restant exact, d'être poète" (I try, in remaining exact, to be a poet). The sentence is taken from a letter Jules Renard, the French novelist and dramatist, wrote to Louis Paillard, who had published an essay on his work. Stevens had come across the line when he read Renard's correspondence, though he also owned a four-volume edition of Renard's *Journal*, which he purchased from his Paris art dealer. He told Henry Church that Renard "constantly says things that interest me immensely" (*L*, 510).

In the 1900 letter, Renard commends his critic for the honest as-

sessment of his autobiographical novel *Poil de Carotte* (1894) and
his collection of essays and tales *Les Bucoliques* (1898):

> Non, *Poil de Carotte* n'est pas un roman. Non, les *Bucoliques* ne sont pas
> des nouvelles, et, la meilleure preuve que l'acte de *Poil de Carotte* est
> humaine, c'est que je ne peux pas en faire une série: il faut que j'attende
> l'humanité. La vie me donne ce qu'elle veut. J'accepte, et je tâche, en
> restant exact, d'être poète. Je m'efforce, non de créer, mais de recréer.
> Et vous savez bien que, de vous à moi, ces mots n'ont pas la prétention
> qu'un niais y noterait. Ce que j'écris, je l'écris par fonction naturelle. Je
> tâche de vivre, les yeux d'abord étonnés, puis clairvoyants.

> (No, *Poil de Carotte* is not a novel. No, the *Bucoliques* are not novellas,
> and the best proof that the work *Poil de Carotte* is human is that I am
> unable to do a sequel: I must wait for humanity. Life gives me what it
> wishes. I accept it, and try, in remaining exact, to be a poet. I do not
> endeavor to create but to recreate. And between us, as you well know,
> these words do not have the claim that a naive person would note in
> them. What I write, I write through a natural process. I try to live,
> first with eyes astonished, then clairvoyant.) [11]

What obviously distinguished these remarks in Stevens' estimation
was Renard's insistence upon writing directly from the experience
of an unpredictable life ("il faut que j'attende l'humanité") and in
fidelity to it ("en restant exact") to become the true poet. Here is
the very exactitude that Wyzewa and his aunt Vincentine willfully
shunned in favor of the "libres rêves." Wyzewa and Renard are two
more manifestations of Stevens' interest in the respective claims of
imagination and reality.

In "United Dames of America," Renard becomes the poetic
counterpart of the "actor that will at last declaim our end." The
poem itself, however, displays little exactitude in defining that
actor. The emphasis is perhaps greater on the act of trying ("Je
tâche . . .") to describe precisely. By deliberate poetic feints, not
altogether successful, the poem probes what shape the hero's face
might take, a face that is at first to be covered by leaves but then
crowned with them in laurels. He must be of the masses, "a central
face," and yet "one face keeps returning (never the one)." While
the need for the central face is vehement ("mouths crying and crying day by day"), that actor, imagined by both hermit and politician, only partially emerges in the last lines of the poem:

11. Jules Renard, *Correspondance,* ed. Léon Guichard (Paris, 1953), 227 (my translation).

Yet one face keeps returning (never the one).
The face of the man of the mass, never the face
That hermit on reef sable would have seen,

Never the naked politician taught
By the wise. There are not leaves enough to crown,
To cover, to crown, to cover—let it go—
The actor that will at last declaim our end. (*CP*, 206)

The title, smacking of Stevens' fondness for the breezy and irreverent, has a direct bearing on the poem. Like the United States
of America, the dames are of the American masses, but are recast
in the slangy species of common women. Yet, the irony contra-
venes: the dame of English aristocracy, the counterpart of the lord
(the word derives from the Latin *domina*), points to the hero-ideal.
From the dames that constitute the "mass," it must be possible,
the title implies, to find the dame of rank who possesses the "central face."

"Reply to Papini" begins with a quotation from the Italian critic,
philosopher, poet, and historian, Giovanni Papini: "In all the solemn moments of human history . . . poets rose to sing the hymn
of victory or the psalm of supplication. . . . Cease, then, from
being the astute calligraphers of congealed daydreams, the hunters
of cerebral phosphorescences" (*CP*, 446). Stevens also cites the
source of the epigraph, "LETTER OF CELESTIN VI, POPE, TO THE POETS
P.C.C. GIOVANNI PAPINI." The letter is one of several addressed by
Papini through the fictitious pope, and they include exhortations
to women, historians, scientists, separated Christians, as well as
poets. Papini, best remembered for his *Life of Christ* (1921), converted from atheism to Roman Catholicism in 1920. *The Letters of
Pope Celestin VI to All Mankind* appeared originally in 1946, and in
each case the pope summons his addressees to the Christian life
and a renewed vocation. Stevens' quotation does not correspond
precisely to the English translation published in 1948. There was a
French translation by Juliette Bertrand, however, that was issued in
the same year, and it is possible that the poet made his own translation from that text. "Reply to Papini" was first published in *The
Auroras of Autumn* in 1950.

The poem challenges the religious orthodoxy of Papini and his
papal spokesman; it is a "reply" in the sense of a rejoinder. Celestin's
"ever-living subject," as Stevens characterizes it, was a sympathetic one—the exaltation of the poet. The letter laments the poet's

waning influence: "Men no longer invoke the love of poetry. And yet never before has there been such a need for men to be transfigured, to be rescued, to be comforted by poetry." It is his next assertion that "Reply to Papini" disputes: "Only through the spiritual world can we hope for recovery and returning strength in the material world." Papini's essay begins with the claim that "God inspires me to speak also to you and I obey."[12] Stevens begins his poem in direct rebuttal: "Poor procurator, why do you ask someone else / To say what Celestin should say for himself?"

The faltering poets whom the pope is seeking to rally must be ultimately directed in their art toward eternal life: "You are, within the limitations of terrestrial expression, imitators of the Redemption, preparers of the Kingdom of Heaven."[13] Stevens' exception to these claims derives from Papini's belittling an earthly existence on its own terms:

> The way through the world
> Is more difficult to find than the way beyond it.
>
> You know that the nucleus of a time is not
> The poet but the poem, the growth of the mind
>
> Of the world, the heroic effort to live expressed
> As victory. The poet does not speak in ruins
>
> Nor stand there making orotund consolations.
> He shares the confusions of intelligence.

The poet's "confusions of intelligence" may appear to Celestin as vapid "cerebral phosphorescences," but the second part of Stevens' poem vindicates them as necessary human actions. Hymns are improper while the world "is still profound and in its depths," unless they be hymns "appropriate to / The complexities of the world," and here Stevens means of course *this* world. These "cerebral phosphorescences" are defended and vivified in the poem's final lines:

> The poet
> Increases the aspects of experience,
> As an enchantment, analyzed and fixed
>
> And final. This is the centre. The poet is
> The angry day-son clanging at its make:

---

12. Giovanni Papini, "To the Poets," *The Letters of Pope Celestin VI to All Mankind*, trans. Loretta Murnane (New York, 1948), 118–19.
   13. *Ibid.*, 121.

The satisfaction underneath the sense,
The conception sparkling in still obstinate thought. (*CP*, 446–48)

As a poem, "Reply to Papini" suffers for its dependence upon its source; it answers a point of view larger than the one contained in its epigraph and hence is inaccessible to the reader. It also tends to succumb in places to an overly expository rhetoric—"The world is still profound," "complexities of the world," "intricacies of appearance," "aspects of experience." It is the single instance in which Stevens' epigraph dominates the poem's direction and works to its disadvantage.

Stevens' epigraph in "The World as Meditation" comes from the Romanian violinist and composer, Georges Enesco. In 1951, twenty conversations with Enesco were broadcast in France, and Stevens apparently saw a transcription shortly thereafter. The poem first appeared in the *Hudson Review* in the autumn of 1952. Bernard Gavoty's edition of those conversations, *Les Souvenirs de Georges Enesco,* was published in 1955. Enesco had described the role of meditation in his own musical creations as a kind of intense concentration and as an unconscious dream. The general faculty of meditation, however, described by Stefan Zweig in his novella *Le Bouquiniste Mendel,* was the ideal Enesco outlined for himself: "Cependant, je possède la première des facultés auxquelles il [Zweig] fait allusion, en ce sens que je porte en moi un rêve permanent; quelque chose frémit dans mon coeur, qui ne s'arrête ni nuit, ni jour. C'est dire que ma carrière de virtuose, si elle m'a pris un temps précieux, n'a pas nui, cependant, à ma vocation de compositeur, et que l'obligation de voyager fréquemment n'a jamais interrompu ma méditation solitaire" (Even so, I possess the first of the faculties to which he [Zweig] makes allusion, in the sense that I carry a continuous dream, something vibrates within my heart— ceasing neither night nor day. I mean that my career as a virtuoso, if it has taken precious time, did not harm, however, my vocation as a composer, and that the obligation to travel frequently never interrupted my solitary meditation).[14]

Stevens' transcription of Enesco's words is not precise; his source apparently derives from the 1951 broadcasts instead of the text published in 1955: "J'ai passé trop de temps à travailler mon violon, à voyager. Mais l'exercice essentiel du compositeur—la médi-

---

14. *Les Souvenirs de Georges Enesco,* ed. Bernard Gavoty (Paris, 1955), 154–55.

tation—rien ne l'a jamais suspendu en moi. . . . Je vis un rêve permanent, qui ne s'arrête ni nuit ni jour" (I have spent too much time
playing my violin and traveling. But the essential exercise of the
composer, meditation, was never suspended in me . . . I live a permanent dream, which ceases neither night nor day). Enesco, for
example, does not contend in the 1955 text that his career and
travel as a violinist have taken "trop de temps," even though they
have absorbed "un temps précieux." Neither does Enesco define
meditation as the "exercise essentiel du compositeur," though he
does earlier cite the words from Zweig's story: "'Toutes nos créa-
tions originales et puissantes sont le fruit d'une concentration'"
(All of our original and powerful creations are the fruit of concentration).[15] Equally important, Stevens changes Enesco's "je porte en
moi un rêve permanent" to "Je vis un rêve permanent." The effect
is to make the habitual and constant dream more intrinsic, something to be lived rather than taken up. Enesco's "rêve permanent"
as a composer is similar to Wyzewa's "libres rêves," leading him to
prefer poetry to prose.

The poem itself incorporates Penelope's meditative vigil while
Ulysses-sun "kept coming constantly so near." She is a composer,
not in the exclusive sense of Enesco as a maker of music, but as
any human perceiver creates the world through relentless mental
exertion and reflection. The poem repeats Enesco's two-stage process, meditation and composition, an inner probing to attain the
mind's object:

> She has composed, so long, a self with which to welcome him,
> Companion to his self for her, which she imagined,
> Two in a deep-founded sheltering, friend and dear friend. (CP,
>    520)

Meditation is here one with imagination, composing both the perceiving self and the selves surrounding it.

The sun, like Ulysses an "interminable adventurer," touches
Penelope's pillow and face at daybreak in early spring. Her "barbarous strength" reaches out to possess it, finding appeasement
but never satiety:

> But was it Ulysses? Or was it only the warmth of the sun
> On her pillow? The thought kept beating in her like her heart.
> The two kept beating together. It was only day.

15. *Ibid.*, 154.

It was Ulysses and it was not. Yet they had met,
Friend and dear friend and a planet's encouragement.
The barbarous strength within her would never fail. (*CP,* 520–21)

The epigraph's "exercice essentiel" broadens into the universal: "The trees had been mended, as an essential exercise / In an inhuman meditation." Enesco's meditation as music and Penelope's meditation creating Ulysses' return are both expanded in the poem to contain the world as meditation. The acts of nature and the seasons can be objects of perception (human meditation), but from another perspective, they are imitations of the mind's makings (inhuman meditation).

The poem is itself a meditation, as if to demonstrate its thesis. Its method is one of questions, repetitions, and tentative conclusions. Its rhetoric imitates Penelope, who imagines her lover and composes herself by memory ("Never forgetting him"), by repetition ("Repeating his name with its patient syllables"), and by thought ("The thought kept beating in her like her heart"). In a world where knower and known are divided, the mind's uncertain but irrepressible urge to know distinguishes its identity. In the end, Penelope's meditation affirms her humanity.

Although Stevens used epigraphs skillfully, they remained occasional in his art. As an apparatus too formal or pedantic, it may have been undesirable, or he may have regarded it as too narrow in proposing a poem's scope or too reductive in summarizing a given work. It is possible that he rarely employed the epigraph because of its emphasis on the *what* of a poem rather than its *how,* always a matter of importance with him. Unlike Eliot and Pound, he had no prevailing interest in a poetic texture of literary allusions. The epigraphs do tell us something about Stevens' habits of reading. They suggest that the idea from which these poems sprang was often a casual insertion, a turn of phrase, within an essay, letter, or poem. The epigraphs are not formal allusions; they do not derive from a systematic reading of classical texts. Rather, they are themselves "pieces of paper," nuances, unrehearsed notions that the poet found personally congenial as they nudged again his own peculiar powers of composition to life.

At the age of twenty-seven, Stevens wrote his fiancée of his love for the written word: "Lately, I have been buying almost any book that struck my fancy. I wish I might line my walls with them and devote myself to study, or rather, reading; for if I have ardor left for anything at all, it is for books" (*SP*, 176). There is a sense in which for the rest of his life he did line his walls with books, and their contributions mark one of the principal origins of his poetry. At various periods in his life, for example, he saw with some regularity *La Nouvelle Revue Française, Revue de Paris, Nouvelles Littéraires, Mesures, Cahiers d'Art, New Statesman, Life and Letters, London Mercury, Kenyon Review, New Republic,* and many others. The detailed annotations and underlining in his copies of Henri Focillon's *The Life of Forms in Art,* Charles Mauron's *Aesthetics and Psychology,* and I. A. Richards' *Coleridge on Imagination,* along with the hundreds of books in his personal library, often referred to in his correspondence and excerpted in his notebooks, corroborate his zealous and careful enjoyment of books.[16]

Although Stevens is not a consistently allusive poet, he does playfully and occasionally direct the poem beyond itself. The models for Crispin in "The Comedian as the Letter C" derive from the *commedia dell' arte,* beginning with the Crispin of Paul Scarron's *L'Ecolier de Salamanque* and including the Crispinus of Ben Jonson's *Poetaster.* Stevens' "Peter Quince at the Clavier" derives ironically from the same character in *A Midsummer Night's Dream.* The "ten thousand Thunders" that acclaim Christ after his victory over Satan in *Paradise Lost* (VI, 836) become "ten thousand tumblers tumbling down" in "Credences of Summer" (*CP*, 376). The interweavings of Yeats's "The Lake Isle of Innisfree" and Heine's "Lyrisches Intermezzo (No. 31)" in "Page from a Tale" and the reference to Marianne Moore—"Marianna's Swedish cart" (*CP*, 368), from her "A Carriage from Sweden"—in "The Prejudice against the Past" all attest to Stevens' diverse though infrequent borrowings and allusions.

The heterogeneity of his reading, apparent in the epigraphs, is further reflected in occasional poetic insertions. Victor Serge's "The Revolution at Dead End" is mentioned in part XIV of "Esthétique du Mal"; "Conversation avec Picasso" from *Cahiers d'Art* occurs in

16. See especially J. M. Edelstein, "The Poet as Reader: Wallace Stevens and His Books," *Book Collector,* XXIII (Spring, 1974), 53–68; Milton J. Bates, "Stevens' Books at the Huntington: An Annotated Checklist," *Wallace Stevens Journal,* II (Fall, 1978), 45–61, and "Stevens' Books at the Huntington: An Annotated Checklist (Concluded)," *Wallace Stevens Journal,* III (Spring, 1979), 15–33; Peter Brazeau, "Wallace Stevens at the University of Massachusetts: Check List of an Archive," *Wallace Stevens Journal,* II (Spring, 1978), 50–52. Much of Stevens' personal library was sold at auction in 1963 by Mrs. Stevens, and many of his books have disappeared from record.

part XV of "The Man with the Blue Guitar"; and Guillaume
Apollinaire's *Le Bestiare ou le Cortège d'Orphée* with illustrations by
Raoul Dufy appears in "Lions in Sweden."[17] "Living In Books
And Living In Paintings" (169) was more than an idle wish when
he entered it in his notebook *From Pieces of Paper.* Books on politics, philosophy, literary criticism, painting, music, and the fine
arts sustained him through the evenings in his room on the second
floor at Westerly Terrace. There is a peculiar biographical pertinence
in the lines from "The House Was Quiet and the World Was Calm":

> The house was quiet and the world was calm.
> The reader became the book; and summer night
>
> Was like the conscious being of the book.
> The house was quiet and the world was calm. (*CP,* 358)

Stevens' partiality for epigrammatic wit was present as early as
his New York journals and continued throughout his life. When
one considers how Rossi's casual description of Swift, the source
of which Stevens himself could not recall for sure, or how the presentation of Teodor de Wyzewa's Aunt Vincentine in a *Revue des
Deux Mondes* essay served Stevens, there is an invitation to speculate on how many other poems, unacknowledged by formal epigraphs, may have taken life from equally unpredictable and unlikely sources. The actual epigraphs suggest the real probability
that that was often the case.

17. Victor Serge, "The Revolution at Dead End (1926–1928)," trans. Ethel Libson,
*Politics,* I (June, 1944), 150; Christian Zervos, "Conversation avec Picasso," *Picasso:
1930–1935* (Paris, 1936), 37 ("Chez moi, un tableau est une somme de destructions");
Ramon Guthrie, "Stevens' LIONS IN SWEDEN, 18," *Explicator,* XX (December, 1961), #32.

# 9 ✑ Correspondence

In one of his "Adagia," Stevens affirms: "Life is an affair of people not of places. But for me life is an affair of places and that is the trouble" (*OP*, 158). The admission is all the more revealing when one discovers that Stevens left the United States only for a couple of brief visits to Canada and Cuba and a trip to California by way of the Panama Canal. The world of his poetry, however, is cosmopolitan, as even the titles divulge—"The Doctor of Geneva," for example, or "A Dish of Peaches in Russia," among numerous others. As we have seen, *From Pieces of Paper* also contains numerous references to foreign places. Stevens' active interest in other environments and cultures was nurtured by extensive reading. He delighted in exploring the unseen lands beyond his native soil; his personal correspondence enlarged that exploration.

In his youth, Stevens looked forward to foreign travel, announcing, for example, in his journal as he left Cambridge in 1900: "I am going to New York, I think, to try my hand at journalism. If that does not pan out well, I am resolved to knock about the country—the world" (*SP*, 70). Six months later, he was still clinging to the prospect of travel, this time to Arizona or Mexico. He added, "Europe is still on the other side of the ocean" (*SP*, 94). But Stevens remained in New York, going on to law school and then practicing with various firms in the city. The burdens and delays in attaining financial security, especially as he looked ahead to marriage, must have made "the other side of the ocean" all the more remote. In letters to Elsie written in the months just before their marriage in 1909, however, Stevens returned to his dream of travel: "We'll be going over there one of these days, I hope. I should mope in Paradise (possibly) if I were to die without first having been to London. —On Sunday, it was Berlin. —I have had my hours for Paris, too—when I could see the Street of Little Stables, and the Street of

Beautiful Leaves, and the Bridge of Arts, and the Church of Our Lady, and the Arch of Triumph—as clearly as I can see you looking out of that frame. —Good Fortune, send us to them all."[1] A few weeks later he was still dwelling on Europe and London, but now there was another suggestion: "London continues to be the ultimate point of romance to me. I wish there were some chap there to whom I could write for things" (*SP,* 234–35). Eventually, there would be Chinese tea and artifacts from Lucy Monroe Calhoun in Peking; dolls for his daughter Holly sent from Japan by Rosamund Cary; "kee-moon" tea from Benjamin Kwok in Canton, China; honey from London sent by Ferdinand Reyher; an Oriental scroll from Peter Lee, a Korean student in America. Over the years, Stevens gained an extensive collection of European books and French paintings. These commodities were precious to him. "For my part," he once told James Powers, "I never really lived until I had a home, and my own room, say, with a package of books from Paris or London" (*L,* 301). The packages from abroad rescued him from the insularity of his daily business life in Hartford.

Besides the parcels, there were hundreds of postcards and letters from friends abroad, people he did not see often. There were some correspondents whom he never met personally. "Ceylon is the sort of place with which one can come to grips and still be fascinated," Stevens wrote Leonard C. van Geyzel, who lived there. "It is like Florida, or, to take something a little more prodigious, like Bengal, as I understand Bengal to be" (*L,* 353). To Barbara Church in France, he wrote: "The postcards from Ville d'Avray came the other day. They did me a lot of good. In fact, I survive on postcards from Europe" (*L,* 797). Toward the end of his life he asked her for more "gypsy cards": "By gypsy cards, I do not mean the ones specifically gypsy, but all of them as tokens of your wandering. I have often seen Seville before but never smelled the heavy fragrance of its orange blossoms. And I have seen Granada but never felt the noise of its mountain water. Also, I have been in Madrid but this time it was a change to get away from the Prado and to go to restaurants and sit by the door and look out at the 18th century. I liked to stop at Bordeaux where other friends of mine have lived" (*L,* 837). It is not an exaggeration to suggest that Ste-

---

1. Wallace Stevens to Elsie Moll [Kachel], January 26, 1909.

vens' closest friends were the ones he knew, not through regular personal contact, but through letters, and even when these friends drew close to the Stevens' home in Hartford, it was his habit to meet them in New York City for lunch or cocktails and return home on the evening train. He kept his friends at a distance, in part to protect his domestic privacy and routine, the ordered world in which business and poetry prospered. For the sedentary poet whose eye was habitually fixed abroad, however, the letters constituted a workshop for the writing of poetry. One sees poems emerging from them.

In several ways, the correspondence with Thomas McGreevy, an Irish poet and art critic, is typical. In 1948, McGreevy first established contact with Stevens; they exchanged letters regularly for the remainder of Stevens' life, though they met, apparently, only once, the year before Stevens' death. Jack Yeats, younger brother of William Butler Yeats, was a close friend of McGreevy's and had completed a book about his several friends' drawings. At Stevens' request, Jack sketched a profile of McGreevy on the title page before he sent the book to Stevens—"You and Mr. Yeats must be a pair of very good-natured men to indulge me this way. I appreciate the kindness of both of you" (L, 596). McGreevy's interest in poetry and art was a natural basis for friendship, and he was later to become, to Stevens' delight, director of the National Gallery in Dublin. There was also a certain exuberance in McGreevy's letters that Stevens enjoyed, as he commented to Barbara Church: "He is, in any event, a blessed creature, sustained by a habit of almost medieval faith and I like the God bless you with which he winds up his letters" (L, 682–83).

It was through McGreevy's letters that Stevens came to write "Our Stars Come from Ireland" in 1948. The poem was written at a time when Ireland had been brought palpably to life in Stevens' imagination, as he said in a letter to Barbara Church: "The Irish seem to have hearts. Besides, Dublin and the whole place look to my eye like the pages of a novel—not one of those frightful continental novels in ten volumes, all psychology and no fresh air, but a novel full of the smell of ale and horses and noisy with people living in flats, playing the piano, and telephoning and with the sound of drunks in the street at night" (L, 609). The first part of the poem is addressed to McGreevy: "*Tom McGreevy, in America,*

*Thinks of Himself as a Boy.*"[2] Stevens had read with interest a poem by McGreevy called "Recessional." Living amid the "outrageous roars" of Switzerland, the poet remembers, as the young Yeats in London had remembered the Innisfree of Sligo, the town of his own youth, Tarbert, and the sound of the sea from Mal Bay thirty miles away. McGreevy's poem concludes:

In tender, less glaring, island days
And ways
I could hear—
Where listeners still hear—
That far-away, dear
Roar
The long, silvery roar
Of Mal Bay.[3]

"Our Stars Come from Ireland," as Stevens later said to McGreevy, celebrates the importance of places as figments of memory, including McGreevy's recollection of Mal Bay and Tarbert:

Out of him that I loved,
Mal Bay I made,
I made Mal Bay
And him in that water.

Over the top of the Bank of Ireland,
The wind blows quaintly
Its thin-stringed music,
As he heard it in Tarbert. (*CP,* 454)

The second quatrain, as Peter Brazeau has shown, reconstructs a stanza from McGreevy's "Homage to Hieronymus Bosch": "High above the Bank of Ireland / Unearthly music sounded, / Passing westwards."[4] The stars of Ireland, of Tarbert and Kerry and Mal Bay, move westward and hover over the Pennsylvania landscape of

2. Stevens sent the first part of the poem to McGreevy on July 28, 1948; it was entitled "Tom McGreevy, Having Emigrated to America, Remembers His Youth." He later decided to allow McGreevy to retain in the title his native Ireland ("Our Stars Come From Ireland") and to introduce himself as the American ("I live in Pennsylvania"). When he added the second part, *"The Westwardness of Everything,"* he changed Part I to *"Tom McGreevy, in America, Thinks of Himself as a Boy,"* and the complete poem was then given the title "Our Stars Come from Ireland."
3. Thomas MacGreevy [*sic*], *Collected Poems* (Dublin, 1971), 49.
4. Peter Brazeau, "The Irish Connection: Wallace Stevens and Thomas McGreevy," *Southern Review,* n.s., XVII (1981), 536–37; MacGreevy, *Collected Poems,* 23.

Stevens' own youth, resulting in a harmony, "These Gaeled and fitful-fangled darknesses / Made suddenly luminous" (*CP*, 455). Stevens later explained to McGreevy the personal meaning of westward motion:

> What you say in one of your letters about your westwardness as a result of living near the Shannon Estuary interested me. The house in which I was born and lived as a boy faced the west and wherever I have lived if the house faced any other way I have always been pulling it round on an axis to get it straight. But that is the least of this sort of thing. After all, instead of facing the Atlantic, you might have faced London and Paris. The poem which I sent you some time ago is one of two. The other is on this very subject: the westwardness of things. The poem does little more than make the point but the point is there to be made. (*L*, 618)

José Rodríguez-Feo was a recent graduate of Harvard when he wrote Stevens in 1944, requesting permission to translate "Esthétique du Mal" for a little magazine, *Origenes,* he had founded in Havana. Little more than a year later, *Origenes* introduced Wallace Stevens to Cubans in Spanish. Stevens' correspondence with Rodríguez-Feo, like the letters to McGreevy, expanded to include a variety of subjects. His new friend was able to introduce Stevens to the work of a number of Cuban artists, notably the drawings of Mariano Rodríguez, and Stevens occasionally visited his exhibitions in New York City. The letters also touch on the mundane, including Rodríguez-Feo's description of his family life in Cuba and his mother's burro, Pompilio: "There still remains in Cuba a nice old woman, who loves her burro and asks Jose to tell me, for Xmas, that Pompilio is well. Saludos, Pompilio" (*L*, 865). On one of the few occasions when they met in the United States, Rodríguez-Feo tried to turn the conversation to literature, but Stevens obdurately preferred to discuss Cuba. Rodríguez-Feo remembers, "'I have the sensation that you're sort of plundering me because when I talk about all these things, all the things come into your poetry.' He smiled and sort of laughed. 'You're a very smart young Cuban fellow.'"[5]

"The Novel" was conceived from a Cuban setting provided by

5. Rodríguez-Feo quoted in Peter Brazeau, *Parts of a World: Wallace Stevens Remembered* (New York, 1983), 142.

Rodríguez-Feo, and the individual named in the poem is José from "vividest Varadero," the coastal town from which Rodríguez-Feo often wrote Stevens. What is especially notable is the fact that the third and fourth stanzas of the poem are almost literal transcriptions of a plea by Rodríguez-Feo's mother that he not accept a position with UNESCO in Paris. The Cuban quotes his mother in a letter to Stevens on September 21, 1948:

> I gave up the job at the Unesco at Paris because mother was afraid I would freeze in the Parisian hotels. She happened to listen in on a conversation wherein a friend of mine described in gruesome details the fate of an Argentine writer. At night he would go to bed, cover himself with blankets—protruding from the pile of wool a hand, in a black glove, holds a novel by Camus. That was the only safe way he could keep in touch with French literary events. Mother was much impressed by the picture of the engloved hand holding a trembling little volume. She begged me to stay away. (*L, 617*)

Like Rodríguez-Feo's mother, Stevens was obviously moved by the description of the Argentine writer, who is drawn in the poem "verbatim from your letter":

> *Mother was afraid I should freeze in the Parisian hotels.*
> *She had heard of the fate of an Argentine writer. At night*
> *He would go to bed, cover himself with blankets—*
>
> *Protruding from the pile of wool, a hand,*
> *In a black glove, holds a novel by Camus. She begged*
> *That I stay away.* These are the words of José.

The poem then describes the sound of the water at Varadero Beach:

> How tranquil it was at vividest Varadero,
> While the water kept running through the mouth of the speaker,
> Saying, *Olalla blanca en el blanco*. (*CP, 457*)

The quotation from Lorca's "Martirio de Santa Olalla" in the last line of the tercet, interestingly enough, had come to Stevens a few months earlier. He acknowledged to McGreevy when the poem appeared in *The Auroras of Autumn*: "Also, in the poem called *The Novel* I use a line from Lorca which you quoted" (*L, 690*). The line, partially misquoted by Stevens, occurs at the end of Lorca's poem:

> ¡Saltan vidrios de colores!
> Olalla blanca en lo blanco.

Ángeles y serafines
dicen: Santo, Santo, Santo.[6]

Stevens' poem goes on to describe the fear born of the "Arcadian imagination" that had taken hold of the Argentine in frigid Paris. At the end, the Argentine has been enlarged to include all men. "The Novel" does not focus on Havana, which Stevens knew first-hand, but on Varadero, which he knew only through the letters and postcards from Rodríguez-Feo. The background of this poem and the circumstances of its creation are perhaps the best illustration of one of the poem's principal conclusions: "Only the real can be / Unreal today, be hidden and alive" (*CP*, 458).

Rodríguez-Feo had played a part in three earlier poems by Stevens, one of which is entitled "A Word with José Rodríguez-Feo." This poem, as Stevens explained, insists that "although the grotesque has taken possession of the subconscious, this is not because there is any particular relationship between the two things" (*L*, 489). Thus, the answer to the question posed in the poem, "Is lunar Habana the Cuba of the self?" (*CP*, 333), is negative. The grotesque is separate, a "simplified geography, in which / The sun comes up like news from Africa" (*CP*, 334).

"Attempt to Discover Life," as Stevens later told Rodríguez-Feo, was prompted by the question "whether the experience of life is in the end worthy more than tuppence: dos centavos" (*L*, 540). The poem, set in a club at a Cuban health resort, begins: "At San Miguel de los Baños, / The waitress heaped up black Hermosas." The somewhat mysterious events and setting are vaguely reminiscent of Eliot's "Sweeney among the Nightingales": a waitress scatters multicolored roses among the patrons; a "cadaverous person" enters, accompanied by "A woman brilliant and pallid-skinned," who is "smiling and wetting her lips." The poem then concludes in the third stanza:

> The green roses drifted up from the table
> In smoke. The blue petals became
> The yellowing fomentations of effulgence,
> Among fomentations of black bloom and of white bloom.
> The cadaverous persons were dispelled.

6. Federico García Lorca, *Antología Poética* (Buenos Aires, 1957), 119.

On the table near which they stood
Two coins were lying—dos centavos. (*CP,* 370)

The bathetic conclusion, and indeed the whole poem, was shaped by Stevens' letter from Rodríguez-Feo in 1946:

> I am at the moment in San Miguel de los Baños—literally Saint Michael of the Baths—a health resort near Habana. Its mineral waters are famous; they are very curative, especially for those who suffer of liver and stomacal troubles. I am resting; there is nothing here to distract one's life: no movies, parties, known people who can pester us with their invitations, etc. It's a lovely little village, surrounded by high lomas (hills). The vegetation is very puritanical in appearance; mostly palm trees—no flowers. In the evening I meet some of the town's capitans (that's how we call here the Chinese) and play dominoes. It's very amusing to watch them play—they are so calm and serious about everything. Sometimes we play billiards and asi [*sic*] life rounds up the perfect day. I do nothing else; most of the time I just sit and watch the modest citizens (really very poor) walk about, selling lotery [*sic*] tickets or marching about the streets with their sad-looking horses to incite some rich sick-visitor to take a hike on horses and win therefore a few pesos.[7]

Stevens changed the "puritanical" vegetation ("no flowers") to include the various rose petals of the poem. It was the image of the "modest citizens (really very poor)," however, that suggested the "cadaverous persons" leaving not the "few pesos" of the letter, but "dos centavos."

"Paisant Chronicle" was written by Stevens as a response to a number of questions about the "major men," an appellation that Rodríguez-Feo had noted in "Notes toward a Supreme Fiction," for example. In several letters, Stevens attempted to clarify his ideas, undoubtedly stirring his own interest in the hero-giant-poet that was a continuing feature of many of his poems. Stevens declared that the "major men" are neither "exponents of humanism" nor "Nietzschean shadows." Rather, they are the creators of the supreme fiction that Stevens defined as "some arbitrary object of belief." The hero-figures can make prevail the fictions that men can accept and by which they can live their lives: "The major men are

---

7. José Rodríguez-Feo to Wallace Stevens, March 21, 1946.

234 WALLACE STEVENS: A POET'S GROWTH

part of the entourage of that artificial object" (*L*, 485). Stevens was dissatisfied with this prose exegesis—as he was with all paraphrases of the ideas in his poetry. A more fruitful attempt was through a poem, and in "Paisant Chronicle," Stevens wrote to Rodríguez-Feo, "I have defined major men for you" (*L*, 489).

In the poem, Stevens distinguishes major men from traditional national heroes and other men who are admired for feats of bravery. The major man is different, embodying the paradox that is at the heart of all of Stevens' poems defining him. He is real enough to be believable, but he is also the man of imagination, the embellisher of reality. He is real and unreal, and, as a result, ideal and finally unattainable. As the poem itself declares, major men are "beyond / Reality" but "composed thereof"; "They are / The fictive man created out of men" (*CP*, 335). As a result, major men can bring to life the fictions of the imagination, without which no man can survive; at the same time, they do not compromise the undistorted reality, without which all fictions are evasive. Like the "central man" of "Asides on the Oboe," major man is "The impossible possible philosophers' man, / . . . Who in a million diamonds sums us up" (*CP*, 250).

The long exchange of letters between Stevens and Rodríguez-Feo was to have major implications for Stevens' poetry—not only in settings ("Attempt to Discover Life") and phraseology ("The Novel"). The correspondence was also a source of stimulation in regard to major concepts in Stevens' longer poetic elaboration. The coming to terms with "major men," at Rodríguez-Feo's request, is one such instance.

In 1937, at the suggestion of mutual friends, Stevens wrote to Leonard C. van Geyzel in Ceylon, asking him to send some carvings, jewelry, and tea as Christmas gifts for his family. Van Geyzel was able to respond to the request, and the poet was elated by the quality and taste of the selections. An exchange of letters ensued, frequently accompanied by books and other articles. It was through van Geyzel that Ceylon came to have a prominent symbolic import in Stevens' own mind and, consequently, in his poems. Some nineteen months after the correspondence began, for example, Stevens reported to van Geyzel: "Ceylon has taken a strong hold on my imagination. These things [other articles sent by van Geyzel] help one to visualize the people in the streets" (*L*, 337). It was also at this time that references to Ceylon began to appear in Stevens' poems. One of the first, "Connoisseur of Chaos," was written about four months after Stevens received the original Christmas package from van Geyzel. Here, "Englishmen lived without tea in Ceylon" (*CP*, 215) appears as one in a series of illustrations showing that "inherent opposites" can create an "essential unity." In "Extracts from Addresses to the Academy of Fine Ideas," Ceylon is a "past apocalypse" (*CP*, 257) that the mind, at last poetically satisfied, can discard. In "Description without Place," the frequently cited reference to "Pablo Neruda in Ceylon" (*CP*, 341) illustrates the transforming power of the imagination: "Things are as they seemed." One of the most exotic references to the island occurs in "Notes toward a Supreme Fiction":

> The elephant
> Breaches the darkness of Ceylon with blares,
>
> The glitter-goes on surfaces of tanks,
> Shattering velvetest far-away. (*CP*, 384)

The images of Ceylon in Stevens' poetry follow no consistent pattern; they are brief and playful interjections of geographical fancy. Through the van Geyzel correspondence that continued for some eighteen years, Stevens shored up that remote island in his poetic consciousness.

Stevens wrote "An Ordinary Evening in New Haven" in the spring and summer of 1949. It was one of his most ambitious undertakings, begun at the invitation of the Connecticut Academy of Arts and Sciences. Through the summer of 1949, the poet received a succession of letters and cards from friends in Europe, and in canto XXVIII, he drew together the various locations to illustrate that "Real and unreal are two in one":

> If it should be true that reality exists
> In the mind: the tin plate, the loaf of bread on it,
> The long-bladed knife, the little to drink and her
>
> Misericordia, it follows that
> Real and unreal are two in one: New Haven
> Before and after one arrives or, say,
>
> Bergamo on a postcard, Rome after dark,
> Sweden described, Salzburg with shaded eyes
> Or Paris in conversation at a café.

This endlessly elaborating poem
Displays the theory of poetry,
As the life of poetry. A more severe,

More harassing master would extemporize
Subtler, more urgent proof that the theory
Of poetry is the theory of life,

As it is, in the intricate evasions of as,
In things seen and unseen, created from nothingness,
The heavens, the hells, the worlds, the longed-for lands. (*CP,*
   485–86)

If the theory of poetry, holding the unity of real and unreal, was also the theory of life, the poet could show that this was so by pointing to the world at hand—New Haven before arrival (unreal to the perceiver) and after (real). He could also direct attention to more remote places, such as Bergamo, Rome, Sweden, Salzburg, Paris. All were unreal to his own immediate experience, but vividly real through the agency of his friends' correspondence.

After the death of Stevens' friend Henry Church in 1947, his widow in many ways replaced her husband in Stevens' affections. It became her practice to spend her summers in Ville d'Avray in France, but to return each winter to her apartment in New York. She became one of Stevens' steadiest correspondents, and he occasionally joined her and her friends in New York for drinks when he was in the city. In the summer of 1949, she traveled extensively through Europe. In Stockholm in June, she sent Stevens a postcard: "On a day's visit to Stockholm—it is cold in Scandanavia but very beautiful. The nights where sunset and sunrise meet are as mysterious and wonderful as poems and fiction try to say. Nobody wants to sleep. The night of 23/24 I spent in a big house by the sea—it was St. John's (St. Hans in danish) night, fires burning all along the coast on the danish, on the swedish side with witches on broomsticks burning on top. Lots of drinking, singing and the[y] all have good happy voices." There had been other descriptions of Sweden from Ebba Dalin, an American married to a Swedish-American engineer. On August 17, 1948, for example, she had sent several pictures of Stockholm with an invitation to visit them.[8]

---

8. Barbara Church to Wallace Stevens, June 25, 1949; Ebba Dalin to Wallace Stevens, August 17, 1948.

In 1949, Barbara Church returned to Ville d'Avray by way of Paris. The "conversation at a café" was described on July 3: "diner [sic] with André Beucler . . . , his wife Nathalie, a beautiful woman, gay and witty too and Laure Lévèque in a little café near Notre Dame on the sidewalks overlooking the Seine. A good diner some very good wine and a sunset just right." Later in the summer, she was traveling with James and Laura Sweeney, and sent snapshots taken in Bergamo, where Sweeney read a paper at an architects' conference. There was a photograph of Barbara Church and Laura Sweeney, both wearing sun glasses ("with shaded eyes"), on the back of which she wrote: "July 1949, Bergamo, If you look hard you can see Laura Sweeney and myself at the foot of the staircase leading to the big Hall of the Palazzo de la Ragione where the architects sessions took place." On the reverse of a second snapshot, her note said: "July 1949, Here I am walking resolutely towards the Palazzo de la Ragione and one of the big sessions." Finally, McGreevy had sent the poet a postcard from Rome several months earlier—a reproduction of the Roman Forum. He later described the city "after dark": "Of the nights nothing, neither content nor discontent but just going to bed with the assumption that I and the Roman morning would be together again in the course of a few hours."[9]

Here was "Bergamo on a postcard, Rome after dark, / Sweden described, Salzburg with shaded eyes / Or Paris in conversation at a café." All the messages, casual and scrawled on commercial reproductions or snapshots, impressed Stevens deeply, lifting him out of his tedium and aiding him in his progress on "An Ordinary Evening in New Haven." He told Barbara Church on August 19 of the pleasure her trip that summer had brought him: "It interests me immensely to have you speak of so many places that have been merely names for me. Yet really they have always been a good deal more than names. I practically lived in France when old Mr. Vidal was alive because if I had asked him to procure from an obscure fromagerie in the country some of the cheese with raisins in it of

9. Barbara Church to Wallace Stevens, July 3, August 13 (with photos), 1949; Thomas McGreevy to Wallace Stevens, January 31, 1949. McGreevy also sent Stevens a postcard dated November 29, 1948, which showed the Roman Forum with dark clouds above it. In January, Stevens acknowledged it: "Your postcard from Rome set me up. Rome is not ordinarily on the itinerary of my imagination. It is a little out of the way, covered by cypresses. It is not a place that one visits frequently like Paris or Dublin" (*L*, 629).

which I read one time, he would have done it and that is almost what living in France or anywhere else amounts to" (*L*, 610).

Another image in "An Ordinary Evening in New Haven" came from an unlikely source. Sister M. Bernetta Quinn was an early, appreciative reader of Stevens' verse. She sent a commentary on his poems to which he, in turn, responded, and she began the practice of sending greeting cards at Christmas and Easter. Her Easter card in 1949 included a reference to the Lion of Judah. Stevens later acknowledged, "I put the lion into something that I was doing at the time" (*L*, 635). Part XI of the poem recognizes the enduring religious image: "We remember the lion of Juda and we save / The phrase." The lion, however, is metamorphosed into a cat, "potent in the sun"; thus the religious reference is reduced to the level of common reality: "And Juda becomes New Haven or else must" (*CP*, 472–73).

Another poem also originated from a card. John Sweeney had been interested in Stevens' work and had arranged for an exhibition of his books in 1951 at Harvard. The following year, while on a vacation in Ireland, he sent Stevens a postcard with a photograph of the Cliffs of Moher in County Clare. The majestic sweep of the cliffs, "like a gust of freedom, a return to the spacious, solitary world in which we used to exist" (*L*, 760–61), provided Stevens with a setting for poetic exploration. As he wrote later to Barbara Church, the photograph "eventually became a poem" (*L*, 770). In "The Irish Cliffs of Moher," a short lyric in couplets and irregular meter, the cliffs are ancient and "Above the real." They become a symbol of solidarity between present and past and are transformed into the image of the father: "A likeness, one of the race of fathers: earth / And sea and air" (*CP*, 501–502).

Shortly before the publication of *Harmonium*, Stevens corresponded with Harriet Monroe's sister. Lucy Monroe Calhoun lived in Peking and arranged to send some jasmine tea to the poet in 1922. His satisfaction was expressed to Harriet Monroe shortly afterward:

> But I also find a package from Peking containing two packages of jasminerie, one of which I have pried open to smell one of the good smells, out of China. It is a very good smell indeed and I am delighted. Nothing could please me more. Do, please, tell your sister, la belle jasminatrice, how grateful I am. I look forward to some subsequent

marvel; but am patient as you required me to be. For a poet to have even a second-hand contact with China is a great matter; and a desk that sees so much trouble is blessed by such reversions to innocence. (*L*, 229).

Stevens reported that the tea arrived on September 23; in an earlier letter to Monroe, he explained that the manuscript of *Harmonium* was to be ready for Knopf by November 1. It is therefore possible that "Jasmine's Beautiful Thoughts underneath the Willow" was written after September 23, "la belle jasminatrice" having metamorphosed into the Jasmine of the title. The poem was not published prior to its appearance in *Harmonium*.

Peter Lee, a young Korean who was studying in the United States and teaching Far Eastern languages at Yale, sent Stevens some of his poems early in 1951. An affectionate correspondence developed, and Lee eventually came to refer to Stevens as his grandfather (*L*, 864). The exchange continued after Lee went on to continue his studies in Fribourg: "To use a classic phrase, I got a kick out of your turning up in Fribourg. I love all this scholar's life which you lead" (*L*, 839). It was precisely the young man's life as poet, scholar, and polyglot that Stevens valued in his friend. Lee became a figuration of Stevens' own notion of the scholar-hero, the pensive man. In a late poem first published in 1952, "Looking across the Fields and Watching the Birds Fly," Stevens speaks of the "new scholar replacing an older one" in the unrelenting search for the fully realized human, "a human that can be accounted for" (*CP*, 519). After writing the poem, Stevens cast Lee and himself in just such roles: "It was wonderful to have your postcard in French. More than anything else it made me understand how much a Korean student, or, if you like, a young Korean scholar, and a somewhat old American student who never had time to become a scholar resemble each other" (*L*, 845). In one of his last essays, "The Whole Man: Perspectives, Horizons," which was published in the *Yale Review* just after his death, Stevens described Lee again as a representation of the "whole man":

Last week I received a letter, greetings on my seventy-fifth birthday, from a young scholar, a Korean. When he was at New Haven, he used to come up to Hartford and the two of us would go out to Elizabeth Park, in Hartford, and sit on a bench by the pond and talk about poetry. He did not wait for the ducks to bring him ideas but always had in mind questions that disclosed his familiarity with the experience of poetry. He spoke in the most natural English. He is now studying in Switzerland at Fribourg, from where his letter came. It was written in what appeared to be the most natural French. Apparently they prize all-round young men in Korea, too. (*OP*, 230–31)

Stevens had always extolled the scholar, like the rabbi, as the pensive man who, allowing for study and contemplation, discovered vision. He is the "scholar hungriest for that book" that is the "hawk of life" (*CP*, 178) in "The Man with the Blue Guitar." In the moonlight of "God Is Good. It Is a Beautiful Night," the head becomes "scholar again" while "seeking celestial / Rendezvous" (*CP*, 285). These earlier poems precede Stevens' friendship with Lee, but in the Korean scholar he found an incarnation of the trope he had developed in these and other poems. And in "Looking across the Fields and Watching the Birds Fly," Stevens summarized one last time that figure that had sprung as an ideal many years earlier.

Stevens' "affair of places" integrally involved his epistolary "affair with people," and the two were not finally as disjunctive as his adage supposed. His imagination was quickened by the exchanges from abroad. Transcribed into descriptive images of the mind's unique fictions, they became the texture of poetry. Two years before his death, he described the interior synthesis of Paris:

> After waiting for FIGARO a long time, several numbers came at the same time. This has brought Paris close to me. When I go home at night, after the office, I spend a long time dawdling over the fascinating phrases which refresh me as nothing else could. I am one of the many people around the world who live from time to time in a Paris that has never existed and that is composed of the things that other people, primarily Parisians themselves, have said about Paris. That particular Paris communicates an interest in life that may be wholly fiction, but, if so, it is precious fiction. (*L*, 773)

The correspondence, an affair with people and places, was also part of the fiction making. A year later, he described to McGreevy the value of his friends whose journeys made real to him the lands they visited: "She [Barbara Church] is one of the marvels of my experience, which, after all, has taken place in a very limited space.

It means a lot to me to know a man in Dublin, to receive letters
from a friend in Italy, to look at the map of Spain [where Barbara
Church was going] and to find that it suddenly becomes as mi-
nutely significant as the map of Connecticut" (*L*, 827). The letters
obviously meant as much to his life as a poet. The early journals
and letters speak repeatedly·of the desire to visit London and Paris,
but, in writing "Autumn Refrain" at the age of fifty-three, he spoke
of the "measureless measures" of the nightingale, "the name of a
bird and the name of a nameless air / I have never—shall never
hear" (*CP*, 160). His daughter speculates that circumstances for
travel abroad were never favorable: "As a young man he couldn't
afford it, and later he was married to someone who was a terrible
traveler and constantly carsick or seasick whenever she went anywhere. After the war I think he was afraid of finding things too
much changed. By that point, of course, he had constructed his
own Europe." [10] It was the substance of that personal construction,
buttressed by his correspondence, that made many of his poems
possible, even as surety bonds and letters from Ceylon made up his
own immediate world of reality and imagination.

10. Holly Stevens, quoted in Suzi Mee, "The Double Life of Wallace Stevens," *Harvard
Magazine*, LXXXII (September-October, 1979), 48.

# III ✒ THE READER

# 10 ✐ Harriet Monroe and
*Poetry: A Magazine of Verse*

"Your praise is mighty," wrote Wallace Stevens to Harriet Monroe when he sent her in 1916 a revision of his play "Three Travelers Watch a Sunrise" for publication in *Poetry*. Most readers of Stevens remember Monroe's editorial liberties with "Sunday Morning," eliminating three stanzas and encouraging the rearrangement of four of the remaining five. We cluck regretfully and wonder at her obtuseness. Monroe, however, nineteen years Stevens' senior, had already begun publishing his poems in 1914 when *Poetry* was only two years old and Stevens, a vice-president of the New York office of the Equitable Surety Company, was still tentatively and experimentally "trying to get together a little collection of verses" (*L,* 180). Monroe's loyalty to Stevens over the next twenty-two years, her pleas for him to go on as a poet, her advocacy of his work, and, behind it all, her keen understanding of his art single her out as the poet's first important reader. When he called Monroe's praise mighty, he was acknowledging both need and gratitude for her response.

Two months before the four war poems ("Phases") appeared in the November, 1914, issue of *Poetry,* Stevens had published a sequence entitled "Carnet de Voyage" in *Trend.* Most of the poems dated back to the 1909 "June Book." And in November, he retrieved a poem from the 1908 "June Book" and wrote an Imagist exercise— again for *Trend.* These were Stevens' first published poems since his undergraduate days. When she received his first submission for *Poetry,* Harriet Monroe apparently had not seen the recent poems in *Trend*—the poet was an unknown.

Emanating from Chicago, *Poetry* was already a formidable force. From the beginning, it represented a publishing goal for the aspiring poet, and, as Stevens said to her later, "sooner or later I shall have something for Poetry, to which I send what I like most" (*L,*

230). Their correspondence, while formal, is unfailingly cordial and, as the years passed, even warm in mutual fondness.[1] Curious to know Stevens better, she acknowledged in the "Notes" at the end of the "Phases" issue of *Poetry* that he was "unknown as yet to the editor."[2] Stevens' first letter to her did little to help: "My autobiography is, necessarily, very brief; for I have published nothing" (*L,* 182).

When she was reviewing *Harmonium* a decade later, Monroe recalled her discovery of Stevens in 1914: "His book reminds me of a day nine-and-a-half years ago when the World War was still new, and we were preparing for the printer our *War Number* of November, 1914. We had selected for it thirteen poems of war from the seven-hundred-and-thirty-seven submitted in competition for our one-hundred-dollar prize, and had even paged up the proof, when a new and irresistible claimant arrived." She elaborated in her autobiography: "I remember my eager reassembling of the page proofs to make room for two pages—all I could squeeze in—by this master of strange and beautiful rhythms."[3] Although he had received no personal invitation from Monroe, Stevens had responded to the announcement in the magazine of a prize for the best poem on war or peace. As we have seen, this aroused his interest. In the case of "Phases," he did not win, and his eleven-poem sequence had been reduced to four because of last-minute space restrictions, but his contact with Monroe and *Poetry* was successfully fixed his first time out. In "Phases," Stevens had also settled upon a central theme that was to become endemic, the "nobility" of death based upon fulfillment in the physical world and repudiation of heaven's "futile thrones." His first publication in *Poetry* was a major advance in his poetic progress.

So heartened, Stevens must have gathered almost immediately another group of poems destined for Chicago. Early in the new

1. Fifty-eight letters from Stevens to Monroe are preserved at the University of Chicago; there are two at the University of Illinois. There are ten letters from Monroe to Stevens at the Huntington Library.
2. *Poetry: A Magazine of Verse,* V (November, 1914), 97.
3. *Poetry,* XXIII (March, 1924), 322; Harriet Monroe, *A Poet's Life: Seventy Years in a Changing World* (New York, 1938), 342. Ellen Williams speculates that Stevens' poems replaced those of Amy Lowell, "who had submitted two long poems, 'The Allies,' and 'The Bombardment.' 'The Allies' got as far as proofs, but was not used in the end" (*Harriet Monroe and the Poetry Renaissance: The First Ten Years of "Poetry," 1912–22* [Urbana, 1977], 144).

year, however, Monroe returned them: "I don't know when any poems have 'intrigued' me so much as these. They are recondite, erudite, provocatively obscure, with a kind of modern-gargoyle grin in them—Aubrey Beardsleyish in the making. They are weirder than your war series, and I don't like them, and I'll be blamed if I'll print them; but their author will surely catch me next time if he will only uncurl and uncoil a little—condescend to chase his mystically mirthful and mournful muse out of the nether darkness. In other words, please send more."[4]

The identity of these poems is unknown, but "Sunday Morning" may have seemed no less "provocatively obscure," and its formal diction and meter can hardly have represented an uncurling and uncoiling. This time, of course, Monroe took the poem, but not without the notorious modifications. The suggestions for cutting were Monroe's, but the ordering of the remaining stanzas appears to have been Stevens'. When he responded in June, 1915, it was without "objection to cutting down," but with the stipulation that "your selection" be in "the following order: I, VIII, IV, V" (*L,* 183). Two weeks later he agreed that VII ("Supple and turbulent, a ring of men . . .") was not "too detached to conclude with" (*L,* 183). Thus the poem's arrangement was determined. Monroe's part of the correspondence has not been preserved, and it is impossible to know how strongly she pressed for the changes. We do know that her dislike of the plate imagery at the end of part V led Stevens to submit alternate lines: "She causes boys to bring sweet-smelling pears, / And plums in ponderous piles. The maidens taste / And stray etc." Although Monroe adopted this version, the alliterative feuding between the liquid *s*'s and the plosive *p*'s leads to self-parody, not unlike Jove and his mumbling *m*'s at the beginning of III, "Large-manner motions to his mythy mind / He moved among us as a muttering king," mocking the inhuman god. If the lines were meant as a subtle retaliation against his editor's impertinence, there was no flinch from Monroe. Not until "Sunday Morning" appeared eight years later were the number and arrangement of stanzas, including the original words of stanza V, restored.

While Stevens was reading proof for the revised "Sunday Morning" the October, 1915, issue of *Poetry* announced a prize of one

---

4. Harriet Monroe to Wallace Stevens, January 27, 1915.

hundred dollars, donated by the Players Producing Company, "for a one-act poetic play. The conditions are that the play be in poetic form—in metrical verse or *vers libre;* that it be American in subject matter, or substance; and that it be actable."[5] Stevens wrote his first of three one-act verse dramas, "Three Travelers Watch a Sunrise," as his entry in the competition. The condition that the play be "American in subject matter" accounts, I think, for the fact that the play, otherwise unmistakably Oriental, is set "on a hilltop in eastern Pennsylvania." For his theme Stevens chose the tension between the art that arises from ideal beauty beyond the stream of history (associated by the Chinese speakers with the seclusion of the court) and the art that is born of "poverty," "wretchedness," "suffering," and "pity" (the "invasion" of humanity). The play endorses the latter by introducing the pitiful figure of Anna, whose lover, "an Italian," has hanged himself in despair of the romance. The three Chinese serve as interpretive cantors.

The judges were Harriet Monroe, the donor of the prize, and the staff of *Poetry,* including a poet named Max Michelson; and the award was given to Stevens. Before the play was published in the July, 1916, issue of *Poetry,* however, Stevens and Monroe collaborated on revisions. The suggestions for changes apparently originated from the notes compiled by Michelson during the competition; they were endorsed by Monroe. Michelson's principal objection was to the presence on the stage of a hanging body, first described in the introduction to the play.

Monroe's revisions marked on the original typewritten draft treat issues of style and clarity, along with routine editorial notations. She reworked selected parts of Stevens' manuscript, crossing out sections and writing in alterations. She enlarged, for example, the descriptions of characters. The First Chinese became "quizzical" in addition to Stevens' presentation of him as "short and fat and of middle age." The Second Chinese, whom the poet saw as "of middle height, thin and turning gray," became "a man of sense and sympathy." "Intent, detached" was added to the description of the Third, whom Stevens had envisioned simply as "a young man." In Stevens' original version, Anna is described twice as she sits "half stupefied" under the tree where her love is hanged.

---

5. *Poetry,* VII (October, 1915), 52.

Monroe deleted the description that would have followed the stage directions in which the Chinese recognize the corpse hanging overhead (*OP,* 139). The following are her canceled lines:

> 1st Chinese (Bewildered)
> The young gentleman of the ballad.
> (The 2nd negro walks toward the body. He pulls away some of the undergrowth. The figure of a girl is seen sitting on the ground under the tree to which the body hangs. Her head is bent forward in her arms, resting on her knees. She appears to be stupefied.[)]
> He was alone without her,
> Just as the young gentleman
> Was alone without her.
> Three beggars, you see,
> Begging from one another.
> (A negro carrying two lanterns approaches cautiously through the trees. At the sight of him, the 1st negro, seated near the Chinese, jumps to his feet. The 2nd negro comes out of the trees and approaches the green handkerchief. They do not see the figure of the girl, which is now quite clear. The 2nd negro places the lanterns on the ground. He removes the handkerchief.)[6]

Five lines from this passage had just been recited before the recognition (*OP,* 139), and Monroe obviously found them redundant. In fact, she reduced Stevens' intended effect of echoing incantation, but the omission does little damage to the text and Stevens accepted it without demurral.

Monroe's recommendations were selective and hardly radical. She sent Stevens the revised manuscript, along with Michelson's suggestions. Stevens was as accommodating as he had been about "Sunday Morning": "You are an encouraging person, if there ever was one and I am grateful to you not only for that, but because, in addition, you give me an opportunity to do what you want, if I can. I shall try."[7] Try he did, as he reworked the play to remove the appearance of the hanging corpse. Ten days later he submitted the new copy to Monroe, and the accompanying letter said:

6. Version A, "Three Travelers Watch a Sunrise" (Typescript with autograph alterations by Harriet Monroe, in Folder 14, Box 39, *Poetry* Magazine Papers, 1912–35, University of Chicago Library), 2, 14–15.
7. Wallace Stevens to Harriet Monroe, May 19, 1916, in Folder 10, Box 39, *Poetry* Magazine Papers.

My object in sending the play to you at once is to make it possible for you to consider its new form in time to form a deliberate opinion about it and to write to me again, if you desire to do so. If you prefer this form, use it. Or if you desire still further changes in it, let me know. Or, last of all, if you have doubts and think the original form the better of the two, again let me know. In the last case, I should like to make a few changes in direction etc. Personally, I like the new form.

The letter closes with the exclamation, "Your praise is mighty" (*L,* 195).

The following three versions of the opening stage directions demonstrate the kinds of variations involved. *Stevens' original description* read: "When the curtain rises, the small stage is dark. The limb of a tree creaks. A negro carrying a lantern passes along the road. The sound is repeated. The negro comes through the bushes, raises his lantern and looks through the trees. He crosses the stage. His lantern light falls on the body of a man hanging to the limb of one of the trees. Only the back of the body is to be seen. The limb creaks. The negro shrinks back into the forest to the left" (Version A). In *Monroe's corrected version,* the text was: "When the curtain rises, the stage is dark. The limb of a tree creaks. A negro carrying a lantern passes along the road. The sound is repeated. The negro comes through the bushes, raises his lantern and looks through the trees. Discerning a dark object swaying among the branches, he shrinks back perturbed, crosses stage, and exits through the wood at the left" (Version A). And *Stevens' revised version* had: "When the curtain rises, the small stage is dark. A negro carrying a lantern passes along the road. The negro sees the broken bushes and enters the opening. He raises his lantern. He sees a green handkerchief spread on the rocks. He approaches, picks up the handkerchief and starts back. The light of his lantern falls on the face of a man. The negro lifts the head slightly and looks at the face. He covers the face again with the handkerchief and returns to the opening. He hears sounds on the road, turns and crosses the stage, and hurries away into the forest to the left" (Version B).[8]

In making her final choice for publication, Monroe ignored almost completely Stevens' second version, preferring the first with her own modifications. Whereas in Stevens' second version the

8. Version A, "Three Travelers Watch a Sunrise," 1; Version B, "Three Travelers Watch a Sunrise" (Typescript, in Folder 14, Box 39, *Poetry* Magazine Papers), 1.

hanging body is omitted entirely, in the published work the body is presented both in the introduction and toward the end when Anna appears seated beneath the tree where her dead lover hangs. Earlier, Stevens described the gradual appearance of the body as "a distinct, although dim, silhouette." Monroe again blurred the image but retained its stark presence: "A dark object, hanging to the limb of the tree, becomes a dim silhouette."[9] Her reason for the change was not arbitrary: the Chinese do not yet recognize the corpse that hangs overhead. Stevens accepted the modification (*OP,* 137).

On the galley proofs later sent to Stevens for further corrections, Monroe jotted at the top of the first page the unlikely location of her editorial pencil: "I have been correcting this at the republican convention, between speeches." (The improbable contrast between Senator William E. Borah's oration and the cryptic rhythms of Stevens' three Chinese could not have been more complete—Monroe called it a "'delicate incongruity.'") For the opening description, Monroe now questioned the use of the word *swaying:* "Perhaps omit swaying—as too definite." Stevens' note beneath hers agrees, "Omit it."[10]

At some minor suggestions, the poet balked. The lantern carried by one of the Chinese, for example, had been designated a "Chinese" lantern by Monroe. Stevens was obdurate: "The lantern is *not* a Chinese lantern," he noted in the margin on the galleys, and his opinion prevailed. "How can one strike an instrument in an insinuating manner?" she had questioned in the galleys, referring to the action of the Second Chinese just before the appearance of the hanging body. Stevens' response was firm: "Please do not change. This may be a heathen mystery but I believe in it." It remained. At the end of the galleys, however, in a final word to Monroe, Stevens approved her choice of the text: "Renewed, consolidated and added thanks. This seems all right. My remark that I liked the second version was a fib designed to give you your choice. But I *did* rather like the green bandanna."[11]

9. Version A, "Three Travelers Watch a Sunrise," 12.

10. Galley proofs, "Three Travelers Watch a Sunrise" (in Folder 14, Box 39, *Poetry* Magazine Papers), 1. Her choice of the word *perturbed,* describing the Negro in the same passage, must have been canceled later in page proofs; "exits" was changed to "goes out."

11. Galley proofs, "Three Travelers Watch a Sunrise," 1, 3, 8. Louis L. Martz has further interesting observations regarding variations between the play as published and the alternate version Stevens prepared in reponse to Monroe's suggestions. See "Manuscripts of Wallace Stevens," *Yale University Library Gazette,* LIV (October, 1979), 54–59.

Although *Three Travelers Watch a Sunrise* is the strongest of Stevens' three short verse dramas, he never reprinted it after its appearance in *Poetry*. Not everyone shared Monroe's satisfaction with it, even in 1916. In her autobiography she quotes a Richard Burton who had written expressing his "'bewildered indignation that such a piece of drivel . . . should have been awarded a prize by you or anybody else.'" Monroe's own enthusiasm was unchecked. When *Three Travelers* was performed at the Provincetown Playhouse in New York four years later, Stevens, though he had the chance, did not bother to see it. "So much water has gone under the bridges since the thing was written that I have not the curiosity even to read it to see how it looks at this late day. That's truth, not pose" (*L*, 216). Monroe, on the other hand, was present for the production and, as she told her readers in *Poetry*, saw it as the very embodiment of the poetic drama as Yeats had recommended in his remarks in Chicago shortly before. The play, she said, was "as perfect as a Greek vase in its assertion of beauty." [12]

It is possible that the poet and his editor at *Poetry* met during the summer of the play's publication, 1916. Stevens made a business trip to the Midwest that took him as far as St. Paul. Late in June he had written that he was "looking forward to a little chat" when he passed through Chicago. In the meantime, Harriet Monroe and Alice Corbin Henderson, also on the staff of *Poetry*, were collecting poems for their *The New Poetry: An Anthology*. Perhaps with *Three Travelers* in mind, Monroe noted in her introduction: "In the nineteenth century the western world—the western aesthetic world—discovered the orient. Someone has said that when Perry knocked at the gates of Japan, these opened, not to let us in, but to let the Japanese out. Japanese graphic art, especially, began almost at once to kindle progressive minds." She saw it as a major influence on "the new poetry." [13] Stevens was represented in the anthology—"Peter Quince at the Clavier," which had appeared in *Others*, and, from *Poetry*, the fourth of the "Phases" poems, now entitled "In Battle," and the abbreviated "Sunday Morning." (When the an-

---

12. Monroe, *A Poet's Life*, 408; "Mr. Yeats and the Poetic Drama," *Poetry*, XVI (April, 1920), 35.
13. Wallace Stevens to Harriet Monroe, June 23, 1916, in Folder 10, Box 39, *Poetry Magazine Papers*; Harriet Monroe, "Introduction," *The New Poetry: An Anthology* (New York, 1917), xi.

thology was reissued "New and Enlarged" in 1923, an additional sixteen poems by Stevens were added.) As early as 1917, Monroe's confidence in Stevens was set, and by the time *Harmonium* was published, it was unshakable.

Stevens' fascination with war poems did not end with "Phases." Not surprisingly during these years, war poetry was popular in the pages of *Poetry* and elsewhere, and on September 1, 1917, Stevens submitted to Monroe a thirteen-poem sequence entitled "Lettres d'un Soldat." As "Phases" had already revealed and as "Examination of the Hero in a Time of War" and "Esthétique du Mal" would show during the Second World War, Stevens invariably treated the dying soldier, who, having performed courageously in battle, is equally valorous in death—he accepts heroically his mortality, satisfied with having enjoyed the assuagements of the physical world. For each poem in this sequence, Stevens chose an epigraph from the letters of Eugène Lemercier, a young French painter who was a soldier in the First World War. Nine of the thirteen poems submitted were accepted and appeared in May, 1918. The decision to delete four of them was, again, a joint one. Stevens happened to be in Chicago on business, and on March 14, 1918, the poet wrote his wife: "Late this afternoon I went up to *Poetry*'s office and saw Miss Monroe about my war-poems. We went over them together and weeded out the bad ones" (*L, 205*). Three poems in the published sequence were later reproduced in the second edition of *Harmonium:* "The Surprises of the Superhuman," "Negation," and "The Death of a Soldier." The remaining six were dropped from Stevens' canon. In 1918, however, the decision was made to eliminate from the original sequence the poem that eventually became "Lunar Paraphrase." Stevens may have found this difficult to accept. The omission is indeed curious, for "Lunar Paraphrase" is superior to most of the poems preserved in the sequence. In addition, the image of the moon as "mother of pathos and pity" consoling Mary, the other mother who stands beside "the body of Jesus," leads organically into the next poem, which begins "There is another mother whom I love." Some continuity in the sequence is thus lost. Monroe must have mounted opposition to the poem when they met on March 14, perhaps on the grounds that it was another instance of the "mournful music" she had decried three years earlier. Just as he refused in the end to abandon the first draft of "Sunday Morning," in spite of his editor, Stevens later found a place for "Lunar Paraphrase" in the second edition of *Harmonium*.[14]

The original holograph manuscript of "Lettres d'un Soldat" gives evidence of specific collaboration. In Monroe's hand is written beside the first poem "W. S. says ♉." It was omitted. The other excluded poems, besides "Lunar Paraphrase," were the twelfth and thirteenth in the series. To the side of the last, Monroe had jotted, "W S says end here if I wish" and a line under the second of the four tercets is drawn. She must have preferred, however, to withdraw the whole poem.[15]

Their March 14 meeting in Chicago to review the war sequence could naturally have led Stevens and Monroe to a discussion of death. He must have blurted out something, for after he returned home he wrote to her that "I've had the blooming horrors, following my gossip about death, at your house. I have not known just what to do. I had hoped to set things right, personally; but find that I am not likely to see you in Chicago for some little time. Accordingly, so that you may not think I am unconscious of the thing, nor indifferent, I write this to let you know that I have been sincerely regretful and hope that you and your family will forgive me" (*L,* 206). There was a tendency on Stevens' part to magnify the significance of certain of his statements in social situations and then to express contrition. In 1949, for example, he begged Allen Tate to smooth over an exchange he had had a year earlier with Cleanth Brooks and his wife, and as late as 1951, still unsettled by the memory, he wrote directly to Brooks who, Stevens remarked, "could not have been more decent about it" (*L,* 634, 706). One suspects a similar fastidiousness on this occasion; the episode, whatever its import, did nothing to discourage Monroe's friendliness.

Stevens wrote his second verse drama, *Carlos Among the Candles,* expressly for performance. Almost twenty years later, he recalled taking the play to John LaFarge's son, Bancel, who did a series of sketches for its production. The sketches notwithstanding,

---

14. Lines 3–4 of "Lunar Paraphrase" were altered slightly. In the holograph manuscript, they read: "Her [the moon's] old light moves along the branches— / Les scaramouches— depending upon them" (MS in Folder 11, Box 39, *Poetry* Magazine Papers). In the 1931 *Harmonium,* they read: "Her old light moves along the branches, / Feebly, slowly, depending upon them."

15. In the fifth poem, Monroe altered "mountain paleurs" to "mountain pallors" (l. 3) and, three lines later, "willow leaves" became "willow trees." There were a few minor changes in punctuation (MS in Folder 11, Box 39, *Poetry* Magazine Papers).

the stage setting was crudely painted "by a school boy." When it was performed in New York by the Wisconsin Players on October 20, 1917, "the principal character forgot three pages of the text which only contained, as I remember it, about ten or twelve pages" (*L*, 291). The play closed after one performance, and the newspaper reviews were unsparing. The embarrassment may have contributed to Stevens' decision three years later to boycott the production of *Three Travelers Watch a Sunrise*. He was prepared to forget about *Carlos*. But Harriet Monroe, having published the first play, wanted the second for *Poetry* as well. Stevens tried to discourage her by sending copies of the reviews. With both bemusement and tenacity, Monroe responded: "Indeed I can't help laughing over what almost any actor might do with *Carlos* (Nijinsky might dance him). But I am not in the least discouraged from desiring to see him in print. So let's go to it."[16] The extant letters do not indicate that Monroe edited the play in any way, and she would never again take liberties with Stevens' texts as she had in the previous three years. The play appeared in the December, 1917, issue.

The associate editor of *Poetry*, Alice Corbin Henderson, was having doubts about Stevens. She wrote Monroe on May 2, 1918: "I don't mean that Stevens' work is not worth while, but he does seem to me lately to have more tendency towards the precieuse or precieux than formerly, he always had it somewhat. I like him, you know, but I am sometimes afraid that he may wear a little thin."[17] *Carlos Among the Candles,* published five months earlier, was indeed the most *précieux* of his work in *Poetry,* but Monroe ignored Henderson's opinion.

Stevens and Monroe managed brief but fairly regular meetings in subsequent years. Stevens' visits to Chicago always involved business assignments, and Monroe was occasionally in the East on literary business. There are records of personal impressions from both. After Monroe's death in 1936, Stevens wrote for *Poetry*'s memorial issue a brief memoir in which he singled out her graciousness:

No one could have been more agreeable, yet she had not a trace of the busy welcomer. She wanted more time so that she might know you better. She would go along to lunch and then invite you to her house

16. Harriet Monroe to Wallace Stevens, November 2, 1917.
17. Alice Corbin Henderson to Harriet Monroe, May 2, 1918, in Williams, *Harriet Monroe and the Poetry Renaissance*, 229.

for dinner. She did the most she could for you and gave you the best she had. To cite not too exalted an instance, I remember that on one occasion she produced after dinner as a liqueur a small bottle of whiskey which she said was something like ninety years old, almost colonial, as if stored up for that particular winter's night.

In *A Poet's Life,* Monroe cited Arthur Ficke's letter of praise for "Sunday Morning." Ficke added: "Have you known Stevens? He's a big, slightly fat, awfully competent-looking man. You expect him to roar, but when he speaks there emerges the gravest, softest, most subtly modulated voice I've ever heard—a voice on tiptoe at dawn! A personality beside which all the nice *little* poets in the world shrink to cheese mites!" Monroe recorded her own impression: "No one who has ever met Wallace Stevens can forget the quiet power of the man—the flicker of humor playing on deep pools of understanding; supersensitive to beauty, but incased in the protective armor of an insurance attorney. I love to remember his low chuckle of delight while we were witnessing together that masterpiece of the 1850's, Anna Cora Mowatt's *Fashion.*" [18]

In 1918, Stevens tried to discourage her from being drawn into a debate with the English poet Edgar Jepson, who had attacked her magazine for a narrow regionalism. In July she had turned the tables on her critic: "If Mr. Jepson admires the fine ironics and sophisticated intuitions and decoratively balanced rhythms of Mr. Eliot, why is he . . . so deaf to the sombre yet whimsical emotional and musical motives of Wallace Stevens?" Stevens, however, found the exchange unoriginal and futile: "Don't you take Jepson too seriously? And Pound, too? I should mourn if you were to become involved in a very uninteresting row with these two. Pound is deliberately capitalizing old stuff all around. It is such a chestnut to peck at: United States art, Great Britain poetry, and so on. . . . But, of course, I live in the country and may not realize the importance of things. I hope soon to be in Chicago, at least to pass through the place and to find out from you then just why various things matter." [19]

In 1919, Monroe may have arranged a meeting between Stevens

18. *Poetry,* XLIX (December, 1936), 155; Monroe, *A Poet's Life,* 390–91.
19. "Mr. Jepson's Slam," *Poetry,* XII (July, 1918), 210; Wallace Stevens to Harriet Monroe, November 5, 1918, in George Hendrick, "Wallace Stevens' Manuscripts at the University of Illinois," *Wallace Stevens Journal,* II (Fall, 1978), 19.

and Carl Sandburg; he asked her to set it up shortly before his arrival. In New York, the poet and his editor typically met for a cocktail or two, and Monroe visited the Stevenses in Hartford on several occasions. Once, Stevens hoped for a meeting in New Haven, "when you make your annual return, like Proserpine, to this region." By 1920, Stevens must have felt secure in Monroe's steady interest and approbation. During a train trip from Indianapolis, he scrawled a series of brief poems, notes really, though he numbered them from I to VI, and mailed them to her. The fifth, for example, "Poupée de Poupées," read:

> She was not the child of religion or science
> Created by a god as by earth.
> She was the creature of her own minds.

The sixth was a personal greeting in French (*L,* 218). They met in Chicago a few weeks later and Stevens, now familiar with the city, took her to a "little Italian place I know." [20]

Lucy Monroe Calhoun, Harriet's widowed sister, lived in Peking, where her husband had been U.S. minister. Her home was an old temple palace. Monroe had visited the Calhouns in 1910 and would return in the 1930s. She had told Stevens about her sister's unconventional life. Once, after she had described the delicate savor of jasmine tea, Stevens asked if Lucy Calhoun might send him a small package of it. Stevens' elation was obvious when it arrived: "Do, please, tell your sister, la belle jasminatrice, how grateful I am." In the next few years, Monroe became a clearing agent between Stevens and her sister, when he requested various Chinese objets d'art. A carved wooden figure of a religious pilgrim was a particular favorite (*L,* 280).

Stevens' most generous appearance in *Poetry* was collected under the title "Pecksniffiana," drawing on the name and personality of the supercilious architect *manqué* in Dickens' *Martin Chuzzlewit,* Mr. Pecksniff. The group consisted of fourteen short poems, among them "Homunculus et La Belle Etoile," "Ploughing on Sunday," "Anecdote of the Jar," and "The Paltry Nude Starts on a Spring Voyage." After delivering the original selection to Monroe in 1919, on his way home from Milwaukee, Stevens offered three

---

20. Wallace Stevens to Harriet Monroe, December 26, 1919, in Folder 10, Box 39, *Poetry* Magazine Papers; Wallace Stevens to Elsie Kachel Stevens, June 5, 1920.

new poems in place of three that he regarded as weak. Instead, Monroe not only accepted the new ones, she retained two of the three Stevens was withdrawing. Only "Piano Practice at the Academy of the Holy Angels" was omitted. (At some later date she wrote "Jewel never published" and "cancelled by the author" on the galley proofs of the unpublished poem.) If in 1915 she had excised stanzas from Stevens' work, she now insisted on publishing poems that he was formally recalling. In the same letter he enclosed a fourth new poem, "The Indigo Glass in the Grass," calling it a "trifle," but suggesting that it might appear after "Of the Surface of Things" in the sequence (*L,* 214). Monroe did not take up her red pencil with the "Pecksniffiana" poems, though "The Indigo Glass in the Grass" did not follow "Of the Surface of Things." In returning proof, he apparently made suggestions about the layout, adding in a note to Monroe his thanks: "You know that I am grateful and do not mean to be finical. I always wonder at the trouble you take, when there must be so much of it to take. In my own case, I am merely hoping to make the design as belle as possible."[21]

"Pecksniffiana" filled the first eleven pages of the October, 1919, issue of *Poetry,* and Monroe extolled Stevens' modernity in her "What Next?" essay: "Shall we, who listen eagerly to Prokofieff, refuse to Wallace Stevens a hearing for his subtle and haunting compositions, as if with wood-wind instruments, in the present number?"[22] Her private comment about "Anecdote of the Jar" ("the jar point") is unknown, though Stevens later acknowledged it as "well made" (*L,* 216). The sequence was an immediate success. "Pecksniffiana" won *Poetry*'s Helen Haire Levinson Prize of $200, and along with the announcement in the November, 1920, issue, Monroe reprinted four of the poems—"Fabliau of Florida," "Peter Parasol," "The Place of the Solitaires," and "The Paltry Nude Starts on a Spring Voyage." Kreymborg selected eight of them, along with "Le Monocle de Mon Oncle," for his *Others for 1919: An Anthology of the New Verse.*

Twelve short lyrics, including "The Snow Man," appeared in *Poetry* exactly two years after "Pecksniffiana"; they had the title

21. Wallace Stevens to Elsie Kachel Stevens, May 6, 1919; Wallace Stevens to Harriet Monroe, August 27, 1919, in Folder 11, Box 39, *Poetry* Magazine Papers.
22. Harriet Monroe, "What Next?" *Poetry,* XV (October, 1919), 35.

"Sur Ma Guzzla Gracile." In that interim, Stevens had not written much poetry. In the letter accompanying the poems, he admitted that he had pruned his poetic stock: "They [the poems] are the result of a good deal of weeding out—or the residue. This has not been a good year for poetry with me." He went on to apologize that the poems had gathered dust: "They read better backwards than forwards in my eye—they've been here so long." Monroe, however, was more approving. This collection, too, was considered for *Poetry's* annual array of prizes, and "Another Weeping Woman," "Tea at the Palaz of Hoon," "On the Manner of Addressing Clouds," and "Hibiscus On the Sleeping Shores" received honorable mention a year later. In her notes on the contributors at the end of the "Sur Ma Guzzla Gracile" issue, Monroe identified Stevens as "a frequent and valued contributor to the special magazines, but he has not yet yielded to the solicitation of his admirers so far as to publish a volume."[23] *Harmonium,* however, was still two years away.

In December, 1921, a new prize was announced in *Poetry:* "In our advertising pages the Poetry Society of South Carolina makes an announcement of great interest to poets. A prize of $250, donated by W. Van R. Whitall, Esq., of Pelham, N.Y., is to be awarded annually, under the Society's auspices, for the best poem sent in competition before Jan. 1st of each year. Mr. Pelham [*sic*] makes sure of a competent choice this year by appointing Miss Amy Lowell to the honor of initiating the award by acting as the first judge." Stevens began immediately "From the Journal of Crispin," informing Harriet Monroe just before Christmas that he had been "churning and churning." He met the New Year's Day deadline, but had to settle for first honorable mention. Hervey Allen tried to reassure him by saying that Lowell had "hesitated a long time."[24] "From the Journal of Crispin" was the longest poem Stevens had written, and it had been undertaken in exceptional haste. When Monroe offered to find a place for it in *Poetry,* Stevens said that he

---

23. Wallace Stevens to Harriet Monroe, January 30, 1921, in Hendrick, "Wallace Stevens' Manuscripts at the University of Illionois," 19; Harriet Monroe, "Notes," *Poetry,* XIX (October, 1921), 57.

24. Harriet Monroe, "Notes," *Poetry,* XIX (December, 1921), 173; Hervey Allen to Wallace Stevens, April 20, 1922.

had promised Pitts Sanborn a long poem for the *Measure* and that he was rewriting and expanding the poem that was becoming "The Comedian as the Letter C." (That poem's first publication, however, was in *Harmonium*.)

Carl Van Vechten and others were also urging Stevens to put together a book-length collection. The recent completion of "The Comedian as the Letter C," a poem of 573 lines, may have convinced Stevens that such a project was feasible. In 1922, Van Vechten took a manuscript Stevens had prepared to Alfred Knopf, his own publisher. Knopf "almost immediately" agreed to publish the volume that became *Harmonium*.[25] Stevens informed Monroe of the news, asking that it be kept confidential, "but I don't know of any one more entitled to first news of it than yourself" (*L*, 228).

The publication of *Harmonium* can have pleased few people more than Monroe. One-third of the poems in the volume (twenty-five of seventy-four) had been published in *Poetry*, and many of them appeared in the two editions of her anthology. When selecting the poems, Stevens admitted to her that "I have omitted many things, exercising the most fastidious choice" (*L*, 232). Among the omissions were the four "Phases" poems and the two verse dramas that had appeared in *Poetry*. The four poems from "Lettres d'un Soldat" would wait until the 1931 *Harmonium*. "Sunday Morning" was restored whole. But poems from the magazine since 1919 were liberally represented: all but two of the "Pecksniffiana" poems and all of "Sur Ma Guzzla Gracile."

"A Cavalier of Beauty," Monroe's review in *Poetry*, was predictably enthusiastic. It was Stevens' "sheer beauty of sound, phrase, rhythm, packed with prismatically colored ideas by a mind at once wise and whimsical" that she saw as *Harmonium*'s dominant feature. Obviously influenced by the looming presence of "The Comedian as the Letter C," she certified Stevens as a humorist: "The hard black stone is there, but laughter washes over it, covers it up, conceals it." Life as "fantastic miracle" is everywhere evidenced. Such an appraisal is typical of the early readings of *Harmonium*, even though they overlook the more somber heft of other poems in

---

25. Carl Van Vechten, "Rogue Elephant in Porcelain," *Yale University Library Gazette*, XXXVIII (October, 1963), 50.

the collection. Monroe spoke of Stevens, not as the neophyte with a first volume, but as a progenitor: "like Napoleon he may say, '*Je suis ancêtre!*' for shoals of young poets derive from him." Later in the year she returned to Stevens' rhythms: "Wallace Stevens is a poet of very different quality from these [Pound, Aldington, H.D., Fletcher, Amy Lowell, Sandburg], one quite unmoved by their kind of realities but feeling keenly his own kind. Intensely individual, he has belonged to no school and taken orders from his muse alone. . . . His rhythms, whether bond or free, are his own. His moods, whether serious or whimsical, are tributes to the queer, audacious, fascinating beauty of the world."[26]

In the years following the publication of *Harmonium,* Stevens the poet fell into a protracted silence as he immersed himself in family and business. With some foresight, Monroe, in her review of the volume, had worried that Crispin's fate might be one with the poet's: "We must hope that the poem ["The Comedian as the Letter C"] is not strictly autobiographical, that Mr. Stevens, unlike his baffled hero, will get his story uttered."[27] Even though he saw his volume through a second edition and did a handful of things for publication, the ten years after *Harmonium* were largely barren. Monroe's interest in Stevens did not relax, however; they continued to correspond and to meet occasionally, and there were the orders for various items she sent to her sister. Monroe was not alone in her inquiries about his work and exhortations to resume. Marianne Moore and William Carlos Williams, among others, also set out to rally him. But the poet told Monroe that his royalties on the first volume for the first half of 1924 had come to only $6.70 (*L,* 243), and early in 1925, he conceded, "I haven't written a thing for months" (*L,* 244). More than seven years later, the message had not changed.

He did, however, break his silence briefly in 1928 to send Monroe a small piece that "I jotted down in New York yesterday." "Metropolitan Melancholy," he explained, was for her "private library" (*L,* 252). And, on the occasion of her seventieth birthday,

26. Harriet Monroe, "A Cavalier of Beauty," *Poetry,* XXIII (March, 1924), 322–27; Harriet Monroe, "The Free-Verse Movement in America," *English Journal,* XIII (December, 1924), 703.
27. Monroe, "A Cavalier of Beauty," 327.

there was another presentation "for yourself alone" (*L*, 260). It was part III of "The Woman Who Blamed Life on a Spaniard."[28] These poems no doubt pleased her, though she must have recognized, too, that they were little more than exercises.

The poetry editor of a Hartford newspaper wrote Monroe, boasting of the Poetry Club of Hartford. Robert Hillyer and others were cited as members, but not Stevens. She printed the comment in a 1928 number of *Poetry* with a brisk corrective: "Here we must remark parenthetically that in our opinion the poetry center of Hartford is in the residence of Wallace Stevens."[29]

The years of Stevens' poetic exile were coming to an end when, in 1932, he offered Monroe "Good Man, Bad Woman" as a "scrap for publication." Her answer was immediate and insistent: "Of course I want your 'scrap' for October—and if you find—or write—any other scraps I beg you to send them on. . . . But that's not important [her fund-raising efforts for *Poetry*] compared with your deserting *your* job. Is there anything—*anything*—I can do to keep you keen for it?"[30] Stevens must have been encouraged when his work was included in a new anthology. With Morton Dauwen Zabel, associate editor of *Poetry,* Monroe edited *A Book of Poems for Every Mood* in 1933. The anthology was not restricted to the "new poetry"—it included Shakespeare, Jonson, Donne, Wordsworth, and many others. A place was found for "Ploughing on Sunday," "Disillusionment of Ten O'Clock," and "Another Weeping Woman."

When Zabel wrote early in 1933 requesting some poems, Stevens was more responsive than usual, acknowledging that many had lately been asking for his work. He had been complying with some of the requests, he said, but warned that it might be some months before there was anything for *Poetry*. He mentioned a special incentive: "Miss Monroe has always been so particularly friendly that I should like to make a fresh effort for her" (*L*, 265). More than a half year later, however, *Poetry* was still waiting, and Stevens promised Zabel that "I shall really try to do something for you" (*L*, 271). Almost immediately he began "Like Decorations in

28. The complete poem was published two years later in *Contempo,* III (December 15, 1932), 1.
29. *Poetry,* XXXII (August, 1928), 296.
30. Harriet Monroe to Wallace Stevens, August 8, 1932.

a Nigger Cemetery"; the fifty-part poem was sent to Zabel six weeks later. "Like Decorations in a Nigger Cemetery," along with "The Idea of Order at Key West," signaled Stevens' vigorous return to his craft. Monroe, who had been visiting her sister in China, recognized at once that the poem took Stevens beyond his occasional exercises she had seen over the previous years: "I can't tell you what pleasure it gave me to see you in *Poetry* again—and to find you there in a mood and a form which reminded me of the country I had come from. For there is in Chinese art a most delicate combination of irony and humor and shy seriousness which one finds so often in your poetry, and now especially in these *Decorations.*"[31]

When that poem appeared in 1935, Monroe was approaching her seventy-fifth birthday, and though she remained as editor, Zabel took on many of the details of running *Poetry*. Stevens' respect and friendship for her were undiminished, but a new figure was coming to occupy the role of mentor and editor. Ronald Lane Latimer, as much as any individual, was responsible for awakening the poet from his long dormancy. As Monroe had done after 1914, Latimer offered encouragement and a new medium for Stevens' work.

When Latimer published *Ideas of Order* through his Alcestis Press in 1935, Monroe wrote one of her last reviews for *Poetry*. Of the volume's thirty-three poems, only "Like Decorations in a Nigger Cemetery" had been published in *Poetry*. But her longstanding familiarity with Stevens' work was obvious, and in place of the humor that she had found so prominent in *Harmonium,* there was now a serenity won from "an impassioned acceptance of life." In quoting six stanzas from "Sad Strains of a Gay Waltz," she noticed a more somber tone, one she had failed to see in *Harmonium*. One wonders if, in citing the references to Claude Lorraine and his "panoramas" in "Botanist on Alp (No. 1)," she remembered her first encounter with Stevens more than twenty years earlier. In the tenth of the "Phases" poems, Stevens had evoked the painter in the same central context: "Peace means long, delicious valleys, / In the mode of Claude Lorraine." Now, she was more than ever confident of Stevens' enduring importance: "The poetry

---

31. Harriet Monroe to Wallace Stevens, March 11, 1935.

of Wallace Stevens will live 'radiantly'—not for the casual crowd perhaps, but for those who love his kind of magic—his rolling or skilfully broken rhythms, his orchestral range of music from the organ to the piccolo, his whimsically philosophic mind, his eye and ear observant to the last queer detail which no one else would notice; in short, his sheer delight in all the strange and miraculous adornments of life on earth that converge for beauty and oddity in the human brain." [32]

Stevens' last letter to Monroe was typical in its expressions of gratitude and fondness; it was exceptional in its disclosure that he had read her review of *Ideas of Order* and had "read it carefully." As a rule he did not pay much attention to reviews. "I am quite staggered by your notice of IDEAS OF ORDER. It was just as if a rich uncle had died and left me everything he had. In any case, I took it home with me last night and read it carefully. It is really very skilful, and I am grateful to you, as I have had so many occasions to be in the past" (*L,* 298–99). Her response was one of surprise—"I thought you never read reviews and had no idea you would read my unworthy effort"—but she was also "pleased and proud." [33]

In the summer of 1936, Monroe was invited to represent the Chicago chapter of PEN (Poets, Essayists, and Novelists of Europe and the Americas) at its international congress in Buenos Aires. She enjoyed the two-week ocean voyage and the ten-day conference. On her way to visit the Inca ruins in Peru, she suffered a cerebral hemorrhage and died suddenly in Arequipa, Peru, on September 26. It is not surprising that on her last trips she was still promoting Stevens' poetry. To the PEN delegates she recommended him, along with a dozen other contemporary Americans, as "names to be ever memorable when the final record of our time is written." [34] In Peking in 1934, as she later recalled in a letter to Stevens, she had read his poetry to students at various universities in that city. After her death, one of her relatives discovered a 1923 document in which she stipulated that the bronze paper weight on her desk be sent to Stevens in the distribution of her property. Early in 1937, it was forwarded to him.

---

32. Harriet Monroe, "He Plays the Present," *Poetry,* XLVII (December, 1935), 153–57.
33. Harriet Monroe to Wallace Stevens, December 13, 1935.
34. Monroe, *A Poet's Life,* 471.

Quoting Whitman, Monroe had reminded her readers on the cover of every issue of *Poetry* that "to have great poets there must be great audiences too." It is not too extravagant to claim that both the magazine and its editor had constituted such an audience for Stevens. There are, I think, four principal reasons that help to account for Monroe's emergence as his primary reader. First is the role of the magazine itself. Already in 1914, when Stevens submitted his "Phases" manuscript, the two-year-old *Poetry* had published generous selections of poems by Yeats, Pound, Williams, Lawrence, H.D., Amy Lowell, and others. Pound, its "foreign correspondent," had reviewed Robert Frost's first volume, *A Boy's Will,* and would introduce Eliot's "The Love Song of J. Alfred Prufrock" in *Poetry* five months before Stevens' own "Sunday Morning" appeared there. *Poetry* was avant-garde, associated with free verse and Imagism, but it was clearly more than an organ for fads and poseurs. In addition, its format was uncluttered and attractive, and Stevens valued that. For all these reasons, he offered his poems to *Poetry* and even allowed the reorganization of "Sunday Morning" in order to appear there. Another feature of the magazine had a peculiar appeal—the regular offering of contests and prizes, ventures that challenged Stevens in a special way.

A second reason for Monroe's decisive role in Stevens' early years has to do with her personality and manner. Before 1919, she had been firm in her editorial decisions—rejecting, selecting in a fragmentary fashion, altering the order of stanzas, revising the diction of lines and phrases. She always consulted the poet, however, and usually managed to leave him feeling persuaded rather than pressured. (In the case of "Sunday Morning" and "Lunar Paraphrase," he patiently waited to restore them in *Harmonium*.) She could be censorious, but it was not without charm. "I was heartbroken that we could not use more of your poem especially the first section," she wrote after selecting four poems from "Phases." In 1915 she rejected some of his work, saying, "Their author will surely catch me next time if he will only uncurl and uncoil a little." Monroe was of course accustomed to dealing with poets whose personalities differed widely, but she must also have found Stevens refreshingly polite and undemanding. She once said that "of all the poets I have ever met, Stevens is the most indifferent as to the fate of his works after they have emerged from his mind."[35] One suspects that even after the 1918 exchange on the subject of death, for which Stevens later wrote his apology, it was Monroe who gracefully uncomplicated the situation.

Third, Monroe's personal support of Stevens' work was obvious. This was especially true after 1919 and during the years of his poetic drought after *Harmonium*. But his winning a prize for *Three Travelers Watch a Sunrise* in 1916, his appearance in her anthology *The New Poetry* in 1917 and her publication of *Carlos Among the Candles* despite the play's failure on the stage, and the Levinson Prize for "Pecksniffiana," all reinforced the notion that Monroe's interest superseded routine editorial courtesy.

Finally, Monroe's consistent reaction to his poems shows her shrewd discernment of the unique modernity of Stevens' work. In an unpublished essay cited by Ellen Williams in her *Harriet Monroe and the Poetry Renaissance,* Monroe once referred typically to Stevens as "a wizard with fine ironies and solitary grandeurs set in curious rhythms." Writing his autobiography in 1937, John Gould Fletcher called Stevens "almost the only ultra-modern 'discovery' about whom she [Monroe] was deeply enthusiastic." He went on to speculate that Monroe prized "certain affinities he showed with Chinese art, about which she was glowingly enthusiastic." Monroe appears, in fact, to have had little interest in philosophical paraphrases of the poems, invariably singling out characteristics of form. Stevens, who issued similar caveats for the rest of his life, obviously approved. Such a view might lead to her excisions of "Sunday Morning," but it also enabled her to sense at once the novelty, the subtle and witty turns and counterturns within even a short poem, the constant parade of bold diction, and "his eye and ear observant to the last queer detail which no one else would notice."[36]

Monroe's death did not mark the severance of Stevens' association with *Poetry*. Thirteen cantos of "The Man with the Blue Guitar" appeared in 1937, and another dozen short poems were placed there in subsequent years. But the excitement that existed during

35. *Ibid.*, 391.
36. Monroe quoted in Williams, *Harriet Monroe and the Poetry Renaissance,* 235; John Gould Fletcher, *Life Is My Song* (New York, 1937), 191; Monroe, "He Plays the Present," 156.

the Monroe years was never recaptured. A decade after her death, Stevens was named winner of the Harriet Monroe Poetry Award. In a letter to the president of the University of Chicago, he reflected on the friendship that had lasted for twenty-two years: "The award is not only a great honor, but, since I knew Miss Monroe well for a good many years, it brings her back with her friendliest smile and the charm she exerted merely by being interested. I am touched by all this more than I can say" (*L*, 529).

# 11 ✍ Stevens on Stevens

"A paraphrase . . . is a sort of murder. It makes one say a good many things that are true only when they are not said this way" (*L,* 360). Stevens' admonition occurs at the end of a long letter to Hi Simons in which, section by section, he had closely paraphrased "The Man with the Blue Guitar." No poet ever disparaged more and indulged more in the practice of self-commentary than did Stevens. In years of correspondence he generously responded to queries about individual poems, their sources, and the intentions that lay behind them. These glosses, the most detailed of which were sent to Ronald Lane Latimer, Hi Simons, and Renato Poggioli, are of only limited value as the poet's formalist criticism of his work. On the other hand, Stevens' annotations disclose a great deal about his attitude toward his craft, the ends he sought, and the relation between the poem's private incipiency and its final formulation as art.

In addition, Stevens' self-commentaries frequently hint at theories of poetic discourse that go beyond the particular poem under discussion. As a theoretician, he is rarely systematic, especially in his letters. But even in the formal essays, his methodology is discursive and impressionistic. Terms such as *imagination, decreation, actuality, reality, romantic,* and *unreal,* for example, are not rigorously defined, and their meanings vary from one essay to another. Stevens is also fond of quoting from various external sources to buttress his own arguments. Usually brief, the quotations are often stripped of their original contexts. The result is that they sometimes suffer minor distortions, as if Stevens were creating his authorities out of some compelling need to reinforce his own less certain propositions. The reader of Stevens' comments on the function of resemblance, the relationship between poetry and painting, or the identity of poetry and style will construct the poet's frame of ideas only piecemeal, from statements and impressions introduced in different contexts and over many years.

The tone of the commentaries varies. If a correspondent appears to have tripped on syntax, for example, Stevens, perhaps impatient but also dogged, comes to his aid: "As to the form of this poem, the initial words 'that I may' = I wish that I might" (L, 360). In other cases, the urge to provide expanded and enlivening connotations for a given passage leads him from the critic's analytic dispassion to the poet's metaphorical exclamation. In pointing out to Simons the importance of the various C-sounds in "The Comedian as the Letter C," Stevens wrote: "Now, as Crispin moves through the poem, the sounds of the letter C accompany him, as the sounds of the crickets, etc. must have accompanied St. Francis. I don't mean to say that there is an incessant din, but you ought not to be able to read very far in the poem without recognizing what I mean" (L, 351). In a later letter, he recaptured the climactic triumph of one of the concluding sections of "The Man with the Blue Guitar": "The point of the poem is, not that this [redefining the self imaginatively] can be done, but that, if done, it is the key to poetry, to the closed garden, if I may become rhapsodic about it, of the fountain of youth and life and renewal" (L, 364). It is as if the critic's return to his poem stirred to life the memory, metaphoric and rhapsodic, of the creating poet.

Stevens' formal repudiation of paraphrase is based on several theories. The first, the untranslatable quality of poetry, is hinted at in the letter to Simons where he speaks of paraphrase as murder. His fear of such restatements was not unlike Dryden's admonition on free translations: "The spirit of an author may be transfus'd, and yet not lost," but "by innovation of thoughts, methinks he breaks it."[1] As Stevens said to L. W. Payne, Jr., an early anthologist: "It is very difficult for me to change things from one category to another, and, as a matter of fact, I dislike to do so. It may or may not be like converting a piece of mysticism into a piece of logic. But the feeling is much the same" (L, 250). Stevens' reaction is the inevitable reluctance on the part of the poet to see his poems reduced to mere summary. A second reason for his distrusting para-

---

1. John Dryden, "The Preface to Ovid's Epistles," *The Poetical Works of Dryden*, ed. George R. Noyes (Cambridge, 1950), 92.

phrase is less obvious. Stevens worried that a poem's appeal could be exhausted by excessive interpretation: "I have the greatest dislike for explanations. As soon as people are perfectly sure of a poem they are just as likely as not to have no further interest in it; it loses whatever potency it had" (L, 294). That concern was repeated five years later: "A long time ago I made up my mind not to explain things, because most people have so little appreciation of poetry that once a poem has been explained it has been destroyed: that is to say, they are no longer able to seize the poem" (L, 346). A final reason for Stevens' resisting paraphrase was his objection to artificial or simplistic systems being imposed upon his poems. Seeking the poet's imprimatur for their readings, critics did not always win Stevens' encouragement: "There's no symbolism in the 'Earthy Anecdote,'" he once explained. "There's a good deal of theory about it, however; but explanations spoil things" (L, 204). He said later, "This group of poems ["Thirteen Ways of Looking at a Blackbird"] is not meant to be a collection of epigrams or of ideas, but of sensations" (L, 251). And speaking about the writing of one section of "Owl's Clover," he added, "I am thinking of using images that are never fully defined. We constantly use such images: any state of mind is in effect such an image. This is part of the rapidity of thought" (L, 319). I will return later to Stevens' theory of poetry as "rapidity of thought," which eludes of necessity the "fully defined" statement. Prose translations of poems threatened their autonomy as poems, risked incurring the reader's disengagement, and confused sensations and ideas. His theory notwithstanding, Stevens succumbed frequently to its violation.

Like a well-tutored formalist, Stevens first insisted upon the poem's independence from the fallacy of intention. The poet, he explained to Simons, could be instructed by his readers: "In the case of a competent critic the author may well have a great deal to find out about himself and his work. This goes to the extent of saying that it would be legitimate for a critic to make statements respecting the purpose of an author's work that were altogether contrary to the intention of the author" (L, 346). Simons, however, disagreed. It would be useless, he replied, for the critic to work contrary to the author's intention, and to work solely from the text was "an ideal proposition rather than a practicable proposition": "Criticism rightfully and necessarily uses every mite of evidence accessible (autobiography, biography, letters by and to the artist, contemporary records and memoirs, collateral works of art, etc. etc.) to make sure of its understanding of the artist before it presumes to judge him. Criticism will even go, if it has the chance, to the artist himself for control of what without control were merely more or less shrewd speculation. Criticism lets no false pride stand against its getting the facts it needs."[2] Stevens took Simons' remarks seriously, and with his parable of the poem as man and shadow, he seems to acknowledge the pluralism of Simons' methodology:

> Obviously, it is not possible to tell one what one's own poems mean, or were intended to mean. On the other hand, it is not the simplest thing in the world to explain a poem. I thought of it this way this morning: a poem is like a man walking on the bank of a river, whose shadow is reflected in the water. If you explain a poem, you are quite likely to do it either in terms of the man or in terms of the shadow, but you have to explain it in terms of the whole. When I said recently that a poem was what was on a page, it seems to me now that I was wrong because that is explaining in terms of the man. But the thing and its double always go together. (L, 354)

Stevens' analogy is not completely clear. He reminds Simons that his earlier view of the poem as "what was on a page" now seems wrong because it is "explaining in terms of the man." The shadow, it seems to follow, consists of all the extratextual components of which Simons had spoken. Stevens then concedes that the "thing and its double," the poem as man and shadow, as text and context, "always go together." In spite of his avowed suspicion and even aversion to the poet's explanations, he seems to be allowing here for their validity.

Almost three years later, still offering critical assistance to Simons, Stevens seemed almost eager: "There are several things in the NOTES that would stand a little annotating" (L, 434). At the same time, the poet insisted on the right to remain invisible as critic. He said to L. W. Payne, Jr., "It is shocking to have to say this sort of thing. Please destroy these notes. I don't mind your saying what I have said here. But I don't want you to quote me" (L, 252);

---

2. Hi Simons to Wallace Stevens, January 14, 1940, in Folder 8, Box 1, Hi Simons Papers, University of Chicago Library.

and to Simons, "These notes are for your personal use. They are not to be quoted" (*L,* 350).

Stevens' motives for cooperating with his critics were diverse. One such involved offers of assistance to translators, as was the case with the earliest letters to Henry Church. As editor of *Mesures,* Church wanted the poet's reaction to some French renderings of Stevens' poems he was about to publish. The letters in the 1950s to Poggioli concerned his translations into Italian. Principally, however, Stevens seem to have looked with favor on the interest his correspondents took in his work and particularly the prospect of their assistance as publishers or as publishing critics. In short, Stevens' cooperation as self-critic was partly motivated by self-interest, and he wrote his commentaries for the enlightenment of his interlocutor, as well as for the benefit of the correspondent's larger audience. Latimer not only announced a plan to write an analysis of Stevens' poems (*L,* 359), but as editor of the Alcestis Press and *Alcestis* magazine, he was an eager publisher during the mid-1930s, when the circle of Stevens' readers was small. Simons began his correspondence with Stevens in 1937, asking for help with a bibliography he was compiling on Stevens' publications. Later, his essay on "The Comedian as the Letter C" for the *Southern Review,*[3] followed by his plan to do a longer critical piece, prompted the poet's avid endorsement: "I hadn't the faintest idea that you were working on the scale that your letter of January 14th indicates. . . . It is unnecessary to say that I shall be glad to do anything that I can to help you, so whenever you have any questions that you want to ask, don't hesitate to write to me" (*L,* 353–54).

Stevens the critic functions as both annotator and theoretician, and I want to examine some of his activities in those roles. The poet's self-proclaimed resistance to self-paraphrase frequently led him into a reformulation of one major and abiding issue: How can a poem, enjoying its own complete statement, yield to commentaries by its creator or by anyone else? Or, how can a poem, which so manifestly exists by the power of its unique form, survive its translations by critics? For Stevens, the role of pure poetry was never far from his consideration; a poem's élan lay in its style and

3. Hi Simons, "'The Comedian as the Letter C': Its Sense and Its Significance," *Southern Review,* V (Winter, 1940), 453–68.

expressiveness. In the end, the relation between a poem's style and its meaning is the principal issue for Stevens as critic, not least because it is the same issue each of his readers confronts.

The greater part of Stevens' reviews of his own work involves simple annotation. Invariably, Stevens' questioner was concerned about individual lines or images within poems and asked for his aid in understanding them. Numbering his responses by title or by section for the longer poems, the poet-critic systematically cataloged his various recollections. There are scores of such summaries throughout Stevens' letters and, more rarely, his essays. We learn, for example, a specialized meaning of "disregarded plate" in "Sunday Morning" from a 1915 letter to Harriet Monroe (*L,* 183). He offers a gloss on the statue in the first part of "Owl's Clover," "The Old Woman and the Statue": "A symbol for art, art being a word that I have never used and never can use without some feeling of repugnance" (*L,* 290). In his long outline of "The Man with the Blue Guitar" for Simons in 1940, he defined such figurations as the "sullen psaltery" (part XVI), the "lion in the lute" and the "lion locked in stone" (part XIX), and "the old fantoche" (part XXX) (*L,* 360, 362). "I did have the Spanish Republicans in mind when I wrote *The Men that are Falling*" (*L,* 798), he told Heringman, whereas "The Snow Man" is an example of "the necessity of identifying oneself with reality in order to understand it and enjoy it" (*L,* 464). For Poggioli's translation into Italian, Stevens volunteered interpretations of the "thin men of Haddam" from "Thirteen Ways of Looking at a Blackbird" and the figure of the rabbi from "The Sun This March" (*L,* 786).

In these illustrations and many others, the poet may provide a contextual base for a given image, as when he defines the rabbi as "the figure of a man devoted in the extreme to scholarship and at the same time to making some use of it for human purposes" (*L,* 786). Other images, however, are without such contexts—the "thin men of Haddam," for example, are "entirely fictitious" (*L,* 786). Occasionally, the remarks are noncommittal: "My recollection of it is that it ["Homunculus et La Belle Etoile"] does not have a definite theory, that it is merely a statement of an impression: one version of man's place in nature" (*L,* 305).

Rarely do Stevens' descriptions strip back the surfaces of his poems and disclose their concealed meanings. If Latimer, Simons, Poggioli, and others sought such radically revealing insights, Stevens' letters must have disappointed them. He is most helpful as a self-critic in his glib analysis of the kind of poetic exercise that is highly metaphorical or parabolic. Here the poet-critic confronts the mischievous and intractable wit of the poem; he cannot hope to tame it, nor does he wish to. But he does offer a frame in which the characters and settings, the brassy exclamations and untoward images, can be placed. He does not so much explain the poem as ratify the reader's own intimations and guesses. The poem neither needs nor benefits from explanation, but the commentary reinforces the reader's own engagement, never exhausting or simply reducing the poem to a final preemptive meaning.

The second poem in the "It Must Give Pleasure" section of "Notes toward a Supreme Fiction" was a favorite of Stevens'. He told Henry Church that he remembered writing the section, that it was "a difficult one to do," but that "as so often happens with difficult ones, it is one that has survived (for me) particularly well" (*L,* 462–63):

> The blue woman, linked and lacquered, at her window
> Did not desire that feathery argentines
> Should be cold silver, neither that frothy clouds
>
> Should foam, be foamy waves, should move like them,
> Nor that the sexual blossoms should repose
> Without their fierce addictions, nor that the heat
>
> Of summer, growing fragrant in the night,
> Should strengthen her abortive dreams and take
> In sleep its natural form. It was enough
>
> For her that she remembered: the argentines
> Of spring come to their places in the grape leaves
> To cool their ruddy pulses; the frothy clouds
>
> Are nothing but frothy clouds; the frothy blooms
> Waste without puberty; and afterward,
> When the harmonious heat of August pines
>
> Enters the room, it drowses and is the night.
> It was enough for her that she remembered.
> The blue woman looked and from her window named

The corals of the dogwood, cold and clear,
Cold, coldly delineating, being real,
Clear and, except for the eye, without intrusion. (*CP*, 399–400)

The poem is full of eccentric images that at first tend to disarm the reader—feathery argentines, frothy clouds, sexual blossoms. There are hints of potential metamorphoses of these images, but the blue woman resists them ("Did not desire") in her surrender to the summer setting. A year after writing the poem, Stevens sent Simons some explanatory notes on it. The blue woman herself, as "linked and lacquered," is almost surreal, and Stevens reinforces this impression by saying she is "probably the weather of a Sunday morning early last April." She seems finally to be both observer and observed in perfect concord and unity. Stevens identifies himself with the woman in desiring no transformations of the scene from her window: "I had the feeling that the 'feathery argentines' were right and that it would not help to change them to something else, any more than it would help to metamorphize [*sic*] this, that or the other (clouds into foam, living blossoms to blossoms without life, heat to a form of heat)." The images that appear strangely incongruous are, in fact, so intended—"this, that or the other." On a summer day, she then remembers the same collection of images during an earlier spring, equally unmetamorphosed. The present scene, Stevens explains, "validated the memory" and gave it an "intensity expressible in terms of coldness and clearness." That intense meaning of the real as "corals of the dogwood" concludes the section; Stevens compresses the scene from the more lush description of summer—"corals . . . cold and clear . . . Cold, coldly . . . Clear." But the assuagements of both seasons are equally real and "except for the eye, without intrusion" of any distorting agency.

Stevens summarizes his remarks to Simons:

One way of making progress is by mere contrast. If the sense of reality makes more acute the sense of the fictive, so the appreciation of the routine, the mechanism etc. intensifies appreciation of the fictive. The law of contrast is crude. Even in a text expounding *it must change,* it is permissible to illustrate *it must give pleasure* without any law whatever. Obviously in a poem composed of the weather and of things drifting round in it: the time of year and one's thoughts and feelings, the cold

> delineations round one take their places without help. Distinguish
> change & metamorphosis. (*L,* 444–45)

These conclusions are present in the poem only implicitly, as if the poet were re-creating the larger frame of mind from which it sprang. With its focus on the "appreciation of the routine" of a summer day, the poem makes possible and intensifies the fictions of other days. It also illustrates the pleasure of a natural scene "without any law whatever." If the supreme fiction must be abstract and must change, the pleasure of the quest for it is spontaneous and undecreed. Stevens' remarks to Simons add little if anything to the poem's own statement; they remind the reader that the vignette of his Sunday in April is itself unrehearsed, its images are no more than "this, that or the other"; the very woman who is the perceiving agent in the poem is the "weather of a Sunday morning"; the past ("corals of the dogwood") and present ("feathery argentines") are one in the satisfactions they bestow.[4]

From time to time, Stevens could be less than candid, sometimes even contradictory, more often, simply forgetful. He was somewhat evasive, for example, when he told Poggioli that he "had no particular painting of Picasso's in mind" (*L,* 786) when he chose the title and principal symbol for "The Man with the Blue Guitar." Picasso's *The Old Guitarist* (1903), with its dominant blues enveloping a guitar player who is cross-legged and with bent head, must have been at least a partial source. Picasso is named in the fifteenth section. Stevens told another interlocutor that the name Ramon Fernandez from "The Idea of Order at Key West" was made of "two every day names. As I might have expected, they turned out to be an actual name" (*L,* 798). Six years later his memory was clearer: "I knew of Ramon Fernandez, the critic, and had read some of his criticisms but I did not have him in mind" (*L,* 798). Joseph Riddel, however, has demonstrated convincingly that there are connections between the poem and Fernandez's essay "Of Philosophical Criticism."[5] When a Yale undergraduate wrote in 1941 for information about "Sea Surface Full of Clouds," Stevens'

---

4. For a useful discussion of this poem and others where Stevens' glosses are pertinent, see Frank Doggett, "The Making of a Thing Yet To Be Made," *Wallace Stevens: The Making of the Poem* (Baltimore, 1980), 21–41.

5. Joseph N. Riddel, *The Clairvoyant Eye: The Poetry and Poetics of Wallace Stevens* (Baton Rouge, 1965), 117–18.

response again seemed disingenuous: "I remember that when I wrote this particular poem I was doing a great deal of theorizing about poetry, but actually I have not the faintest recollection of what theory prompted that particular poem" (*L*, 390). In "Notes toward a Supreme Fiction," the following passage occurs:

> The bees come booming
> As if—The pigeons clatter in the air.
>
> An erotic perfume, half of the body, half
> Of an obvious acid is sure what it intends. (*CP*, 390)

When asked about the meaning of "obvious acid," Stevens seemed genuinely forgetful: "I don't actually recall what I had in mind when I said 'obvious acid', but it is clear that the meaning is visible change" (*L*, 434). Poggioli's plea for help with the reference to the Franciscans in part XXIX of "The Man with the Blue Guitar" drew a similar but understandable reply; the poem had been written more than sixteen years before. "You have me up a tree on this one. I suppose, although I really do not remember that I was, that I was trying to make a choice of a priestly character suitable for appearance in the context of the poem" (*L*, 784).

Although these comments refer mostly to details in the long works, and the questions were raised years after Stevens had written the poems, his lapses were not always those of memory. Responding to Poggioli's queries on "hoo-ing the slick trombones" (part X) and "amorist Adjective aflame" (part XIII) in "The Man with the Blue Guitar," he returned explanations for both in June, 1953. A later rereading of the poem, however, caused retractions. The former, which he first defined as "making Bing Crosby: performing in an accomplished way" (*L*, 783), was now seen to be "nonsense" and "laziness of my part, for which I apologize" (*L*, 790). Both "hoo-ing" and "slick" were intended pejoratively, he clarified—not at all "an accomplished way." And the "amorist Adjective aflame" was not a metamorphosis "into blue as a reality" (*L*, 783), as he had earlier pronounced; that reading was "a bit too expansive" and "misleading." More accurately, the phrase was meant to depict "the intensity of the imagination unmodified by contacts with reality" (*L*, 785). Again, in reply to Latimer's uncertainty about the "sisterhood of the living dead" in "To the One of

Fictive Music," Stevens labeled it "a muse: all of the muses are of that sisterhood" (*L*, 297). One day later, however, he was bothered sufficiently to qualify the explanation: "To explain is to translate, and the translation contained in yesterday's letter was rather loathsome. No muses exist for me. The One of Fictive Music is one of the sisterhood; who the others are I don't know, except to say that they are figures of that sort. I felt as though I should have to say this to you in order to enjoy Thanksgiving properly" (*L*, 298). Another act of self-revision took place a few years later after he had defined the "monster" in "The Man with the Blue Guitar":

> That I may reduce the monster to
> Myself, and then may be myself
> In face of the monster. (*CP*, 175)

He explained to Simons: "As I go on with the thing, I am a little horrified by it. Take, for instance, what I said yesterday about the monster. Certainly I never converted the monster into the sort of extension that you are looking for; I never said to myself that it was the world. These things are intact in themselves" (*L*, 361). These acknowledged errors indicate that interpretations could be as spontaneous as the impulse from which the poems themselves derived.

There is obviously a danger in relying too much on Stevens' commentaries. In addition to his lapses of memory and self-corrections, there are other instances in which his suggestions varied from one account to the next, altering, and in some cases contradicting, previous conclusions. Stevens' discussion of the "sea of ex," for example, led to a shift in definition. The "sea of ex" appears at the end of part XVIII of "The Man with the Blue Guitar," and it follows a series of analogies related to a "dream" of "things as they are":

> A dream (to call it a dream) in which
> I can believe, in face of the object,
>
> A dream no longer a dream, a thing,
> Of things as they are, as the blue guitar
>
> After long strumming on certain nights
> Gives the touch of the senses, not of the hand,
>
> But the very senses as they touch
> The wind-gloss. Or as daylight comes,

> Like light in a mirroring of cliffs,
> Rising upward from a sea of ex. (*CP*, 174–75)

Stevens' syntax in this single sentence is complicated by his fondness for analogies through apposition in which the elements are defined minimally. The section might be schematized as follows:

|   | | | |
|---|---|---|---|
| | "the object," "things as they are" | becomes | "a dream . . . in which / I can believe" |
| *as* | | | |
| | "hand" on "the blue guitar" | becomes | "touch of the senses, not of the hand" |
| *as* | | | |
| | "cliffs" beside sea | becomes | "light in a mirroring of cliffs" from "sea of ex" |

The three processes involve a transformation of ordinary sense perceptions into (1) the imagination's dream, (2) nontactile senses, and (3) brilliant matinal mirroring. Thus, Stevens' note to Simons in 1940 defines the "sea of ex" in the third transformation as "pure irreality": "Sea of Ex. The imagination takes us out of (Ex) reality into a pure irreality. One has this sense of irreality often in the presence of morning lights on cliffs which then rise from a sea that has ceased to be real and is therefore a sea of Ex" (*L*, 360). When he returned to an explanation of this canto thirteen years later, however, his reading had altered. What was "pure irreality" of "a sea that has ceased to be real" had now come to be regarded as unstimulating and pejorative: "A sea of ex means a purely negative sea. The realm of has-been without interest or provocativeness" (*L*, 783). But the poem itself hardly sustains the latter dismissal of the "sea of ex." The second paraphrase, coming sixteen years after the poem's creation, is simply a reinterpretation that may be the result of oversight or may even correspond to the original intention. In any case, it violates the poem's apparent statement, disrupting the parallelism of the three-stage analogy. If the sea of ex is a "purely negative sea" and a "realm of has-been without interest," then its counterparts, the believable dream and "touch of the senses, not of the hand" are necessarily impugned. That conclusion is borne out neither by the poem nor by the earlier explanation.

In a letter to Sister Bernetta Quinn in 1952, Stevens took exception to her student's interpretation of the "angel of reality" in "Angel Surrounded by Paysans." He insisted that the angel should not be taken as the "angel of imagination": "Will you thank the writer for me and say that in Angel Surrounded by Paysans the angel is the angel of reality. This is clear only if the reader is of the idea that we live in a world of the imagination, in which reality and contact with it are the great blessings. For nine readers out of ten, the necessary angel will appear to be the angel of the imagination and for nine days out of ten that is true, although it is the tenth day that counts" (L, 753). He reiterated the point to the poet Mona Van Duyn after reading the Stevens issue of *Perspective* in 1954: "The Necessary Angel is not the imagination but reality" (L, 852). An examination of the poem discloses that Stevens' comments are only partly consistent with its statement. The angel is explicitly identified in line 3 as "the angel of reality"; as an angel, though it might appear *in propria persona* to be imaginary, here it has no "ashen wing" and lacks its usual "tepid aureole." Rather, the angel is "one of you," as he identifies himself to one of the countrymen, and "in my sight, you see the earth again." The sound of the earth reheard through the powers of the angel, however, suggests another quality, its imaginary potency. An angel is itself a curious representation of reality. In the poem, the "tragic drone" of the world is made to "Rise liquidly" and metamorphose into "watery words awash" through the "sight" and "hearing" of the angel. More directly, the angel at the end of the poem is revealed as "a man / Of the mind" and a vanishing "apparition," all qualities that might more properly be associated with the function of the fictive imagination:

> Am I [the angel] not,
> Myself, only half of a figure of a sort.
>
> A figure half seen, or seen for a moment, a man
> Of the mind, an apparition apparelled in
>
> Apparels of such lightest look that a turn
> Of my shoulder and quickly, too quickly, I am gone? (*CP*,
>     496–97)

"Angel Surrounded by Paysans" moves from the image of the speaker as "angel of reality" to the figure "seen for a moment" as "apparition" and "man / Of the mind." And if the angel mediates a view of the "earth again," it is one of an earth transformed "By repetitions of half-meanings." The language of the poem itself, showing an evolving figuration, has greater authority than does the later interpretation. One has the impression that as Stevens wrote, the poem became more complex than he had first intended, and in his memory of the poem he continued to adhere to that point of origin.

In both of these instances, the connotation of "sea of ex," and the necessary angel, Stevens as critic is forced into reductive and sometimes conflicting paraphrases in his effort to appease his questioner. The poem's vitality has simply outdistanced the poet's plan in its making, and his attempt to recover it leads him to uncertainty and inconsistency.

If Stevens could be forgetful, whether deliberately or not, and even contradictory in his notes on his poems, he could also be self-critical. Rereading and rethinking poems from earlier years led not only to expostulation but also to occasional self-reprimand. Especially in his detailed commentaries on "Owl's Clover," Stevens' longest and least successful extended poem, he found occasion for an apology: "The trouble here is that the lines are over-concise" (*L,* 374); he added, "Very likely, the transition from one phase of the poem to another, at this point, is too immediate" (*L,* 375). Charges against the poems that Stevens regarded as ill founded, however, could elicit a testy defense. Harriet Monroe felt the poet's riposte when she questioned the reference to Voragine in the first line of "Colloquy with a Polish Aunt."[6] "Voragine may warrant a charge of obscurantism on my part," the poet began, "or of stupidity on the other fellow's part, as the wind blows. Jacques de Voragine or Jacopo da Voragino is the immortal begetter of the Legenda Aurea, which, as the best known book of the Middle ages, . . . ought to be fairly well-known even to book reviewers" (*L,* 216).

Stevens' self-evaluation also led to a discussion of his preferred works. He told William Rose Benét in 1933 that "The Emperor of Ice-Cream" was his favorite poem (*L,* 263). After the publication of *Ideas of Order* in 1935, the poet wrote to Latimer that the poem in that volume he liked most was "How to Live. What to Do," because it "so definitely represents my way of thinking" (*L,* 239).

6. Monroe's original letter has not been preserved, and it is difficult to discern whether the charge of obscurantism was hers or one which she supported.

"Sailing after Lunch," from the same volume, was also recommended. In choosing it as the opening poem, he told Latimer that
"perhaps it means more to me than it should" (*L,* 277). Four years
later, when Henry Church was arranging for the French translations, Stevens wrote, "If you want to translate another poem and
really want a suggestion from me, one poem that I have always
liked is FABLIAU OF FLORIDA" (*L,* 341). "Domination of Black" was
his apparent choice for Whit Burnett's anthology *This Is My Best*
(1942), but Stevens' correspondence with Burnett, which was published in 1979, discloses a selection of eighteen poems for the anthology. Because of the deadline, Burnett had room for only one
and chose "Domination of Black." Stevens' complete selection, "a
personal choice and not a critical choice," included, in addition to
the published poem: "Earthy Anecdote," "In the Carolinas," "The
Snow Man," "The Load of Sugar Cane," "The Emperor of Ice-
Cream," "Sunday Morning," "Anecdote of the Jar," "To the One
of Fictive Music," "Dance of the Macabre Mice," "The Pleasures
of Merely Circulating," "The Man with the Blue Guitar" (sections
V, XV, XVII, XVIII, XXVIII), "Country Words," and "Asides on
the Oboe."[7] Later in his career, when Poggioli was selecting the
poems to be translated into Italian, Stevens urged him to consider
"A Rabbit as King of the Ghosts," "Credences of Summer," and
"Large Red Man Reading"—they were "poems I like very much"
(*L,* 778). A year and a half before his death, he wrote to Sister Bernetta Quinn that "I like a few things in Harmonium better than
anything that I have done since" (*L,* 807), but he admitted his
fondness for "Metamorphosis," "the Yillow, Yillow etc. poem"
(*L,* 753), in an earlier note to her. When invited to read some
poems at the University of Massachusetts, he recommended the
second part of "Notes toward a Supreme Fiction": "I would just as
lief read that ["It Must Change"] as anything since there are three
or four parts of it that I like very much. I don't particularly like the
first one or two parts."[8]

In 1950, Stevens agreed to a suggestion from Knopf to look
back over his various volumes for the purpose of compiling a *Selected Poems.* The project was later abandoned—Stevens was then

    7. Glen MacLeod, "A New Version of Wallace Stevens," *Princeton University Library
Chronicle,* XLI (Autumn, 1979), 23.
    8. Wallace Stevens to Robert G. Tucker, February 24, 1954.

unwilling to agree to a more comprehensive *Collected Poems,* and the editors at Knopf found the list he submitted too much a miscellany. Nonetheless, on this occasion Stevens selected eighty-six poems from his six volumes, and he obviously chose the ones he regarded as strongest. His preface insisted that the list did not express "a final choice." It remains a selection of favorites nonetheless. He chose thirty-one from *Harmonium,* fourteen from *Ideas of Order,* two from *The Man with the Blue Guitar and Other Poems,* seventeen from *Parts of a World,* fourteen from *Transport to Summer,* and only eight from his new volume, *The Auroras of Autumn,* which would appear in September.

Earthy Anecdote
In the Carolinas
The Paltry Nude Starts on a Spring Voyage
The Plot Against the Giant
Domination of Black
The Snow Man
Le Monocle de Mon Oncle
Ploughing on Sunday
Fabliau of Florida
The Worms at Heaven's Gate
On the Manner of Addressing Clouds
Of Heaven Considered as a Tomb
The Place of the Solitaires
Depression before Spring
The Emperor of Ice-Cream
Sunday Morning
The Virgin Carrying a Lantern
Bantams in Pine-Woods
Anecdote of the Jar
The Bird with the Coppery, Keen Claws
Life Is Motion
Gubbinal
Two Figures in Dense Violet Night
To the One of Fictive Music
Hymn from a Watermelon Pavilion
Peter Quince at the Clavier
Thirteen Ways of Looking at a Blackbird
Nomad Exquisite
Sea Surface Full of Clouds
Indian River

Tea
Sad Strains of a Gay Waltz
Dance of the Macabre Mice
Meditation Celestial and Terrestrial
Lions in Sweden
The Idea of Order at Key West
The American Sublime
The Sun This March
Botanist on Alp (No. 1)
The Brave Man
Re-Statement of Romance
The Pleasures of Merely Circulating
Like Decorations in a Nigger Cemetery
A Postcard from the Volcano
Gallant Chateau
The Man with the Blue Guitar
The Men That Are Falling
Poetry Is a Destructive Force
The Poems of Our Climate
Dry Loaf
The Man on the Dump
On the Road Home
Country Words
The Dwarf
A Rabbit as King of the Ghosts
Girl in a Nightgown
Connoisseur of Chaos
The Sense of the Sleight-of-hand Man
Variations on a Summer Day
Martial Cadenza
Asides on the Oboe
Montrachet-le-Jardin
Metamorphosis
The Search for Sound Free from Motion
God Is Good. It Is a Beautiful Night
Esthétique du Mal, III, VII, VIII, XIII, XIV
Flyer's Fall
Debris of Life and Mind
Late Hymn from the Myrrh-Mountain
A Completely New Set of Objects
Men Made Out of Words
Thinking of a Relation between the Images of Metaphors

The House Was Quiet and the World Was Calm
The Red Fern
Extraordinary References
A Lot of People Bathing in a Stream
Credences of Summer
Notes toward a Supreme Fiction
   It Must Be Abstract, I, VII, X
   It Must Change, IV, V, VII, VIII
   It Must Give Pleasure, II, IV, VII, IX, X
   Soldier, There Is a War
The Auroras of Autumn, VIII, IX
In the Element of Antagonisms
The Beginning
A Primitive Like an Orb
Puella Parvula
An Ordinary Evening in New Haven, I, VI, IX, XI, XII
   XVI, XXII, XXVIII, XXX, XXXI, XXIX
Things of August, II, III, VII
Angel Surrounded by Paysans[9]

Late in the following year he made another selection for the Faber edition of his poems. Most of the poems were the same ones chosen in the previous year, but there were also a few additional ones.

Infanta Marina
Cy Est Pourtraicte, Madame Ste Ursule, et Les Unze Mille Vierges
Another Weeping Woman
From the Misery of Don Joost
A High-Toned Old Christian Woman
Tea at the Palaz of Hoon
Disillusionment of Ten O'Clock
Evening without Angels
Notes toward a Supreme Fiction (in entirety)
Large Red Man Reading
This Solitude of Cataracts
Final Soliloquy of the Interior Paramour[10]

A handful of poems wore less favorably with their creator. As we have seen, "The Sail of Ulysses," read at Columbia but never published in his lifetime, was suppressed, and "Owl's Clover" was

9. Wallace Stevens to Alfred A. Knopf, May 15, 1950.
10. Wallace Stevens, *Selected Poems* (London: 1953).

withheld from the *Collected Poems*. Three poems were withdrawn from the second edition of *Harmonium* and two others from *Parts of a World* were not reproduced in the *Collected Poems*. In 1938, after Latimer proposed a collected volume, Stevens said that "I might want to eliminate a few things: for instance, I think that THE COMEDIAN AS THE LETTER C has gathered a good deal of dust" (*L*, 330). In 1955, when Oscar Williams was planning his *The New Pocket Anthology of American Verse*, Stevens suggested that "Mrs. Alfred Uruguay" was "questionable. . . . If I took anything out, it would be that." [11]

It is well known that Stevens proposed as the title of his first volume *The Grand Poem: Preliminary Minutiae* (*L*, 237), but Knopf persuaded him to accept *Harmonium*. More than thirty years later, he preferred *The Whole of Harmonium* (*L*, 834) to *The Collected Poems of Wallace Stevens*, but Knopf's judgment again prevailed. He seemed to favor *Aphorisms on Society* over *Owl's Clover* as the title of his third volume, and he considered *The Man, That's All One Knows* before settling upon *Parts of a World* for the later one. [12] When the *Collected Poems* was published in 1954, the last section of poems, all previously uncollected, were to have been gathered at Stevens' wish under the subtitle "Amber Umber" (*L*, 833). Richard Eberhart pointed out to him, however, that the words appeared in Christopher Fry's *Venus Observed,* and Stevens withdrew the designation in favor of "The Rock."

As Stevens' interest became fixed upon an individual poem, and he examined anew its issues and imagery, he occasionally moved beyond being an annotator. The opportunity to enlarge upon a favorite idea or theory suggested by the poem under review led to new critical formulations. Even here, his observations were relatively brief, but the poet suddenly gave his correspondent a glimpse at the broader habit of mind from which the poem had sprung. This is the case with such basic premises as the role of the

---

11. Wallace Stevens to Oscar Williams, January 28, 1955.
12. Elsie Stevens had a question about *The Man, That's All One Knows.* She asked him whether "Knows" was to be spelled "Nose," and Stevens decided that the title had better be *Parts of a World.* Wilson E. Taylor, "Of a Remembered Time," in Frank Doggett and Robert Buttel (eds.), *Wallace Stevens: A Celebration* (Princeton, 1980), 96.

imagination and the function of the poet's fictions in place of religious belief.

In one section of "The Man with the Blue Guitar," Stevens poses the possibility of an "absence in reality" as the imagination vitally issues and returns from one poem to another. In the second half of the section he pulls up, however, to question the absence of reality and then to deny it:

> Poetry is the subject of the poem,
> From this the poem issues and
>
> To this returns. Between the two
> Between issue and return, there is
>
> An absence in reality,
> Things as they are. Or so we say.
>
> But are these separate? Is it
> an absence for the poem, which acquires
>
> Its true appearances there, sun's green,
> Cloud's red, earth feeling, sky that thinks?
>
> From these it takes. Perhaps it gives,
> In the universal intercourse. (*CP*, 176–77)

The "issue" back and forth between poetry and reality was, of course, one of Stevens' touchstones, one to which he was to return often in both the poems and the essays. To Simons, though, he restated the dependence of the "universal intercourse": "Poetry is a passion, not a habit. This passion nourishes itself on reality. Imagination has no source except in reality, and ceases to have any value when it departs from reality. Here is a fundamental principle about the imagination: It does not create except as it transforms. There is nothing that exists exclusively by reason of the imagination, or that does not exist in some form in reality. Thus, reality = the imagination, and the imagination = reality. Imagination gives, but gives in relation" (*L*, 364).

In many poems Stevens returns to the issue of religious belief, or, more exactly, what will substitute for its loss. In his explanations he enlarges on the subject as elaborately as he had in the essay "The Noble Rider and the Sound of Words." "Winter Bells," he told Simons, was designed to show how "the strength of the church grows less and less until the church stands for little more than propriety." The poem offers no speculation on the values of humanism, but to his correspondent Stevens was compelled to expound:

> My trouble, and the trouble of a great many people, is the loss of belief in the sort of God in Whom we were all brought up to believe. Humanism would be the natural substitute, but the more I see of humanism the less I like it. A thing of this kind is not to be judged by ideal presentations of it, but by what it really is. In its most acceptable form it is probably a baseball game with all the beer signs and coca cola signs, etc. If so, we ought to be able to get along without it. I make this comment because the poem is an illustration of what I have just called a habit of mind. (*L*, 348)

A part of "Owl's Clover" returned to the alternatives to religious belief. Commenting later upon them, Stevens also provided a summary of his recent poems: "If one no longer believes in God (as truth), it is not possible merely to disbelieve; it becomes necessary to believe in something else. Logically, I ought to believe in essential imagination, but that has its difficulties. It is easier to believe in a thing created by the imagination. A good deal of my poetry recently has concerned an identity for that thing" (*L*, 370).

In preparing his responses to the various questions from his early critics, Stevens was ever aware that the poems themselves and his explanations were in a sense working at cross-purposes. That in turn led to the constant justification of style and form and the continuous repudiation of isolated "meanings." So fundamental was this proposition to Stevens as an active poet that, as critic, he could never allow himself to ignore it for long. As a result, the critical theory that recurs most frequently in his various self-commentaries is his apology for poetic style.

"People ought to like poetry the way a child likes snow" (*L*, 349), Stevens once told Simons. By that, he meant that the poem's freshness depended upon its spontaneity, its exuberant playfulness, its simplicity, and its wit. The poem could sacrifice logical precision to a higher end, one that might from time to time seem eccentric, peculiarly private, or even willfully obscure. But the delight of a child in snow had its counterpart in the mind's sportive turns. In submitting his explanations, Stevens found himself forced into superimposing upon some poems a rationality, a chronology, or a narrative frame that the works themselves eschewed. He responded to this dilemma with a corrective suggestion in a letter to van Geyzel, when the latter had cited a friend's reaction to "The Emperor of Ice-Cream": "When people think of poems as integrations, they are thinking usually of integration of ideas: that is to say, of what they mean. However, a poem must have a peculiarity, as if it was the momentarily complete idiom of that which prompts it, even if that which prompts it is the vaguest emotion" (*L,* 500). In this statement Stevens discloses, as directly as anywhere in his work, a theory of personal composition and a view of how his own poetry functions. There was a similar observation for a student, Signe Culbertson, in 1955: "'I do try to have a definite meaning,' he said. 'But any sense that one gets out of a poem is legitimate. Communication is more a showing of the pleasure which the poet felt when he wrote his line than an understanding of the sense he was intending.' (Then, for my puzzled look, an explanation) 'I am no convincer, you understand. I see no point in trying to influence the age's mind at this late date.'"[13] His acclaimed aphorism that "poetry must resist the intelligence almost successfully" (*OP,* 171) is a restatement of the same notion. A poem is the "momentarily complete idiom" of an idea, image, or experience out of which it began; as such, it is not an "integration of ideas," but the indulgence in an impulse, a glimpse of an image, or the wisp of a feeling that could be shaped into the idiom of the poem.

In several places in his letters, Stevens found himself face to face with the tangle presented by a reader who wanted the "integration of ideas" for a certain poem and his own recollection, if indeed it was subject to recall, of "the vaguest emotion" that had originally given it birth. "Like Decorations in a Nigger Cemetery," first published in *Poetry* in 1935, is like "Thirteen Ways of Looking at a Blackbird" and "New England Verses" in its clipped and aphoristic style. Its fifty sections, most of which are three or four lines long, are self-contained propositions, characteristically pithy and seemingly random. As Helen Vendler notes, "In at least a fifth of the poem the stanzas are syntactically incomplete, and verbs have been

13. Signe Culbertson, "An Interview with Wallace Stevens: One Angry Day-Son," *In Context,* III (May, 1955), 11–12.

dispensed with."[14] The epigrammatic quality of the poem also derives from the circumstances of its composition—Stevens walking to his office in Hartford. Stanza XXXVI is typical:

> The children will be crying on the stair,
> Half-way to bed, when the phrase will be spoken,
> The starry voluptuary will be born. (*CP*, 156)

Stevens' gloss is direct: "Death is like this: A child will die halfway to bed. The phrase is *voice of death;* the *voluptuary* is the child in heaven" (*L*, 349). The stanza does not state, as the paraphrase does, "Death is like this"; nor do the adjacent stanzas discuss death. The transition from children "crying" to the birth of the "starry voluptuary" may or may not involve the same individuals; the transition itself is effected by a "phrase," and the "phrase" defined in the note as "*voice of death*" is consistent with the poem, but only implicitly. One might also be justified in calling it the phrase uttered by the poet, a parent, or the constellations themselves. Moreover, the three clauses are connected by commas without a clarifying semicolon, contributing further to the absence of closure. Stevens' interpretation does not invalidate the alternate readings. As a result, Stevens' résumé is more precisely the disclosure of an associative pattern of thought, the charting of the poem's original impulse in the poet's mind as much as its final embodiment as a poem. The pattern of connection between the poet's first notion and the poem's final articulation is obviously indirect—associative rather than literal mirroring, tentative rather than definitive, tossed off rather than fleshed out. Stevens' choice was a strategic one; he was willing to sacrifice whole meaning ("Death is like this:") to the effect of rapid but loose association (crying children, phrase, starry voluptuary).

Stevens was conscious of the risks in such a process. The difficulty Simons was having with "On an Old Horn," for example, led to this self-evaluation:

> I took a look at it . . . this morning, to see what the difficulty could be. I think I know what it is. Sometimes, when I am writing a thing, it is complete in my own mind; I write it in my own way and don't care what happens. I don't mean to say that I am deliberately obscure, but I

---

14. Helen Hennessy Vendler, *On Extended Wings: Wallace Stevens' Longer Poems* (Cambridge, Mass., 1969), 69.

do mean to say that, when the thing has been put down and is complete to my own way of thinking, I let it go. After all, if the thing is really there, the reader gets it. He may not get it at once, but, if he is sufficiently interested, he invariably gets it. A man who wrote with the idea of being deliberately obscure would be an imposter. (*L*, 403)

It may or may not be that the reader "invariably gets it" in precisely the sense intended by the poet. But the reader does partake of the leaps, in stanza XXXVI, from tears to starry voluptuary, and for a poem such as this, operating through the cumulative force of epigrammatic flashes, it is enough.

In poems that contain expositions longer than mere aphorisms, Stevens is fond of creating poetic parables about fictional creatures who enact symbolic dramas. These are usually confined to a single section of the poem. Both action and character are frequently only half-realized, resisting a consistent allegorical parallel. The "blue woman" pondering her "feathery argentines" in "Notes toward a Supreme Fiction" is an example. In his essay "Effects of Analogy," Stevens distinguishes between the allegories of John Bunyan, in which "the other meaning divides our attention and thus diminishes our enjoyment of the story," and La Fontaine's *Fables*. The latter are superior as art:

> In La Fontaine, there is a difference. We are not distracted. Our attention is on the symbol, which is interesting in itself. The other meaning does not dog the symbol like its shadow. It is not attached to it. Here the effect of analogy almost ceases to exist and the reason for this is, of course, that we are not particularly conscious of it. We do not have to stand up to it and take it. It is like a play of thought, some trophy that we ourselves gather, some meaning that we ourselves supply. It is like a pleasant shadow, faint and volatile. (*NA*, 109)

That secondary meaning that "we ourselves gather" through a "play of thought" is very near the effect of Stevens' own poetic parables.

One long poem, "Owl's Clover," perplexed one of Stevens' business associates, Stevens T. Mason. He wrote the poet in 1936, complaining that the reviewer in the New York *Times* had understood the poem in a way that had discouraged his own inadequate attempts. Stevens' response made it plain that the poem, far from possessing a single allegorical meaning, could be read in many ways:

Not everything that Mrs. Walton said in her article in the New York Times was true. How could it be, since she had only the book itself to go by, and since, as I have just said, one's real subject in such a book is not the nominal subject but the poetic subject. Nevertheless, she had the general idea and a good many of the details. Some one said not long ago that a poem consists of all the constructions that can be placed upon it. Its measure is the variety of constructions that can be placed upon it: the variety of meanings that can be found in it.[15]

One of the final sections of "The Man with the Blue Guitar" creates a drama of fanciful characters, costumes, and lighthearted exclamations:

> He held the world upon his nose
> And this-a-way he gave a fling.
>
> His robes and symbols, ai-yi-yi—
> And that-a-way he twirled the thing.
>
> Sombre as fir-trees, liquid cats
> Moved in the grass without a sound.
>
> They did not know the grass went round.
> The cats had cats and the grass turned gray
>
> And the world had worlds, ai, this-a-way:
> The grass turned green and the grass turned gray.
>
> And the nose is eternal, that-a-way.
> Things as they were, things as they are,
>
> Things as they will be by and by . . .
> A fat thumb beats out ai-yi-yi. (*CP,* 178)

In this parable of particulars—*he* (nose, robes, symbols) and *world* (fir trees, liquid cats, revolving grass)—the symbolic assignments are not fully defined. As poetry, the lines turn on the tone of jocular exuberance, nursery-rhyme insouciance, childish delight ("ai-yi-yi"). But as *parable,* the lines are not only illuminated by the paraphrase, they are very nearly dependent upon it. Just as he did with "Like Decorations in a Nigger Cemetery," Stevens provided Simons an outline for the action of the poem. The unnamed man who turns the world upon his nose is a "man of imagination."

15. Stevens quoted in George S. Lensing, "Wallace Stevens and Stevens T. Mason: An Epistolary Exchange on Poetic Meaning," *Wallace Stevens Journal,* IV (Fall, 1980), 36.

The liquid cats, oblivious to such enlivening pranks, represent people who "go about their accustomed jobs, unconscious of what is occurring." Stevens continues: "The figure (he) with his robes, the cats, the being and begetting are merely paraphernalia used to produce an effect of comedy. The poet is a comedian. . . . Anyhow, one is trying to do a poem which may be organized out of whatever material one can snatch up. The fat thumb, etc. = stupid people at the spectacle of life, which they enjoy but do not understand." Stevens candidly defines some of the objects in the poem as "merely paraphernalia" with no other purpose than to generate "an effect of comedy." Indeed, "any material one can snatch up" is apropos. The poem is itself an illustration of its theme: "When the imagination is moving rapidly, it identifies things only approximately, and to stop to define them would be to stop altogether" (*L,* 361). Even so, in my own reading, the fat thumb and the sound it makes are associated with the poet strumming the blue guitar as he appears in other sections of the poem. The "ai-yi-yi" sound is the same one made in line 3 by the man Stevens identified to Simons as a "man of imagination." The poet explained, however, that the "fat thumb" is "stupid people at the spectacle of life, which they enjoy but do not understand."

The parabolic quality of the poem upon which such an argument turns is secondary to its comic ventriloquism, the unpredictable antics in a circus sideshow. One observes how the tetrameters reinforce the poem's revolving ("They did not know the grass went round") and self-proliferating ("The cats had cats"; "And the world had worlds") cosmos. Caesuras perform a similar function. Rhymes are integral to the poem's childlike pageantry—sounds "fling" about much like the objects on the comedian's nose. In "The grass turned green and the grass turned gray," the alliterative shifts mimic the literal turning of the grass. The Pennsylvania Dutch exclamation at the end of the poem, "ai-yi-yi," forms a reversal of the sound of " be by and by." The poetic result is hardly nonsense, even if the world presented is imaginatively irrational. The poem aims, as Stevens told Simons, for "an effect of comedy." It is little wonder that Stevens dreaded its prose summary.

The poems of parabolic wit are most frequently incorporated into Stevens' longer poems, and their very nature and method should discourage his readers from a constant temptation—the reduction of the poetic statement to paraphrase, to an imposed "integration of ideas." It does not follow that these poems resist a frame of ideas or that they are composed of nonsensical mannerisms; rather, the frame is a highly protean one, constantly readjusting itself from line to line and from image to image. And the poem's delight in that readjustment is its ultimate *raison d'être*. As Stevens said to Simons on another occasion, "This is not just an explanation; I remember very well that this is the sort of thing that produced the poem. To a person not accustomed to the vagaries of poetic thinking the explanation may seem to be a very strange affair, but there you are; its strangeness is what gives it poetic value" (*L,* 404).

In poems of any length and especially those from *Harmonium,* Stevens' pleasure in the expressiveness of poetry is constant. "Bantams in Pine-Woods," "The Comedian as the Letter C," and "Sea Surface Full of Clouds," for example, are typical verbal spectacles. When Latimer reminded Stevens in 1935 of the "decorative" quality of his verse, the poet did not disagree: "I have delayed answering your letter because I was on the point of saying that I did not agree with the opinion that my verse is decorative, when I remembered that when HARMONIUM was in the making there was a time when I liked the idea of images and images alone, or images and the music of verse together. I then believed in *pure poetry,* as it was called" (*L,* 288). Two months later, however, he assured Latimer that "there must be pure poetry and there must be a certain amount of didactic poetry" (*L,* 302–303), and on the dust jacket for the trade edition of *Ideas of Order,* the author summarized, "The book is essentially a book of pure poetry." Three and a half years later, to Henry Church, Stevens reiterated: "I am, in the long run, interested in pure poetry. No doubt from the Marxian point of view this sort of thing is incredible, but pure poetry is rather older and tougher than Marx and will remain so" (*L,* 340). By pure poetry Stevens seems to have meant the kind of verse unencumbered by didactic or propagandistic statement, a poetry in which the manner of the telling superseded all other considerations. The poem was no transparent medium toward something beyond itself. As he said in his essay "The Irrational Element in

Poetry," the choice of a subject was unpredictable, and so was the poem's development. "One is always writing about two things at the same time in poetry and it is this that produces the tension characteristic of poetry. One is the true subject and the other is the poetry of the subject. The difficulty of sticking to the true subject, when it is the poetry of the subject that is paramount in one's mind, need only be mentioned to be understood" (*OP,* 221).

Litz has argued persuasively for Croce's role in forming Stevens' final attitude toward *la poésie pure.*[16] Indeed, the poet once asked Church if it were "possible to discuss aesthetic expression without at least discussing Croce" (*L,* 385). Stevens himself had recommended John Sparrow's *Sense and Poetry: Essays on the Place of Meaning in Contemporary Verse* to Stevens T. Mason, who had written to describe his problems reading "Owl's Clover." Both Croce and Sparrow were sympathetic to the aims of pure poetry but were aware of its limitations for a poet and suspicious that it could be attained absolutely.

In Croce's essay "The Defence of Poetry," from which Stevens quotes in "The Noble Rider and the Sound of Words" (*NA,* 16), Croce rejects that kind of verse that "excludes, or pretends to exclude, from poetry all the meaning of words, concentrating on the mere sound." But sound can be an end in itself as a poem: "Pure poetry, in the pure sense of the term, is certainly 'sounds', and certainly it is not sounds which have a logical meaning like the sounds of prose. That is to say, it does not communicate a conception, a judgement, or an inference, nor the story of particular facts. But to say it has no logical meaning is not to say it is a mere physical sound without a soul."[17]

Sparrow's book, too, says that "it is possible to recognize and share another's mood without the intervention of intelligible speech." He adds, however, that it is invariably a futile goal for the poet, and he is constantly impatient with those poets who pretend otherwise: "When a writer thus allows purely personal associa-

---

16. A. Walton Litz, "Wallace Stevens' Defense of Poetry: *La poesie pure,* the New Romantic, and the Pressure of Reality," in George Bornstein (ed.), *Romantic and Modern: Revaluations of Literary Tradition* (Pittsburgh, 1977), 111–32.

17. Benedetto Croce, *The Defence of Poetry: Variations on the Theme of Shelley,* trans. E. F. Carritt (Oxford, 1933), 19, 22.

tions to dictate to him his choice of ideas, without reference to any community of association between himself and his readers, he is running a grave risk of writing for himself alone."[18]

One of Stevens' most comprehensive explanations of the conflict between a reader who seeks "a simple, rational meaning" of a poem (in this case, "The Emperor of Ice-Cream") and his own conviction that a poem conveys "imaginative or emotional ambiguity or uncertainty" occurs in a statement he prepared for the *Explicator* in 1948, and I want to quote from it at some length:

> Things that have their origin in the imagination or in the emotions (poems) very often have meanings that differ in nature from the meanings of things that have their origin in reason. They have imaginative or emotional meanings, not rational meanings, and they communicate these meanings to people who are susceptible to imaginative or emotional meanings. They may communicate nothing at all to people who are open only to rational meanings. In short, things that have their origin in the imagination or in the emotions very often take on a form that is ambiguous or uncertain. It is not possible to attach a single, rational meaning to such things without destroying the imaginative or emotional ambiguity or uncertainty that is inherent in them and that is why poets do not like to explain. That the meanings given by others are sometimes meanings not intended by the poet or that were never present in his mind does not impair them as meanings. On the inside cover of the album of Mahler's Fifth Symphony recently issued by Columbia there is a note on the meanings of that work. Bruno Walter, however, says that he never heard Mahler intimate that the symphony had any meanings except the meanings of the music. Does this impair the meanings of the commentators as meanings? Certainly this music had no single meaning which alone was the meaning intended and to which one is bound to penetrate. If it had, what justification could the composer have had for concealing it? The score with its markings contains any meaning that imaginative and sensitive listeners find in it. It takes very little to experience the variety in everything. The poet, the musician, both have explicit meanings but they express them in the forms these take and not in explanation.[19]

Like Croce, who insisted that the poem "has no other equivalent than the melody in which it is expressed, and that may be sung but

---

18. John Sparrow, *Sound and Sense: Essays on the Place of Meaning in Contemporary Verse* (New Haven, 1934), 81.

19. "18. Stevens' THE EMPEROR OF ICE-CREAM," *Explicator*, VII (November, 1948), n.p.

never rendered into prose," Stevens also turns to the musical analogy. Mahler's symphonies could not be reduced to a "single meaning." Both poet and musician could be explicit, but their meanings
lay in the "forms these take and not in explanation." Croce and
Sparrow, in fact, ratified for Stevens two principal conclusions
within the framework of "pure poetry." First, a poem could justify
itself in terms of its sounds alone. Under certain limited conditions, the rhetoric of a poem or a part of a poem could be sustained
on the music of its cadence, the boldness of its diction, the innocence of its own exclamation. Second, and more important, there
was a *via media* between the two extremes: what Michel Benamou
calls Mallarmé's "paradise of perception . . . outside nature" and
beyond referential language, and the poem as "single, rational
meaning."[20] In the end, the issue for Stevens was not the choice of
form to the exclusion of meaning, but rather which the poet
thought was paramount: "In spite of M. Brémond, pure poetry is
a term that has grown to be descriptive of poetry in which not the
true subject but the poetry of the subject is paramount" (*OP*, 222).

In his essay "Two or Three Ideas," Stevens went back to *From
Pieces of Paper* to declare that "the style of a poem and the poem
itself are one" (*OP*, 202). There was also a second proposition—
"the style of the gods and the gods themselves are one." Those
gods, he explained, made up a "delicious subject," and their "style"
seemed near his own. In the first place, they "give to the subject
just that degree of effulgence and excess, no more, no less, that the
subject requires." As such, what "appears to be whimsical . . .
turns out to be essential." Enthroned in their paradise of style, the
gods abide there, in fact, as creations of the "style of men" (*OP*,
212–13). Their theology is the splendor of their metaphorical
garb. But the "effulgence and excess" that Stevens relishes in their
style, and the "whimsical" that turns out to be the "essential" are
the very ingredients of his own poetic form—the style that is the
poem.

Throughout his various prose observations on the poems, Stevens invariably returned to his interest in "the poetry of the subject," urging his reader not to probe for a final meaning. The purpose of "Domination of Black," for example, was "to fill the mind

20. Michel Benamou, *Wallace Stevens and the Symbolist Imagination* (Princeton, 1972), 71.

with the images & sounds it contains. A mind that examines such a poem for its prose contents gets absolutely nothing from it" (L, 251).[21] In 1933, Stevens recalled his special fondness for "The Emperor of Ice-Cream" because it contained "something of the essential gaudiness of poetry" (L, 263), and twelve years later he told van Geyzel that the "concupiscent curds" from the poem "have no genealogy; they are merely expressive" (L, 500). His use of the phrase "animal eyes" in "Gubbinal," he explained to Latimer in 1935, was "purely stylistic." He denied any further significance: "I am not aware that this sort of thing has any philosophic function" (L, 287). Canon Asprin, from "Notes toward a Supreme Fiction," "is simply a figure, not a symbol" (L, 427), he told Henry Church. "The Curtains in the House of the Metaphysician," he reminded Simons, was a poem of "long open sounds." He added, "I suppose this was written at a time when I felt strongly that poems were things in themselves" (L, 463).

Stevens' fondness for the sounds of poetry accounts for the bravura of many of his words and lines. In the summer before his marriage, he repeated for Elsie a story told by his friend from Reading, Edwin De Turck Bechtel: "Bechtel told me a good story to-night. It was about a Pennsylvania Dutchman that went to the World's Fair. When he had been there a day he wrote a post-card to his wife; and this is what he said: 'Dear Maria: -I-yi-yi-yi-yi! I-yi-yi-yi-yi! I-yi-yi-yi-yi! Sam.' That's the best story I've heard for a long time" (L, 784). Stevens' poems are, as we have seen, filled with similar utterances.

For translations of his poems especially, Stevens was far more interested in capturing the *frisson* of his verse than its literal equivalence. He commended Pierre Leyris for picking up "the fanfaronnade" (L, 338) of "Ploughing on Sunday" in his French version. He offered his own suggestions to Henry Church for the rendering of "Disillusionment of Ten O'Clock" and "The Emperor of Ice-Cream":

> But what I had in mind was something bizarre. Personally, I like words to sound wrong. Of course, I have not an ear for that sort of thing in French. If *cercles* is permissible, I should rather use it, because there is

21. See also Wallace Stevens, "Why He Selected 'Domination of Black,'" in *This Is My Best*, ed. Whit Burnett (New York, 1942), 652.

something tame about *ronds*. Perhaps it is not possible to transpose a feeling for words from one language to another. I think I can illustrate this in THE EMPEROR: In the third line, *Des Laits libidineux,* if good French, carries over the feeling of concupiscent curds far better than *Des crèmes délectables.* Moreover, while *gamines* may be the better word, isn't *souillons* a good deal more forcible? (*L,* 340)

Here he avoids literal translation to promote the essential quality of the two poems as "forcible" and "bizarre." Committed to the single effect of words, he could justify neologisms, such as "tournamonde" from "An Ordinary Evening in New Haven": "Curiously, this word, to which I paid considerable attention when I used it, originated, in my mind, in the word mappemonde. I then got around to tournemonde, which would be a French neologism and I then changed it arbitrarily to tournamonde. I think that the word justified itself in the sense of conveying an immediate, even though rather vague, meaning" (*L,* 699).

Stevens' defense of his work in terms of its variously contrived effects ("sensations," "images & sounds," "gaudiness," "Feeling of the words") underscores the importance of a special craft to him, the sound of a poem, how it was arranged on the page, and how it engaged the reader in all its attributes. Such concerns do not invalidate his many remarks on the meaning of poems; in absolute terms, Stevens was never a maker of pure poetry. But, as he told John Pauker, "from my point of view, the quality called poetry is quite as precious as meaning. The truth is that, since I am far more interested in poetry than I am in philosophy, it is even more precious. But it would take a lot of letter writing to get anywhere with this" (*L,* 389–90).

The tension that Stevens identified between the "true subject" and the "poetry of the subject" began in the poet's desire to elude patent didacticism but never to sacrifice it out of hand, to display his personal pleasure in language, but as public utterance and not private indulgence. That tension carried over into the texture of the poem itself and gave it vitality. That is why, finally, Stevens shrank from paraphrase and explanation—because such statements purported to resolve the tension, usually on the side of an integration of ideas and at the expense of their rhetorical garb. The value of Stevens' paraphrases is not what they explain about the poems but what they disclose about the poet: his anxiety that *in* explaining, he violated the tension between "true subject" and "poetry of the subject." That anxiety is apparent, I think, in his defensiveness when he presented his explanations, and in his evasions, contradictions, and outright refusals as well. The anxiety was least when he could explain in terms of the poet's private intention, *before* the "poetry of the subject" rewrote the "true subject." The poetry of the subject remained its own *raison d'être*. That "violence from within" which is the imagination, says Stevens in "The Noble Rider and the Sound of Words," has to do with nothing less than self-preservation. "That, no doubt, is why the expression of it, *the sound of its words* helps us to live our lives" (*NA*, 36; italics mine).

# Afterword

Three weeks before leaving Harvard in 1900, the president of the *Harvard Advocate* published one of his final poems before suppressing indefinitely his craving to be a poet. For the previous three years, he had enjoyed the pleasure of extensive reading in English, French, and German literature. He had found encouragement in his own work from George Santayana, and, as an editor himself, he had exercised judgments on the work submitted by his fellow undergraduates. His notebook had become the repository for his own earnest and acute observations as an incipient poet. Never before or after this brief interlude did Wallace Stevens breathe the heady winds of the poet's atmosphere so unreservedly. That valedictory poem was "Ballade of the Pink Parasol." Although camouflaged by the pseudonym Carrol More, the poem of the twenty-year-old Stevens is unmistakably the voice of the later and more modern poet. "Ballade of the Pink Parasol" is full of images— "the old-time wig," "the dark spadille," "the slippered feet," "the old calash," "the light sedan," and "the painted fan." All these evocations of adventure, color, and insouciant pleasure are absent, however, and in each stanza the poet questions their disappearance. The poem ends:

> Prince, these baubles are far away,
>     In the ruin of palace and hall,
> Made dark by the shadow of yesterday—
>     But where is the pink parasol? (*SP,* 67)

The poem pushes Stevens beyond his other undergraduate work and to the brink of his birth as a modern poet, although that emergence was, as we know, stillborn. The movement toward this first discovery and the later recoveries of the pink parasol are my subject here—as Stevens put it years later, "*Poesis, poesis,* the literal characters, the vatic lines."

The disclosures of Stevens' "growth" as a poet are personal and unique, but they are also predictable and even inevitable. It is not surprising, for example, to discover the role his notebooks had in the making of poems. His reading and his correspondence with friends, especially those living abroad, are likely conduits to poetry as well. Figures such as George Santayana, Harriet Monroe, Ronald Lane Latimer, and Alfred Knopf, who offered crucial encouragement for Stevens, have their counterparts in the lives of other poets. At the same time, many of the peculiarities of Stevens' life are singular: the early conflict with his father Garrett over his personal ambition and the continuation of that conflict during the years he studied law and began to practice it; his interest in art and artists, from Japanese color prints to Marcel Duchamp; his investigation of the work of fellow poets Donald Evans and William Carlos Williams; his experience as an attorney for an insurance company in traveling throughout the South and the Midwest. Such circumstances and predilections shaped decisively the direction of his poetry. The marriage of poetry and business in Stevens' life led to his unmatched habit of composing verse while walking to the office, just as he rescued other hours for poetry from his work for the Hartford Accident and Indemnity Company.

Stevens once praised an early essay on his poetry but added that "what he [the author] does not see is the sort of world in which I am living" (*L,* 292). He was suggesting, I think, the inevitable incompleteness of the critic's view of the poet. The exclusion of the critic from much of the poet's private world closes him off from many attributes of the poems, especially in trying to understand their making. In addition, the strands of experience, intelligence, and impulse that converge in the writing of a poem scarcely conform to logical analysis and, even to the poet himself, are concealed in mystery. The same is true in a different way of the poet's progenitors. Even though, as we have seen, the young Stevens began in the shadow of Wordsworth and Keats, he was not being merely evasive when he explained to Bernard Heringman, "While, of course, I come down from the past, the past is my own and not something marked Coleridge, Wordsworth, etc. I know of no one who has been particularly important to me. My reality-imagination complex is entirely my own even though I see it in others" (*L,* 792).

Still, Stevens knew that the critic's task could not be abdicated. To Simons he conceded that the critic did have the right to pursue what Simons called "every mite of evidence." His analogy of poem and man/shadow was discussed earlier, but I wish to reproduce it here, only because it is Stevens' fullest defense of the need to probe a poet's "growth":

> Obviously, it is not possible to tell one what one's own poems mean, or were intended to mean. On the other hand, it is not the simplest thing in the world to explain a poem. I thought of it this way this morning: a poem is like a man walking on the bank of a river, whose shadow is reflected in the water. If you explain a poem, you are quite likely to do it either in terms of the man or in terms of the shadow, but you have to explain it in terms of the whole. When I said recently that a poem was what was on a page, it seems to me now that I was wrong because that is explaining in terms of the man. But the thing and its double always go together. (*L,* 354)

If the page of verse is the man who walks beside the river, then his reflected shadow, the man's double, is that far less tractable world defined by Simons as "autobiography, biography, letters by and to the artist, contemporary records and memoirs, collateral works of art, etc. etc." Man and shadow, poem and poet's world, are indivisible, and, as Stevens puts it, "you have to explain it in terms of the whole." No critic will realize that mission perfectly: he cannot see the whole "world in which I am living." I have here assayed a portion of that world, and inevitably I have excluded many things as well. The man and his shadow dart in and out of many corners; they appear in bold relief and then flicker and fade. One pursues them only because of the poems he left behind. Stevens' poet-guitarist described himself, like the man walking along the river, as a "shadow," one "hunched / Above the arrowy, still strings" of the guitar in his hands. But such a shadow was no mirage, either to himself or his beholder; he was a "maker of a thing yet to be made" (*CP,* 169).

# Index